'A lovely, urgent, serious bo~~k~~ ~~re-thinking about L~~
and life all over again' Tessa

'By turns troubled, tender,
Lawrence's vivid talent and

'Refreshing and unexpecte
thinking hard and seriously about the role of reading in a world
characterised by fracture, is powerfully made' Daisy Hay,
*Financial Times*

'A perceptive book ... a critical biography but also a pandemic
memoir – a story about how an author can inform and change
your life ... Feigel's intensity and intimacy are engaging' Blake
Morrison, *Guardian*

'Feigel's book is itself Lawrentian: sprightly, capacious, passionate,
inquisitive and complex' Tomiwa Owolade, *New Statesman*

'To be able to meet the world unillusioned but undismayed is
what Lawrence did for Lara Feigel, and it is what she hopes he can
do for us as a result of her bracing and honest book. Each chapter
homes in on a major topic and Feigel has something fresh to say
in every case ... Some of the sharpest, shrewdest discussions I
have seen of Lawrence for a long time' Paul Dean, *Critic*

'Lara Feigel wrestles with Lawrence, resents him, adores him and
even tries to learn from him, all while Covid rages; it makes for
a daring and unconventional bibliomemoir that might change
the way you feel about sex, motherhood, work, illness and faith'
Samantha Ellis

'A fiercely intelligent engagement with Lawrence, half memoir
and half critical biography, in which Lara Feigel comes in at a
series of oblique angles to reach some startling judgments. I was
highly impressed' D. J. Taylor

'Feigel's Lawrence is an untimely, urgent teacher of life and its passions. Agile, surprising and compulsively absorbing, *Look! We Have Come Through!* is the perfect tonic for the cynical, jaded spirit of our time' Josh Cohen

'Both an analysis of what makes Lawrence so troublingly intoxicating, and an account of what happens when we succumb to the writers we admire. Clear-headed, yet also strangely intuitive, what makes Lara Feigel's writing so seductive is the way she seems to absorb Lawrence's influence so deeply into herself that he becomes her own' Katharine Kilalea

LARA FEIGEL is a Professor of Modern Literature and Culture at King's College London. Her three most recent non-fiction books, *The Love-Charm of Bombs* (2013), *The Bitter Taste of Victory* (2016) and *Free Woman: Life, Literature and Doris Lessing* (2018), and her first novel, *The Group* (2020), were all published to critical acclaim. She is also the author of *Literature, Cinema and Politics*, 1930-1945 and the editor (with Alexandra Harris) of *Modernism on Sea: Art and Culture at the British Seaside* and (with John Sutherland) of the *New Selected Journals of Stephen Spender*. She is a Fellow of the Royal Society of Literature and writes regularly for the *Guardian* and other publications. Lara lives in Oxfordshire.

www.larafeigel.com
@larafeigel

# LOOK! WE HAVE COME THROUGH!

## Living with D. H. Lawrence

## Lara Feigel

BLOOMSBURY PUBLISHING

LONDON · OXFORD · NEW YORK · NEW DELHI · SYDNEY

BLOOMSBURY PUBLISHING
Bloomsbury Publishing Plc
50 Bedford Square, London, WC1B 3DP, UK
29 Earlsfort Terrace, Dublin 2, Ireland

BLOOMSBURY, BLOOMSBURY PUBLISHING and the Diana logo are trademarks of
Bloomsbury Publishing Plc

First published in Great Britain 2022
This edition published 2023

A catalogue record for this book is available from the British Library

Library of Congress Cataloguing-in-Publication data has been applied for

ISBN: HB: 978-1-4088-7753-1; TPB: 978-1-4088-7756-2; PB: 978-1-4088-7755-5;
EBOOK: 978-1-4088-7754-8; EPDF: 978-1-5266-5032-0

2 4 6 8 10 9 7 5 3 1

Typeset by Newgen KnowledgeWorks Pvt. Ltd., Chennai, India
Printed and bound in Great Britain by CPI Group (UK) Ltd, Croydon CR0 4YY

To find out more about our authors and books visit www.bloomsbury.com
and sign up for our newsletters

For Patrick

# Contents

Introduction                                               1
1 Unconscious                                             19
2 Will                                                    43
3 Sex                                                     65
4 Parenthood                                              91
5 Community                                              117
6 Religion                                               147
7 Nature                                                 173
8 Apocalypse                                             201

*Note on Sources*                                        235
*Notes*                                                  237
*Acknowledgements*                                       247
*Index*                                                  251

# Introduction

I've got no idea about the names of the birds that wake us here in the mornings. I don't even know how to tell their calls apart. The little chirrups, the squawks, the glissandos that are easier to call song. But thankfully, I have D. H. Lawrence to guide me. 'It seems when we hear a skylark singing as if sound were running into the future, running so fast and utterly without consideration, straight on into futurity.' Is that a skylark I hear? Or did the future they ran into so recklessly turn out to be a future in which they died out?[1]

I am here, waking in a village in West Oxfordshire with two children and the ghost of D. H. Lawrence, because two weeks ago England went into lockdown and there was a scrambled game of musical chairs. We were to be enclosed within our households for several months. But what constituted a household? If we were to be thrown back into the nuclear families we had thought some combination of feminism and modernity had overcome, how were those not in families to arrange themselves? If you didn't already live with your partner, you were encouraged by the government either to move in with them or to say goodbye for months. So in the days that preceded lockdown, I hastily rented out our London flat and rented a cottage in Oxfordshire. We would be among the lucky few to have a garden; we would be near enough to my partner that we could just about describe ourselves as one household. I locked down with him, with my two-year-old daughter and eight-year-old son, and with D. H. Lawrence.

Lawrence is a necessity: I have agreed to write a book on him. This seems to me the moment for a new approach to Lawrence, now that we're no longer mired either in the Lawrence worship led by F. R. Leavis in the 1950s or in the repulsion and condemnation led by Kate Millett in the 1970s. But Lawrence is necessary to me in another way, too. I am frightened by this loss of familiar community, this cutting off from conversation, this uncertainty about whether I am still part of the academic community I had an ambivalent relationship with in the first place. I have turned to Lawrence for urgent literary companionship, hoping that he will help me make sense of the new world we have found ourselves in. He promises to be well-suited to this. He was so adept himself at isolated living, so good a writer on extreme forms of proximity, so perpetually an outsider yet so foundational to his culture. And he is turning out to be an ideal guide as I navigate my new closeness to birds and flowers.

It was a decade ago, as I turned thirty, that I first formulated the idea of writing a book on him, and six years ago that I promised a book on Lawrence to my publisher. The catalyst for all this was a job interview. At a time when I was applying for every possible academic job, I accidentally got myself shortlisted for a lectureship in D. H. Lawrence studies at Lawrence's nostalgically despised alma mater, the University of Nottingham, though I hadn't read a Lawrence novel for fifteen years. My last attempt at reading him had been when I got halfway through *Sons and Lovers* in impatient adolescence. No one had suggested I should read him as an undergraduate – we were still living in Millett's shadow. So now I had three weeks to go straight from ignorance to expertise. I read *Women in Love*, and was irritated at first by all the wombs and loins, the flames and consummations I recalled from my last attempt. Then I came to the descriptions of sex. There is Ursula, kissed by Birkin, unsure at first because he seems so far away, and 'it was like strange moths, very soft and silent, settling on her from the darkness of her soul'. And then we see them swooning together, deciding to wander off, 'somewhere we can be free – somewhere where one needn't wear much clothes'. Now when he kisses her, 'her arms closed round him again, her hands spread upon his shoulders, moving slowly there, moving slowly on his back, down his back slowly, with a strange recurrent, rhythmic motion, yet moving slowly down, pressing mysteriously over his loins, over his flanks. The sense of the awfulness of riches that could never be impaired flooded her mind like a swoon.' They both write their letters of resignation and prepare to embark on an experiment in mutual freedom.

I swooned alongside her. It wasn't that I was seduced by Birkin – I found his more pompous pronouncements as irritating as Ursula does. I was falling for the dialogue between Birkin and Ursula, the feeling that this was what a relationship could be, this delving into the unknown together with talk and touch. I turned out to love Lawrence's prose, with its endless circlings – 'moving slowly there, moving slowly on his back, down his back slowly' – the awkward off-kilteredness and uncertainty that is suddenly resolved, in the sumptuous clarification of that 'awfulness of riches'. And I shared Ursula's restless energy, her feeling that life promised so much but delivered so little, that there must be forms of connection that went beyond the words – love, sex – that we use. I admired Lawrence's writing of women. It seemed to me that few male novelists of his generation really thought about women, about their childhoods and adolescences and marriages, about their lives as daughters and as mothers, with the intensity and sensitivity that Lawrence did in this book, and in *The Rainbow*, which I read next, even if he sometimes got things wrong. Outrageous as it may seem, it felt to me that those repetitions and circlings were the rhythms of female thought. I liked the way that no one was ever still. No feeling was ever fixed, no view settled, before they were on to the next mood. I liked the way that relationships for him constitute constant gyrations of connection and alienation: it felt true to my lived experience.

This was the moment of conversion that so many readers – among them so many women – have had, both in Lawrence's company (women frequently offered themselves to him, and his wife Frieda took them aside to tell them, not wholly inaccurately, that he was homosexual) and away from him. Visiting Lawrence's shrine in Taos in 1939, W. H. Auden mocked the 'cars of women pilgrims' traipsing up to the Lawrences' former ranch each day 'to stand reverently there and wonder what it would have been like to sleep with him'. Here was I, seventy years later, ready to journey to Nottingham and wonder the same. What's more, I would dress as Ursula. I turned up to my interview in bright-green stockings.[2]

But I didn't write about him straight away. And in the years that followed – years in which I had my first child and found myself drawn to writers of motherhood – I moved away from him, relieved not to have ended up as a lecturer in D. H. Lawrence studies. Yet images and phrases from Lawrence kept coming back to me. I still admired Lawrence's courage in writing openly about sex and bodily life (he was the first English writer to do so), and there were whole categories of experience that his writing continued to define. I decided to teach a Lawrence course and proposed a Lawrence book to my publisher. With my students, I read Simone de Beauvoir's and Kate Millett's coruscating critiques, and found it harder to feel that Lawrence spoke for me as a woman. Beauvoir loved his 'cosmic optimism'; she fell for the scenes that I fell for, feeling that for Lawrence 'the sexual act is without annexation, without surrender of either partner, the marvellous fulfilment of each other', admiring his lovers because 'blending into each other, they blend into the trees, the light, and the rain'. But then she decided that in fact 'Lawrence passionately believes in male supremacy', substituting the cult of the phallic for that of the Goddess Mother, granting all powers of thought and action to men. Twenty years later, after the 1960 trial of *Lady Chatterley's Lover* had chided and lauded Lawrence for championing the whole embodied life of men and women, the brilliantly enraged American feminist activist Kate Millett turned Beauvoir's ambivalence into something more angrily certain in her 1970 *Sexual Politics*, castigating Lawrence for propounding his 'personal cult, "the mystery of the Phallus"' and in doing so bringing about a counter-revolution against women.[3]

Reading Millett, I was overwhelmed by the fierce cogency of her critique. I had been uncertain about *Lady Chatterley's Lover* before I read her and now I was convinced by her argument that it was a book that reduced women to passive objects and reviled the female genitals. Millett's book was written with such sureness and vim that I was becoming as curious about Millett as about Lawrence, partly because I had a sense, as with Beauvoir, that she loved his writing as well as hating it, and was disappointed that he didn't love women enough. This was what I wanted to write about now and, during a research trip to New York, I rushed off upstate to meet her at the farm she had long since set up as a women's colony, there to find a surprisingly benign though very frail host, glad to show me the flowers planted by Doris Lessing and the tree by Simone de Beauvoir, and so pleased with her lovely view of her lovely lake that we sat outside in pouring rain, going in only when the lightning started. She was as embattled as Lawrence – successive builders had been sent away because they were Republicans, so much of the farm was in disarray – but she no longer had anything to say about him and it had been years since she'd read his books. She had made a life living and working alongside women writers and no longer had any need to read or to argue with men.

When I met Millett, I was pregnant with my daughter and was in the midst of splitting up with my husband. I found it a relief to enter the all-female world that Millett and her wife had created and was tempted to abandon Lawrence and to join them. This feeling became stronger when I read *Kangaroo* and *The Plumed Serpent* and was repelled by Lawrence's political ideas (his hatred of democracy) and his racial views (his hierarchy of races). I saw that his prejudices were everywhere; that even in the books I loved this was a vast mind wheeling through all its possibilities at every moment and that this was always going to include his prejudice. I turned away again and wrote a novel about a group of women.

Now, rereading *The Rainbow* as we settle into the countryside, I can see that the feeling of repulsion is part of the larger feeling of being pulled in every direction that reading Lawrence involves for me, as it has for so many of his readers. I feel closer to him again, partly just because this landscape feels close to the landscape he described in Nottinghamshire. I like to imagine that on the farms around me, farms that we wander through when my son becomes bored enough in our cottage that he is prepared to go for a walk, there is the 'intercourse between heaven and earth' that he described: 'sunshine drawn into the breast and bowels, the rain sucked up in the daytime, nakedness that comes under the wind in autumn, showing the birds' nests no longer worth hiding'. I have been reading Lawrence's first novel, *The White Peacock*, and finding that he described this period, the end of winter turning to the beginning of spring, uncannily well. The snowdrops were just coming out here when we arrived, and I read about them now, 'like drops of manna scattered over the red earth'; white flowers pale above the shadows; tears, according to Lawrence's characters, of the druids.

I have never located myself easily in this landscape, though for years I've left the city whenever I can, almost as claustrophobic as Lawrence was when surrounded by buildings. 'Are there any other Jews there?' a friend writes from London, and though I assure him that it's a perfectly cosmopolitan place, I can't yet be sure of this. I have Lawrence, though, a rootless exile, a wanderer, albeit one who refuses to use his christened name of David partly out of dislike for the ancient Hebrew King (he thought he was too egotistical, and too narrowly monotheistic, though he was drawn to the sensuality of his naked dance before God). Here, in this cottage that has features of the houses Lawrence grew up in, I will be able to watch the seasons change alongside him. In the sitting-room bookcase, amid the crime fiction and recipe books that come with the house, I have shelved the only bag of books I brought in my hurried packing: eight volumes of Lawrence's collected letters, his essays, his poetry, his novels and stories. Lawrence was always looking for people to lock down with, and taking them away to remote places in Cornwall or New Mexico. He usually fought with them, finding them too wilful (especially if they were women) or driving them away with his rage, or with the ghoulish spectacle of his fights with Frieda, however much he entertained them with his capacity for mimicry. Here we are together then. I can survive his rage and his lectures if I remind myself that he'll soon be contradicting himself. We will lock down together.

*

There has been a century of people using Lawrence as a guide to life. Frieda said it after his death. You have to understand, she told a critic, in 1951, 'he changed the outlook on sex for all time and you can "live" by Lawrence – he is a "way of life"'. He asked for it: he talked about his world-view as a religion and set himself up as a priest. 'My great religion is a belief in the blood, the flesh,' he wrote in a letter in 1913. 'We can go wrong in our minds. But what our blood feels … is always true.'⁴

People don't just read Lawrence, they have their lives changed by him. And so many of them recorded it, whether it was the women he had actually slept with, the women he had known ('I can only remember how he elevated one and keyed one up to higher and higher reaches of vision and understanding,' wrote the American writer and patron of the arts Mabel Dodge Luhan, who was responsible for getting him to New Mexico), or the women who had merely read him. Before she wrote her erotic fiction, the American writer Anaïs Nin wrote a study of D. H. Lawrence in 1932, where she praised his 'androgynous writing', saying that 'his intuitive intelligence sought the core of women' and that this was 'the first time that a man has so wholly and completely expressed woman accurately'. And there were the men – most prominently F. R. Leavis, an idealistically dogmatic Cambridge don only ten years younger than Lawrence, who shared his disillusionment with the First World War and hatred of the machine age, and in the years after his death became his major academic champion. In his 1955 book on Lawrence, Leavis characterised his work as 'an immense body of living creation in which a supreme vital intelligence is the creative spirit – a spirit informed by an almost infallible sense for health and sanity'. Lawrence's enthusiasts weren't all white, though so far all of his prominent female fans have been. Lawrence had a fan base in the writers of the Harlem Renaissance, with the Jamaican-American writer Claude McKay describing Lawrence as his favourite modern writer and reporting that in Lawrence he found 'confusion – all of the ferment and torment and turmoil, the hesitation and hate and alarm, the sexual inquietude and incertitude of this age, and the psychic and romantic groping for a way out'.⁵

This is also why people have hated him: they worry that he has the power that his disciples ascribe him. T. S. Eliot suggested in *After Strange Gods*, his 1934 grandiose moan in the face of cultural change, that given Lawrence's 'incapacity for what we ordinarily call thinking', and his 'sexual morbidity', his work could appeal only to 'the sick and debile and confused'. Eliot had changed his mind by the time of the 1960 trial of *Lady Chatterley's Lover*. Before it started, he wrote to the defence team that he was glad to have the chance to show that he no longer agreed with all his earlier opinions, 'some of which I now regard as being immature, ill-considered, and too violent'. During the trial, he paced the corridors, waiting to be called as a witness for the defence. The prosecutors could find no writers prepared to speak for their side, but the prosecuting barrister had the full backing of the establishment when he asserted that the book would lead readers to 'a wholly false conception of what proper thought and conduct ought to be in times when some proper conception is so vitally needed'.[6]

If Eliot's early views on Lawrence were, as he put it, too violent, then wasn't this because of a corresponding violence in Lawrence? Lawrence went into writing as a fighter. He loved to be hated, though he hated to be silenced. It's because of the excesses in his writing that critics have responded with such extremes of love and hate, often oscillating between the two. The feminists didn't all hate him, even after Millett's book came out. The queen of cool in American letters, Susan Sontag, announced rather improbably in the 1960s that her whole project was to be a female D. H. Lawrence, and in 1972 she still spoke up for Lawrence as the most 'convincing, genuine, singular voice in our language' of their century. Less surprisingly, the truculent feminist Doris Lessing had fallen headily in love with Lawrence in adolescence, reading him while wandering around the Rhodesian bush. For the Chatterley trial she described him as 'probably the greatest writer produced in this country, this century'. In 2002 she dismissed Millett's concerns as irrelevant. 'What do we care about his pronouncements on the sex war?' she asked, prepared to defend Lawrence's assertion that 'lovemaking, sex, is serious, a life-and-death thing', prepared to admit that Lawrence's men want their women to be passive, but suggesting with typical belligerence that modern women 'do not seem particularly happy having their way'. By this time Lessing had no interest in insisting, like Leavis, on his health, and was prepared to follow Eliot in seeing him as sick, debile and confused. It was his unhealthiness that interested her, and she saw his tuberculosis as the key to his visionary language. 'He was fiery and flamy and lambent, he was flickering and white-hot and glowing – all words he liked to use. Consumption is a disease that over-sensitises, unbalances, heightens sexuality, then makes impotent; it brings death and the fear of death close.'[7]

Angela Carter, too, defending Lawrence from his feminist detractors, focused on his more floridly insane characteristics. A generation younger than Lessing and a contemporary of Millett's, Carter was more at home in feminism than Lessing but more playful in her provocations than Millett. For Carter, as for Nin, it was Lawrence's capacity to capture female experience that was most impressive, but she saw this less as a sign of his heterosexual love for women than of his being himself a woman in flimsy disguise. 'D. H. Lawrence is infinitely more feminine than Jane Austen, if one is talking about these qualities of sensitivity, vulnerability and perception traditionally ascribed by male critics to female novelists,' she wrote in a letter in the late 1960s. 'D. H. Lawrence's tragedy was he thought he was a man.' After Millett's critique, Carter responded by insisting that Lawrence was a feminist himself. 'Oh, but he's a sister,' she shouted out mischievously at a Women Writers' panel. And in a 1975 essay called 'Lorenzo as Closet-Queen', she suggested that 'Lawrence personated women through externalities of dress', revelling in lace and feathers and most of all in stockings – 'defiant, brilliant, emphatic stockings'.[8]

Unlike Lessing, Carter wasn't wholly inclined to disagree with Millett, though she made light of it. Perhaps Millett was right, she suggests here, 'he only wanted to be a woman so that he could achieve the supreme if schizophrenic pleasure of fucking himself, since nobody else was good enough for him'. We can feel that

Lawrence has shrunk for Carter, since that 1960s letter, becoming more human and more comical. It's true that Lawrence loved female clothes and wrote about them more often than he wrote about female bodies. He revelled in the female gaze. Carter's was a moment of beginning again in thinking about Lawrence that still feels exciting now. And it's because Millett was right about Lawrence as well as wrong, because Lawrence did need to be rescued from his own imaginative excesses, and from the areas of his work where his imagination failed to transfigure his prejudices (though not, I now think, *Lady Chatterley's Lover*), that it's thanks to Millett and her contemporaries that we can read him again now, freed to start again and read him on our own terms.

Certainly, no one now would make a case for Lawrence based on his health and sanity. And it's telling that Lawrence has brought out sanity in so few of his critics. There's something very extreme about all these responses, from Nin to Eliot to Leavis to Millett, something far in excess of ordinary criticism, because these are books that seem to demand to be talked about as living beings – as flawed, passionate exercises in life.

In the year that follows my move to Oxfordshire, I will discover that there are other women who were locked down with Lawrence when I was, all of them brilliant, none of them wholly sane. There's Rachel Cusk, whose remarkable novel *Second Place* transposes Mabel Dodge Luhan's memoir about her time with Lawrence in Taos on to a marshy seascape, 'full of desolation and solace and mystery', in contemporary Britain. A woman writer invites a Lawrence-like painter known as L to stay, and finds him challenging her sense of reality and of her own identity, attempting to destroy her will. There's Alison MacLeod, whose novel *Tenderness* is a large-hearted celebration of *Lady Chatterley's Lover*, written from the intertwined perspectives of Lawrence himself, his lover Rosalind Baynes, and his readers from Jackie Kennedy to the prosecution and defence teams at the trial. Lawrence's novel propels the action and, in keeping with the huge ambition of the book, there's even a scene from Constance Chatterley's point of view. And there's Frances Wilson, whose biography of Lawrence is a bravura exercise in imaginative interpretation, an attempt to map Lawrence's life onto Dante's *Divine Comedy*, so that we see Lawrence and Dante as companions on the journey from inferno to paradise.

All of these women evoke Lawrence as a physical presence, turning him into a speaking, physical being. They all seem to be able to picture him in a way that I find hard to do. Though my mind is so caught up in his, he remains a ghost to me. I wonder what they call him in moments of intimacy. Cusk sticks to L. Wilson may go all the way and call him Lorenzo. MacLeod probably does too, when she's inhabiting his lovers' points of view, but as a novelist she maintains a respectful distance and calls him 'the exile'. It's strange, but I think fitting, that he was a man who ended up having no name. As a child, he was known in the family as 'Bert', his middle name, partly because of his own dislike for his first name. David could have been a name to see him through life, but Bert wasn't. He couldn't go to aristocratic lunch parties as Bert. So he became Lawrence at school, and started using it at home as well. 'Do call me Lawrence,' Jessie Chambers recalled him saying to her on their first proper meeting, aged fifteen, after she had said that she thought Bertie was a girlish name, 'I'd like it better.' He was Lawrence, and he was DHL – that was how he signed his letters even to his mother, sisters and lovers, from the age of eighteen. Then, in Italy, Frieda came up with Lorenzo. It's a name well-suited to his image as a Priest of Love, perhaps well-suited to the traveller to far-off places too, but rather brilliantly inappropriate to the puritan, the reader of Hardy, the man of the Midlands. I don't think that Lawrence ever used it to refer to himself; in his head he seems to have had no name, perhaps too frightened by the extraordinary nominative power of words to allow himself one. For me, he has no name, and neither does he really have a body, however much I read about his surprisingly silky red beard, his thin white flanks.[9]

He is easy to characterise. Images come to mind: the skinny Lawrence fighting with the fulsome Frieda, biffing each other as they yelled out insults; the social climber charming aristocratic hostesses with his tales of the mines or his explanations of botany; the pale, luminous man, awakening women in bed, telling them to cast off shame; the giggling performer, playing Gawd-a-Mighty in a charade. Yet there's a sense that he was absent – that he was always the man writing away in his notebook in the corner of a room who the poet H.D. recalls in her memoir, allowing other people to invent him in his absence. He wrote constantly about his own experiences, but he eschewed introspection (he hated psychoanalysis) and didn't believe in personality, thinking that selfhood should be more than our superficial characteristics. So if you're going to turn Lawrence into a character in a book, perhaps you should be attempting a Lawrentian character, a man of moods rather than a man with a novelistic personality.

These women do not say what they made of Lawrence during lockdown in particular, but presumably they found, as I have, that his sense of illness as primarily a psychic event, a response to rage or chagrin, influenced their sense of the virus that has been ravaging our world. 'I am not a mechanism, an assembly of various sections,' Lawrence wrote in 'Healing', a late poem.

And it is not because the mechanism is working wrongly,
That I am ill.
I am ill because of wounds to the soul, to the deep,
    emotional self.

Presumably they wondered, as I have, what he would have made of this pandemic, and thought that he might have said we had willed it into being, that by denying the existence of death we had made it necessary for death to reveal itself, that by excessively medicalising life we had created the conditions for a total takeover of life by medicine, and that these were the conditions in which we were more likely to get ill. 'One is ill because one doesn't live properly – can't,' Birkin says in *Women in Love*, a book that Lawrence hoped would make us healthy, saving us from illness by teaching us to live.

Lawrence wasn't dismissive of the Spanish flu that ravaged Europe in 1918 (and killed 150,000 in Britain): he was happy to self-isolate during the weeks he was ill with it ('I have never been so down in the mud in all my life,' he wrote). But there was nothing then like a national lockdown. In some moods, he might have seen the kind of lockdowns we have lived through as ideal, halting the spread of machine civilisation, enabling us to hide away. But I think he would have raged against the state control it has been a symptom of, astonished that the government could presume to tell him how many hours a day he could spend in exercise, who he was allowed to eat lunch with or to go to bed with.[10]

It is surely not a coincidence that all four of us chose to lock down with Lawrence. He is so well-suited to the intense closeness of lockdown, because intense closeness is always such a feature in his writing. He invites it from readers – so many of us have felt personally addressed by him. And his characters are often too close, mimetically engrossed in each other or captivated by an idea of themselves they have got from another person and can't escape from.

Back to our first rural spring: back to that cottage in a village in an England we know to be industrialised but can make-believe, as Lawrence could in Eastwood, still to be agricultural. Reading about Lawrence as the world settles into a kind of ghastly silence and the birds flare into song, what I am hoping to get is, in part, a guide to the modern world I have briefly escaped. It's a world that he resisted at every turn but that I believe he played a part in bringing into being. In the 1920s, he complained that the feelings of his age, the men and women of his age, were those forged a century earlier by the French Enlightenment, by Rousseau and Diderot, whose rather different thinking he elides here. In Lawrence's account, the thinkers of eighteenth-century France were determinedly good, rational, free beings, whose insistence on irreligious rationality prevented them from worshipping anything and whose insistence on 'nice' feelings turned them into liars. In the 2020s, we might say that the feelings of our age, the men and women of our age, are those created a century earlier by D. H. Lawrence. We believe in embodied life and bodily freedom; we believe in nature, and want to protect it from man. If the opposite remains true – if there are drives to pollute nature, to deny the body, to replace men with machines – then this may simply be the dialectic of modernity. And certainly, Lawrence typified the modern. He was determined to find ways to portray the teeming energy of a world in constant flux.[11]

In Lawrence's 1918 essay 'Poetry of the Present', he writes that 'in the immediate present there is no perfection, no consummation, nothing is finished'. He says that he wants to find a way to write the present, and this is where he writes about that skylark running into the future, rushing towards us. 'The bird is on the wing in the winds,' he writes, 'flexible to every breath, a living spark in the storm, its very flickering depending upon its supreme mutability and power of change.' This is what, astonishingly, he finds ways to write in his fiction as well as his poetry. All the repetitions, the long sentences that begin in one place and end somewhere quite different, are exercises in writing the flux of the present moment. It can be exhausting reading a Lawrence novel because no character or relationship is ever fixed; they are always moving towards the next mood, living sparks in the storm. The British critic Al Alvarez (himself rather a macho, nature-loving Lawrentian figure) writes that 'Lawrence's characters are always in motion, moving beyond their emotions, their states, even their convictions' and that therefore it makes more sense to talk about the rhythms than the form of a Lawrence novel. It's this capacity for constant motion, for writing (as Virginia Woolf put it about her own writing) to a rhythm instead of a plot, that makes Lawrence so good a guide to modern life, however much he railed against most of the changes he saw around him.[12]

In Lawrence's vision of the modern world, the new generation of women are at once a source of threat and of great possibility. Reading Millett, you might think that Lawrence hated modern women. But surely part of what frightened Millett was that she could see her own roots in Ursula and Gudrun Brangwen. Lawrence didn't just portray modern women – he brought them into the world, offering Ursula and Gudrun as models for a generation of women readers. He started right at the beginning, showing their genesis in *The Rainbow*, where the men are contented to exist in the cyclical blood knowledge of the seasons, but the women ask for something more. They look out from 'the heated, blind intercourse of farm-life' to the spoken world. 'They were aware of the lips and the mind of the world speaking and giving utterance, they heard the sound in the distance, and they strained to listen.'

Lawrence mocks suffragettes in his novels, dismissing the feminists of his generation in part because he was so ambivalent about democracy and couldn't see why anyone would want to vote. But he identified intimately with the Brangwen women, who ask for something more from the world than the rhythms of procreation that have contented their grandmothers. A visionary like her creator, Ursula has a revelation of life's potential in a botany lesson at university. Looking at cells under the microscope, she suddenly sees the possibility of self-consummation. 'Self was a oneness with the infinite. To be oneself was a supreme, gleaming triumph of infinity.' Her life from this point becomes a quest for self-realisation that would make no sense to her grandmothers, though they themselves might serve as models for self-realisation to her. By the opening of *Women in Love*, Ursula and Gudrun are both pretty sure that they do not want to marry or have children. Might getting married be an experience, Gudrun asks Ursula? 'More likely to be the end of experience,' Ursula retorts. She is determined to throw off the past and to see herself as thronging with the potential of the present moment: 'What had she to do with parents and antecedents? She knew herself new and unbegotten.' Lawrence would frequently find modern womanhood a source of repulsion rather than reverence. His own modern woman, Frieda, often became too much for him, and he gave Constance Chatterley a more old-fashioned set of desires. But he understood what was at stake for women, understood that being a living spark in the storm of the present moment posed more urgent and often more dangerous challenges for women than men.

Living alongside Lawrence, what I want to gain from him is, perhaps most of all, a sense of what it means to accept our lived experience as one of perpetual change. 'Not I, not I, but the wind that blows through me!' he wrote in his 'Song of a Man Who Has Come Through', which he published in *Look! We Have Come*

*Through!*, his great, passionately fluctile volume of poems about his early months with Frieda. I want to understand what it meant for him to feel himself constantly blown by the wind, and how he came to accept the struggle he saw as entailed by it. 'Fight, fight. That is life,' he wrote in the essay on Herman Melville in *Studies in Classic American Literature*, and this was how he saw life himself. Part of this was an acceptance of ambivalence in its fullest sense: an acceptance that hate is never far from love, that every thought calls for its opposite, that 'all vital truth contains the memory of all that for which it is not true'. This isn't the extreme partisanship we get on social media today. It's a version of strong-mindedness that's desperate for wholeness, and full of spiritedness and good humour. It's because of the partisanship of our own times that we have so much need of him. We need someone capable of holding every side of the argument within his mind as real, energetically alive propositions, someone capable of questioning his own thoughts, even as he allows himself to be polemical. My hunch is that Lawrence was such a crucial figure to his moment, the moment just before the roaring twenties showed everyone that they were modern, that his ideas have remained part of our world as it has developed, embedded in our cultural landscape, ready to be excavated again.

I have always lived with contradictions. It has driven some of the people I've loved mad that I find it necessary to think one thing but also its opposite, to be one thing while also attempting to be another. It seems to me quite natural to be a committed mother, but to yearn to escape your children into a world of silence; to be a wife, but to believe in sexual freedom; to believe in democracy, but also to fear mass rule; to believe in education for all, but also to think that we may be better off uneducated. Lawrence seems to point the way towards a world where ambivalence is not merely undecidedness but is a force towards the truths that Lawrence didn't believe to be relative. He had beliefs that survived the dialectic: belief in the body and its wants, belief in the necessity of struggle, belief in gods in a godless world, belief in nature not as something we create but as something that should be given the space to create us.

I'm aware that I would probably drive him to fits of rage. He didn't like many literary critics and he didn't like many wilful women, however many meals he ate at their supper tables. But I believe in criticism, believe that writing about writing has value, that books call out to be written about as well as read. If the novel is the 'one bright book of life', then criticism of the novel becomes a guide to how life is put together and lived. It is such an exhilarating and athletic imaginative exercise to take on big, complex, teeming books and to labour to understand the depths of thought and feeling, the formal edifice, the ethical and political drives. One hope from locking down with Lawrence is to use this time to think through what I see as the purpose of literary criticism – and whether, in the midst of today's crises, it remains a worthwhile pursuit. Certainly Lawrence himself believed that criticism had a purpose. 'The proper function of a critic is to save the tale from the artist who created it,' he wrote in *Studies in American Literature.*[13]

We often say that our lives have been shaped by books, but in my case this is not a superficial statement and the process has not been wholly sane. Books have played a crucial part in forming me as a wife, mother and lover. I can't be sure that I'd have married or divorced when I did, had children when I did or loved them as I have without the constant dialogue I've had with dead writers. I'm not sure this is a good thing – I certainly wouldn't recommend it for everyone – but I don't think I'd have survived psychically without it. This isn't to say that I see books as a force for good, or for the health and sanity that Leavis saw in Lawrence. There can be ethical gains in engaging with literature. When I picture a world without books – when I worry, for example, that my son doesn't read – I picture a world with less openness to the otherness of other minds. But what books have given me is not just a capacity for empathy but something madder and more destructive: a willingness to dwell with my own capacity for negative feeling, for doubt, sadness and anger. This in turn has given me resources for survival, making me more prepared to accept failure, whether it's the failure of a marriage, or the failure to have children when I wanted them, or the failure to find the kinds of community

I desire. Books have also shown a way to integrate the madness and destruction into a liveable life. Fight, fight, as Lawrence put it, though perhaps to accept the place of struggle isn't always to be embattled. Lawrence feels like the writer who can crystallise what reading is for me. He himself lived primarily for the written word, however much he extolled bodily over mental life. And he was always open to failure and to complication and contradiction, yet determined to keep striving, energetically engaged with all the major questions of our lives.

Lawrence wrote a late poem, 'Thought', riffing on the act of thinking itself. 'Thought, I love thought,' this begins. He despises the 'jiggling and twisting' of already existent ideas but loves the welling up of unknown life into consciousness, rather as the cells emerge onto Ursula's microscope. 'Thought is the testing of statements on the touchstone of the conscience,' he goes on:

> Thought is gazing on to the face of life, and reading what
> can be read,
> Thought is pondering over experience, and coming to a
> conclusion.
> Thought is not a trick, or an exercise, or a set of dodges,
> Thought is a man in his wholeness wholly attending.

What would it mean to read Lawrence in our wholeness, to ponder over experience alongside him? What would it mean to do this while saving the tale from the artist who created it? These are the challenges that he sets for us.

# I

# Unconscious

What if the unconscious is not in the head but in the belly button? It's a pleasurable thought experiment, but for Lawrence it was deadly serious. Deadly, because this was a matter of life and death for him. We live so much in our heads, he thought, that we are only half alive, dying a living death. He wanted us to quicken with blood-consciousness instead of making do with the more deadening mind-consciousness. He wanted our bodies to vibrate in response to the vibrations of nature. And this meant thinking with our stomachs.

For Lawrence this is where it all begins. It's in the 'round little abdomen' that the first cries of the baby are heard; this is the 'wakeful centre' from which little blind puppies and kittens utter their first cries. So it seems to me that it's here that I must begin my thinking about Lawrence. As April lingers, bringing to the countryside a sudden burst of cold that sends us back inside, with duvets piled high again at night, I try to turn my mind towards my stomach as Lawrence and I set out on our mutual reckoning.[1]

I like his writing about the stomach partly because I too have always liked stomachs. Reading Lawrence makes me pay particular attention to the stomachs in our household. My own is still taut when held upright to attention but wrinkled when I allow gravity to pull it downwards if I bend or sit. This is a stomach that has been stretched twice by new life as a seed expands to become a plum, a peach, and then a kicking, hiccuping creature with a belly of its own, eventually leaving its host stomach baggily loose when ties are severed and a new belly button is formed, pulsing with a new, unconscious life.

Lawrence didn't have much to say about the discarded stomach of the mother, because it was the infant belly button that interested him, and the nerve system – the solar plexus – beneath it. Those first cries of the baby are instinctive and unconscious. That's why Lawrence situates the unconscious in the solar plexus. He hated what he took to be Freud's notion of the unconscious, which he saw as merely an 'inverted reflection' of our conscious life, a shadow cast from the mind. Lawrence's unconscious was determinedly independent of the mind and its tricks. In his cranky but strangely moving 1921 polemic, *Psychoanalysis and the Unconscious*, he said that the mother understood both the belly button and the unconscious better than the philosopher because she had experienced the moment when the child became single.

> She knows the strange, sensitive rose of the navel: how it quivers conscious; all its pain, its want for the old connection; all its joy and chuckling exultation in sheer organic singleness and individual liberty.

There are two stomachs in this house that I have seen in that state, seen as the cord is cut and the navel clamped shut with a brightly coloured peg. One of these remains pleasurably round even now, still preceding G's almost-three-year-old body as she potters busily around the house, defining her shape even as her limbs lengthen out of toddlerhood and into childhood. The other is tauter, a muscular board of clenched energy as H gathers himself inward and then projects himself out in a burst of will, insisting on his singleness and liberty. Between these acts of onward-bound assertion, my son still has more joyful interludes of childish stomach life. 'Tickle me,' he urges P, asking for his belly to be made to chuckle again. And then, together, all four of us tickle the stomach of the cat, a soft white belly amid the thicker brown fur of her torso, when she wriggles with pleasure, showing it off. 'There's Bundikins,' I say, and she squirms in delight, as pleased with her stomach as G is with hers.

Lawrence was right, I think, that there are feelings felt most in the stomach. Nervous fear, most obviously, or ticklish delight, but also less obviously bodily feelings. Isn't love, often, a kind of mushiness of the stomach? Is that why I feel so attached to P's stomach in its waxy softness? I like resting my head there, or touching it with my mouth, as Connie does with Mellors in *Lady Chatterley's Lover*, asserting possession while enjoying its separateness. What better place could there be for the unconscious than here, between the head and the genitals, neither in the realm of thought nor of sex, yet so satisfyingly fleshy.

The focus on the stomach was a fairly late development for Lawrence. He began with a less located notion of unconscious life as blood-consciousness. 'My great religion,' he wrote in that 1913 letter, 'is a belief in the blood, the flesh, as being wiser than the intellect. We can go wrong in our minds. But what the blood feels and believes and says, is always true.' Over the next few years, he started to use the term unconscious more often and more precisely. It's worth pausing to notice how surprising it is that he should have cared so much about defining the unconscious, given that he wasn't psychoanalytically inclined, given that no other novelist of his generation put this much thought into it (we don't get fully worked-out theories of the unconscious from Woolf or Joyce). But Lawrence had such a large sense of his mission as a novelist. 'I think, do you know, I have inside me a sort of answer to the *want* of today: to the real, deep want of the English people, not to just what they fancy they want. And gradually, I shall get my hold on them,' he wrote from Italy in 1912. And that involved having a whole theory of the relationship between the mind and the body.[2]

Lawrence was preoccupied by bodies, partly because it took him so long to feel comfortable with himself as a sexual being and partly because he was so often ill. Languishing with the colds and flus that seem to have sent him to bed for weeks at a time from an early age, he saw the mind as at the mercy of the body. His novels know that bodily life can take over at any moment, and that the characters' conscious thoughts are belied by the truths known by their bodies. Miriam and Paul, looking at an enormous orange moon in *Sons and Lovers*, both half know that Paul's 'blood' is 'concentrated like a flame in his chest', that his heart beats heavily and the muscles in his arms contract. But she expects 'some religious state in him' and he is too fearful to recognise that he wants 'to crush her on to his breast to ease the ache there'.

It was this passionate awareness of desiring bodies, singing unheard beneath the clamouring mind, that sent Lawrence into theorising the unconscious. By the time that he published *Sons and Lovers* in 1913, he'd had some version of Freudian theory expounded to him by his German lover, Frieda Weekley. This version was probably unreliable and certainly sketchy, but Frieda was well-schooled in psychoanalysis by her previous lover, Otto Gross, whose love letters she took with them on their first travels together for Lawrence to read.

Lawrence was twenty-six when he encountered the heady combination of Frieda and Freud in 1912. There couldn't have been a better moment for him to hear about psychoanalysis, and there couldn't have been a better person to tell him about it. He was an ambitious young writer who people already saw in a visionary light; a self-taught intellectual who wanted to engage with the largest minds of his day but was also disposed to be contemptuous and truculent. At the same time, he was in the midst of a personal transformation, sure that with Frieda, for the first time he'd found a way for body and mind, sensuality and spirituality to come together. He willingly accepted Frieda's suggestion that his unconscious was released at last. Revising his novel, he allowed the psychoanalytic insights already there to be brought out, making Paul and Mrs Morel's relationship more explicitly Oedipal. It's a very Freudian kind of disavowal we are witnessing in that scene between Paul and Miriam. Lawrence tells us that 'the fact that he might want her as a man wants a woman had in him been suppressed into a shame'.

Yet almost immediately, all this seems to have been too much for Lawrence. He hated the psychoanalytic reviews of *Sons and Lovers*. He seems to have been intimidated by Frieda's intellectual circles and worried that Freud was right. Quickly he started to hate Freud, as he was coming during these years to hate Jesus, seeing both as rivals in their quests to redeem humanity. And so Lawrence found himself writing not just one but two gnarly, argumentative books about the unconscious. He published *Psychoanalysis and the Unconscious* in 1921 and then, when it didn't seem to have any effect in dethroning the Freudian unconscious as the prevailing myth of his times, he tried again, writing up identical ideas (with new cosmological flourishes) in *Fantasia of the Unconscious* the following year. 'I may as well say straight off that I stick to the solar plexus,' he wrote in the foreword, advising 'the generality of critics to throw it in the wastepaper basket without much ado.' These were the great years of high modernism: Eliot was writing *The Waste Land* and Joyce was writing *Ulysses*. Yet Lawrence chose to write not one but two books about the unconscious, picking a one-sided fight with the Freudian unconscious, which he denigrated as 'truly a negative quantity and an unpleasant menagerie' of sexual sordidness.

Intellectually, Lawrence and Freud had more in common than Lawrence would ever admit. They were both committed to diving inwards, far into the psyche, as a first step in solving the problems of humanity. They both saw the mother-baby-breast trio as a vision of human plenitude. But Freud was signed up to rationality and to science, even if his case studies had as many speculative leaps as Lawrence's essays, and quite a lot more room for doubt. Lawrence, who hadn't read the case studies, doubled down on Freud's scientific reasonableness in his characterisation of him, contrasting it with his own pugnacious and vigorous dashes into determinedly unmapped territory. Lawrence had rejected materialism after he'd rejected religion; he hated scientists who left the more mystical elements out of their accounts of human life and he misleadingly turned Freud into a symbol for them. Lawrence wasn't even trying to get psychoanalysis right; instead he was propounding his own very distinctive, intellectually volatile theory on the back of an argument with the argot of the day.

Although Lawrence hadn't read Freud himself, he'd read other thinkers of his times more receptively. He developed his floridly elaborate theory of the nervous system by amalgamating the ideas of contemporary neurologists and theosophers (occultist philosophers who made much of the Hindu chakras). We can hear the French philosopher Henri Bergson, with his idea of *élan vital*, in the background too, offering a model of a flow of consciousness that streams through the body, rather like blood. Lawrence's notion of blood-consciousness continued – 'Blood-consciousness overwhelms, obliterates, and annuls mind-consciousness,' he wrote in his 1924 *Studies in Classic American Literature* – and he saw blood-consciousness as powered by the nerve centres in the stomach, which the blood in turn helped to fuel.

Lawrence was creating an ethics of action, driven by the body, and he had models for thinking that courageous action could come directly out of bodily life. There was the labyrinthine, self-revising philosopher of will to power and cultural regeneration Friedrich Nietzsche, who Lawrence loved when he read him in Croydon in 1907, and who writes in *Thus Spake Zarathustra* that there is a 'mighty lord' called a self that dwells in the body behind our thoughts and feelings: 'There is more sagacity in thy body than in thy best wisdom.' Nietzsche advocated blood-knowledge and he thought, like Lawrence, that writing should emerge out of it: 'Of all that is written, I love only what a person hath written with his blood. Write with blood, and thou wilt find that blood is spirit.' And there was the shape-shifting transcendentalist poet Walt Whitman, another of Lawrence's ambivalent early loves, who in 'Song of Myself' sings his belief 'in the flesh and the appetites, / Seeing, hearing, feeling, are miracles, and each part and tag of me is a miracle', calling the scent of his armpits 'aroma finer than prayer'. For Whitman, as for Lawrence, the soul was found in the flesh, and was formed for action. Lawrence took this soul and called it the unconscious, situating it in the belly.[3]

The house we are renting in our Oxfordshire village has a grate, built in the nineteenth century. The black metal hood remains dusty, even if you try to clean it, with reddish-brown dust. This is not mining country, but when I touch the coal left in the grate, and it flakes off, black, in my hands; it is easy to imagine a miner bending here to wash in a pot of water warmed by the fire. I picture

Lawrence, born into a home with such a room, such a fire, lifting his tiny newborn mouth to cry, to suck from his mother's nipple. I am glad to be with him in this setting.

Lawrence's fight with his imaginary version of Freud isn't, in the end, all that interesting. His cranky theorising was rarely as revealing or as insightful as his novels. But I am still drawn to the largest insights in his books about the unconscious, drawn to his choice of the solar plexus as the seat of the unconscious. Lawrence designated the unconscious as an active bodily organ. It's the belly, both as the source of hunger and as a nerve system, that Lawrence sees as directing the little newborn mouth, 'blind and anticipatory', to seek the breast. How can a mindless little mouth find the breast? 'It needs no eyes nor mind. From the great first-mind of the abdomen it moves direct ... propelled to the maternal breast by vital magnetism.'

I don't think he'd have seen many newborn babies in that first moment. But he may have recalled watching his younger sister Ada, born when he was almost two, and he may have heard about babyhood from Frieda, who was the mother of three small children when Lawrence met her. Reading him brings back for me that first moment of contact that contains, in varying degrees, the strangeness of meeting a new person and the uncanny recognition of encountering someone long known in a new context. With my daughter, this was a comparatively familiar experience, so there was less of the strangeness and I remember it as a moment of astonished, exhausted relief. She was naked except for the yellow peg on her newly formed belly button, and there were midwives putting on a nappy. But I lay back, triumphant that this longed-for snuffling creature had finally emerged and that the tiny mouth knew what to do. This time round I didn't worry about the mechanics, and I knew that it was meant to hurt. After years of willing the baby into being, and a day of hard physical labour getting her out, I could relax, confident that I could now trust in the instincts of the newly encountered mouth. It's at this point for Lawrence that the baby becomes a self. She is exerting a new, voluntary power, acting wilfully for the first time, and her individuality is brought joyously into being.

Lawrence liked thinking and writing about birth, and I think he did it well. Defining and locating the unconscious was part of a search for origins for him. He wanted to get back to what came first, and it was part of his quest to release the essence of primordial experience. It's perhaps not surprising that he imagined his own birth and early days in those memorable scenes in *Sons and Lovers*. Before the birth, Mrs. Morel dreads this baby because she, like Lawrence's mother, has come to despise her miner husband, and does not therefore want another child to bind her into this marriage. Once the child is born, she does feel the tug of love, but her heart is unexpectedly heavy with fear, 'almost as if it were unhealthy, or malformed'. She feels as though 'the navel string that had connected its frail little body with hers had not been broken'. She is struck by the tenderness of the navel, that sensitive rose. Then she thrusts the baby into the sun and he lifts his little fist. This is the moment of separation, the moment when she must let him become a separate being, allowing his instincts to lead him into life.

Watching my daughter peering into the grate, I think of Lawrence as a small child, busy helping his parents or just getting in their way. There are hooks on the beams here, where food would once have hung. There's a little alcove next to the fire where implements could be stored. The Lawrence family homes in Eastwood (they'd moved twice by the time he was six, making their way up the social scale to the point where they had a rural view and a garden of their own) were neat and clean, even though Arthur Lawrence came home every day black with coal and stood bent over in front of the fire while his family washed him, allowing the sinuous miner's body described so many times by Lawrence to emerge. Mrs Morel, in *Sons and Lovers*, is forever washing the floors, and washing up, helped by her sons as well as her daughter. They liked – all of them, even the feckless father – having things in their proper place, and Lawrence continued to wash floors willingly throughout his adult life. He had a kind of party piece: making aristocratic women wash their own floors while their servants looked on in amazement. He claimed that you don't really know your own floor until you've got down on your hands and knees and washed it.

Lawrence later presented himself, as a small child, as caught between the unconscious life he found in nature and the conscious life imposed on him by humans. His mother, he complained repeatedly, loved him too much, too sentimentally and demandingly. She expected too much of him, forcing him into a consciously loving relationship, forcing him to witness and take sides in the battle of wills that constituted her marriage to his father. The Lawrence marriage is much mythologised. The dancing, drinking father, the refined, piano-playing mother. In fact, Arthur seems to have drunk no more than other miners. In later life, Lawrence blamed his mother for becoming so obsessed with the idea of Arthur as a drinker that she prevented him from living according to his nature. But as a child, he adopted her views, disliking his father, loving his mother back, eagerly competing with his older brother to be her loving companion in a way that he'd later see as stifling his living, unconscious urges. He loved her too much, and then he blamed her too much. But he was probably right that it was because of their bond that he wasn't able properly to love a woman while she was alive.

If Lawrence became obsessed with the unconscious, then it was because he saw his acceptance and understanding of the unconscious as crucial to his breakthrough as both a man and a novelist. All this emerged out of his intense, mutually shattering relationship with Jessie Chambers, who would be portrayed retributively and hurtfully as Miriam in *Sons and Lovers*. Jessie is another much-mythologised figure in Lawrence's biography, part of a poor but bookish farming family who lived across the woods at the Haggs Farm, immortalised as Willey Farm in *Sons and Lovers*. By the time he was sixteen, Lawrence walked or cycled to the Haggs Farm most days, reading literature and philosophy with Jessie, teaching her French and maths, going for long, reflective walks in the countryside. They saw each other at chapel too: together they were part of a group of friends whose social life centred on the lectures and discussions there. Jessie was beautiful, with dark eyes and dark hair that framed her face in short curls. She was in a period of rebellion against her family, who she blamed for not educating her enough, and was grateful for the education she got alongside Lawrence, who she loved with a self-sacrificing, devotional love. Some onlookers assumed this to be a sexual relationship, but in fact they didn't kiss – they didn't even hold hands. 'There was no question of it at that time,' Jessie noted, when Lawrence suggested in a 1912 version of 'Paul Morel' that Paul's fingers touched Miriam's.[4]

Lawrence tended to blame Jessie for their sexual squeamishness. I can't love you, Paul tells Miriam in the final version of *Sons and Lovers*, 'can't physically, any more than I can fly up like a skylark'. He says that it's because she is too spiritual, too pure, blessed or burdened with 'an eternal maidenhead'. A few years before writing the novel, Lawrence had talked to Jessie in the same way, telling her that it was because of her spiritual purity he couldn't marry her. 'Look, you are a nun,' he wrote to her. 'I give you what I would give a holy nun. So you must let me marry a woman I can kiss and embrace and make the mother of my children.'[5]

He did know that Jessie couldn't take all of the blame. Reading Schopenhauer's *Metaphysics of Love* aloud to Jessie in his early twenties, and encountering a description of how everyone will 'ardently desire those who are most beautiful', he confessed that he didn't in fact ardently desire anything: 'I see what is most beautiful but don't desire it.' His sexual ignorance in adolescence was astonishing. A friend remembered him being 'innocent of the facts of life when he was fourteen or fifteen years old'. Another recalled him being bewildered and then repulsed by a conversation at the Haggs Farm about taking the cows to the bull, and refusing to believe (in his early twenties) in the existence of female pubic hair. In *Sons and Lovers*, Paul tells Miriam that they have been 'too fierce in our what they call purity'. 'Don't you think that to be so much afraid and averse is a sort of dirtiness?' Paul worries here that he's put all his natural bodily feelings into a cage inside his mind, which it can only escape in perverted form.[6]

Paul goes on to find a less idealistic, more instinctive form of love with Clara, his married lover. There are some quietly beautiful, sensual scenes describing their bodies together. He is aroused by her skin, her strong pale throat, the firmness and softness of her upright body. Sex with her provides the consummation he's longed for, allowing their bodies to meet without interference from their thoughts. During one encounter, in the dark by the canal with lapwings (called peewits here) screaming in the field above them, he sees her 'dark and shining and strange, life wild at the source staring into his life, stranger to him, yet meeting him'. It's not going to last: she's a step on his journey into adulthood, and she is still working out what to make of her own marriage, but she's teaching him to live in greater proximity to his unconscious in a way that his mother, who burdened him with an ideal of motherhood and sonhood, could never do. That's why the son, always more Freudian than Lawrence liked to think of himself, has to kill off his mother, to free himself from his love for her. He poisons her, as Lawrence and his sister poisoned their own mother, wanting to relieve the pain of cancer. Then he retreats into illness and emerges, purified, ready to live from the body his mother denied him.

What Lawrence is describing here is both the birth of the artist and of the sensual man. For Lawrence, the two were vitally connected. That's what made him so ruthless with Jessie. He saw that he needed her help to make him a writer, and it was under her watch that, aged twenty, he wrote his first poems, shy at first about his ambitions, worried about what people would say – 'That I'm a fool. A collier's son a poet!' He needed her uncritical enthusiasm for his writing, needed her to know that this is what he was doing, writing away secretly at his kitchen table when his parents thought he was studying. 'I its creator, you its muse,' he wrote to her about the first draft of *The White Peacock*, and that's what she was prepared to be, far less complicatedly than any of his subsequent women. Having styled himself as DHL, he needed to become him, and he needed Jessie to help him do so. She later described how he would bring her his drafts and 'wait restlessly until we were out in the fields and he could begin to talk about his writing'. He was writing now, but his early efforts make it painfully clear that he knew his own limitations. *The White Peacock* and many of his early short stories portray young men trapped by their own detachment, unable to love or to inhabit their own bodies. Writing was a way to make sense of this predicament, and of the difficulty of being too educated to be at home in the world of the colliers (Mrs Bates, in 'Odour of Chrysanthemums' is a particularly powerful example of this) but not yet accomplished enough to find a new social sphere. He needed in turn to escape both predicaments, to find a new world to be at home in and to gain sensual experience. Encouraged by his mother, he had to leave Jessie behind.[7]

In a single year, in 1908, he rejected Christianity, separated himself from Jessie and took a teaching job in Croydon. He would look back on this as the time when he freed himself for bodily, unconscious life, and freed himself for writing. He had sex with a series of women, often keeping more than one on the go at a time, offering them his body and taking theirs, determined to learn to live sensually. It's appropriate, though painfully so, that it was Jessie who got him published in the midst of this. He had made one abortive attempt to gain recognition by sending his work to G. K. Chesterton, but then gave up, declaring, 'I don't care if I never have a line published.' He was frightened of rejection and he relied on Jessie to face it for him. He encouraged her to send his poems to Ford Madox Hueffer at the *English Review*, and was happy to accept the mantel of greatness that Hueffer immediately laid on him. Jessie knew at this stage that she had no future with the man she nonetheless continued to help on his way, even to the point of once agreeing to have sex with him. He continued to experiment with other women, briefly getting engaged to his friend Louie Burrows, and then in 1912, he found Frieda.[8]

Now he had a mission: to save the nuns from themselves, to escape the dirtiness of purity, to live according to the instincts of his blood. And he saw his centring in on unconscious life as crucial to his new triumphs as a novelist. There are far more uses of the term 'unconscious' in *Sons and Lovers* than in *The White Peacock*, and they are far more interrogatory of what unconscious life might involve. Paul is 'unconsciously' jealous of his brother William, and tells Miriam that her 'unconscious self' asks him to talk, even if consciously she wants them to be silent together. Miriam knows, 'in her heart of hearts, unconsciously', that Paul is trying to get away from her, before she allows herself to know it consciously. Paul is 'unconsciously angry' when Miriam says she is going to come to chapel with him and Clara. There is so much unconscious anger and resentment here that we might ask ourselves if Lawrence's unconscious is finding a way provocatively to act out his own resentful envy towards Freud. Other mentions of the unconscious suggest an escape from mental life. Paul and his mother are happy while he sketches and she reads, but 'both unconscious of it'. He then takes the drawing he has 'produced unconsciously' to discuss it consciously and gain knowledge of what his unconscious has achieved.

By the time that he wrote *Women in Love*, Lawrence had come to associate a psychoanalytic way of thinking about the unconscious with modernity. Part of what makes Ursula and Gudrun modern women is that they have a more Freudian unconscious life than their parents and grandparents, whose 'blood intimacy' was a form of blood-consciousness. Ursula and Gudrun say one thing and mean another; not only this – they analyse their own hidden motives and those of other people. This all becomes explicit in the long, psychologically complex scene in 'Excurse' where Birkin gives Ursula the rings he has bought as a kind of pledge. Ursula responds ambivalently: they are lovely, but she worries about committing herself to him, and she reveals that they are too small for her. Birkin is 'angry at the bottom of his soul'. He is responding unconsciously to her hidden thoughts, and she half knows this – that's why she breaks into anger when he says that he's going to visit Hermione (his former lover), and throws the rings in the mud. She walks off and Birkin is bathed in Lawrentian darkness: 'the terrible knot of consciousness that had persisted there like an obsession was broken'. Ursula returns with a flower, and Birkin is torn between wanting to cry and feeling bored by emotion. He feels peace at last, 'folding her quietly there on the open lane'. This is a non-consciousness that is portrayed as a relaxation of the soul: 'his soul was strong and at ease'. Gradually, Ursula and Birkin will learn to share in Lawrentian unconsciousness, their souls will commune together. But this doesn't stop them either from being motivated by unconscious impulses that are far more Freudian than anything Ursula's grandparents would feel. For Lawrence, Freud was a historically located figure, responsible for crystallising what had happened to intellectual and emotional life over the preceding decades.

It's telling that, having begun with poetry, Lawrence had gone on to write novels. He thought that more of life could be brought into the novel form, and more of life's contradictions. His need to write was a need to channel his combinations of enthusiasm and rage, and to take the raw material of his life and turn it into something richer. In the novel, with its possibilities for invention and metamorphosis and reinterpretation, he found a form where he could be deeply affirmative but also excoriating, where he could make a difference to the world while also separating himself from that world. It mattered to him to write freely. Given that he hated life to be cerebral, he hated the thought of himself as a careful compiler of words. He wanted his writing to be a kind of birdsong, written out of the stomach or the blood. In the preface to *Fantasia of the Unconscious,* he says that he has written his novels and poems out of what sounds like his unconscious: they 'come unwatched out of one's pen'. He is writing now a more conscious analysis of the insights his unconscious revealed. In favour of this interpretation, his singular prolificity could be called on to attest to unconscious inspiration being at play. Over the course of twenty years, he wrote eleven novels, nine books of stories, 900 pages of poems and eight plays. This must be more than the annual output of any other writer. He wrote by hand in frantic bursts, starting again from the beginning rather than revising. Most of his novels were written in spurts where he was drafting around 5,000 words a day. This wasn't carefully formulated, conscious composition. Arguably, his own narrative of his life is right. His instincts – what he called his unconscious – were repressed in childhood, and then let loose in adulthood, and a vast outpouring of words was the result, words that he would see as written with his body and that many readers feel they read with their bodies as well.

It is May here now. The woods are full of bluebells, the fields yellow with buttercups. The colours seem otherworldly in a landscape that was recently brown and green. It is a long time since I've spent the whole of May away from the city and it can feel too much, the shining perfection that we wake up to every day, alongside the news of people dying in their thousands in hospitals and suffering in the lockdown. I feel this especially driving along country roads, where the verges spill outwards, exploding with white cow parsley, and the trees lean out towards me in their different shades of green. Lawrence described the spring in the English countryside with such joy, such specificity, in the early novels that I've been reading here: the hawthorns blooming in *The White Peacock*, the 'new, glamorous world' of Miriam's farm in springtime in *Sons and Lovers*, where 'tiny buds on the hedges, vivid as copper-green, were opening into rosettes; and thrushes called, and blackbirds shrieked and scolded'. I forget myself, lying on the shady lawn of our house that is covered with daisies, surrounded by a cluster of trees, too many for this small garden, towering above me, giving me the feeling of being in a wood.

A friend once told me I had no unconscious. I have never quite known what she meant but I think it's that she thought I expected other people to behave too rationally. Reading about the unconscious, I have begun to feel less that I don't have one than that I don't know what or where it is. There are writings where Freud makes it sound like it has a physical location, hiding away in the brain like a conman, waiting to tell us things we don't want to hear. P, more keen on Lacan than Freud, tells me that it doesn't have a location, that we are in the realm of the unconscious whenever the symbolic – the realm of language – comes up against the real. Reading Lawrence on the unconscious is tricky because he is explaining a complex idea while demonstrating his hatred of ideas. The unconscious is necessarily obscure, whether you like it or not, and this bothered him, as it bothers me, and it doesn't help me that a disproportionate number of my closest friends have staked their lives on the unconscious, whether as psychoanalysts or psychoanalytically inclined writers, which leaves me feeling that they all know what and where it is, while I am unable to follow them. I feel exhausted by words at the moment – by the verbal demands of Lawrence, my students, my children – and I like Lawrence's suggestion that the unconscious is one place where we can escape words altogether because, for him, we have an unconscious before we speak, before we recognise ourselves in the mirror or become aware of our relationships with others. I hope that this self-forgetfulness on the lawn might count as unconsciousness for him, though I worry that I'm meant to feel more alive, more instinctive, more hungry. Am I meant to eat the garden?

Birkin does, in his way, in *Women in Love,* happy and exhausted on the wet hillside after escaping the murderous blow of Hermione. The blow, direct and wilful, with a sharp paperweight, has almost killed him, leaving him barely conscious. It's in this semiconscious state, 'moving in a sort of darkness', that he's able to feel himself a part of the nature that surrounds him and that enables the kind of more alive, hungry unconsciousness that Lawrence located in the solar plexus. Lying on the hillside, overgrown with bushes and flowers, he finds that looking isn't enough for him.

> He wanted to touch them all, to saturate himself with the touch of them all. He took off his clothes, and sat down naked among the primroses, moving his feet softly among the primroses, his legs, his knees, his arms right up to the arm-pits, lying down and letting them touch his belly, his breasts. It was such a fine, cool, subtle touch all over him, he seemed to saturate himself with their contact.

Birkin takes his bearings from Whitman here. 'I will go to the bank by the wood and become undisguised and naked,' Whitman writes in 'Song of Myself,' 'mad for it to be in contact with me.' Whitman's 'respiration and inspiration' is fed by the sniff of green leaves and dry leaves, but Birkin goes further, moving on to the fir trees and thistles, seeking a harsher, more active contact with nature.

> To lie down and roll in the sticky, cool young hyacinths, to lie on one's belly and cover one's back with handfuls of

fine wet grass, soft as a breath, soft and more delicate and more beautiful than the touch of any woman; and then to sting one's thigh against the living dark bristles of the fir-boughs; and then to feel the light whip of the hazel on one's shoulders, stinging, and then to clasp the silvery birch-trunk against one's breast, its smoothness, its hardness, its vital knots and ridges – this was good, this was all very good, very satisfying. Nothing else would do, nothing else would satisfy, except this coolness and subtlety of vegetation travelling into one's blood. How fortunate he was, that there was this lovely, subtle, responsive vegetation, waiting for him, as he waited for it; how fulfilled he was, how happy!

Lawrence's sentences are as saturated as Birkin is. It's the repetitions again. 'Them all, them all'; 'among the primroses, among the primroses'; 'to lie, to lie'; 'softly, soft, soft'. These are the sentences that divide his readers, that repel some with their excess and entice others with their sensuality. Why do I find them so satisfying? Why does no one else write like this? They are hypnotic, inviting us to drench ourselves in them as Birkin does in the foliage, or to bend as they bend, lying and rolling in the stickiness alongside him. And then, and then, and then. He makes us listen to the words as they repeat in our minds, ordinary words given poetic force by the rhythms. It's a ludicrous image, a grown man rolling naked around in the flowers, scratching himself with the bristles. But Lawrence makes it feel both ordinary and inevitable, primordial, man as he might have been, if he wasn't taken over by the tortuous perversions of mental life. Nature here seems as alive as Birkin is – he is learning to be more alive by consuming the 'living dark bristles of the fir-boughs' and by allowing the vegetation to travel into his blood. He is left fulfilled, satisfied, happy.

These are such ordinary words, usually inadequate as descriptions of ecstasy, but Lawrence gives them back their intensity. It may be wrong to see Lawrence as writing unconsciously when there is such an intense effort of craft and technical dexterity on display here. In his best writing Lawrence gives us the feeling of a first draft – it does feel as though it's written at speed – while amazing us with his technical brilliance. It's a combination he pulled off more reliably as he honed his craft – the late poems give this feeling far more than the early ones. And in a passage like this, we get a sense of how he managed it, as he evokes the rhythms of a mind at rest in his prose.

It feels convincing that Birkin is driven by his stomach here. The stomach sends us out into the world, gathers intense, active experience, and then digests what it has found. It's a machine for destroying matter, turning it into energy, pulling everything into its vortex, as Nietzsche and Whitman and Lawrence all do in their writing. It's not surprising that Lawrence's unconscious is noisy and hungry, that his characters should hunger for life and for a more living reality with such physical appetite, or that he loved writing about eating. He mocked people for being too refined in their eating, too out of touch with their unconscious. There's a pleasure for him in the messy munching of the tortoise in his poem 'Lui et Elle'. She opens her mouth suddenly, like curved scissors, 'gulping at more than she can swallow, and working / her thick, soft tongue, / And having the bread hanging over her chin'. His poem 'Figs' opens with an account of 'The proper way to eat a fig, in society', which is to split the fig in four, take the blossom with your lips and throw away the skin. The vulgar way is 'just to put your mouth to the crack, and take out the / flesh in one bite'. The irony here is surely that the proper way is if anything more suggestively sexual than the vulgar way. Opening it in four, you expose the 'glittering, rosy, moist, honied, / heavy-petalled four-petalled flower'. There's a side of Lawrence that clearly loves this. It was a poem written just after he'd had an affair in Italy that involved eating figs with a very proper woman (her name, Ros, may be recalled by the 'rosy'), and he's delighted by their erotic potential. But he wants to make the point that purity can be dirty and that there's more naturalness in the easy sensuality of the quick gobble.

Hardly anyone merely eats in a Lawrence novel; Lawrence gives us the details of how they do it. In *Sons and Lovers*, Mr Morel eats nosily and carelessly. When he's angry, and wants to punish his more refined family, he accentuates this: 'He ate his food in the most brutal manner possible, and, when he had done, pushed all the pots in a heap away from him, to lay his arms on the table.' Clara eats in a 'slow, dignified' manner, Miriam eats in a 'deliberate, constrained way, almost as if she recoiled a little from doing anything so publicly'. Mrs Morel eats in silence. They have all lost touch with their unconscious and with their devouring stomachs. Mr Morel is the closest any of them come to the baby's easy devouring or the tortoise's gulping, but he uses this as a source of cruelty.

In *Women in Love*, Gerald admires Gudrun's delicate, finickity eating (she pulls her food apart with 'fine, small motions'), while Birkin finds it irritating, seeing it, rightly, as a sign that she is repressing the hunger for life that he knows to be consuming her from within. Ursula eats more heartily – she always has. When she was a child in *The Rainbow*, her father fed her the nicest bits from his plate, 'putting them into her red, moist mouth', and made her birds out of jam on pieces of bread and butter that she ate with 'extraordinary relish'. He was glad of this because he himself was an easy eater. 'He took big mouthfuls, big bites, and ate unconsciously with the same abandon an animal gives to its food.' This is high praise from Lawrence!

I have put little morsels into the red, moist mouths of my children. Sometimes I still do with G – there is still the feeling that our bodily experience is shared, where H recoils from the notion of shared food with its pooled germs. With both of them, those early instincts for sightless touch and feeding have become less palpable, present more as muscle memory between us. If there's anyone who makes me aware of the role of the unconscious in consumption, then it's the cat, who, released into the countryside after spending her first nine months in a city flat, catches a mouse. Previously she's played with colourful, squeaking toy mice on sticks, pouncing with what feels like an excess of precision and determination, given the circumstances. Now it becomes clear that she has been a killing machine in waiting all along.

She brings the mouse inside alive and toys with it, allowing it to escape and catching it triumphantly again with soft white paws. I find the whole escapade disturbing – the quivering grey creature is so small, so fast, so afraid – and wish it were over but feel that I can't intervene in this process by which her nature is revealing itself. 'The final aim of every living thing, creature, or being is the full achievement of itself,' Lawrence wrote in his essay on Thomas Hardy, thinking about the poppy in the field with the gorgeous excess of its red colouring, the hare with its 'magical spurt of being' when it runs, and the singing of the bird in spring. Perhaps if we didn't have Lawrence here with us, the mouse would escape alive. As it is, I have to take its little intact body outside the next morning.[9]

It takes two more mice, caught on successive nights, before she realises that she can eat them. This is a modern, over-civilised cat and her unconscious has been thwarted by the unnaturalness of her life. I am in bed asleep, so P watches alone as, over the course of several hours of letting go and catching, playing eventually becomes eating, and she finds herself biting off the mouse's head. She finds that it's tasty enough to reveal that this is the point, this is why she was determined to catch her prey. Slowly, methodically, she eats her way through the rest of it. She spends the whole of the next day in luxuriant sleep.

Lawrence was so aware of food partly because he was always in danger of getting too thin. His instinct for feeding was not as animalistic as he would have liked it to be. When Lawrence characters are ill, they stop eating, and there's a sense of life dwindling as they do so, as it did for Freud's melancholic patients, who seem invariably to have lost their appetites. Paul, sick with bronchitis, eats no dinner. Constance Chatterley has been a golden, healthy girl in her youth, like Frieda. But sex-starved and idea-stuffed, she loses weight, becoming 'thin and earthy-looking' with a scraggy, yellowish neck sticking oddly out of her jumper. Looking at herself in the mirror she finds that her belly has lost the 'fresh, round gleam' it had when she was young and is now 'going slack, and a little flat, thinner, but with a slack thinness'. It's only when Mellors cooks for her that she regains her appetite. If illnesses are afflictions of the psyche for Lawrence, it's not surprising that the stomach can no longer function when people are ill. The diseased mind takes over and the body gives up.

We go every few days to watch the lambs in the fields near our house. My son and I want to feed them grass, as we once did at a children's farm. But they run away from us, more matter-of-factly than fearfully, summoned back by their mothers when we come too close. Instead we have to watch them from a distance, watch them wagging their tails as they feed, two at a time, from their mother's udder, watch them running around together, leaping higher by the week.

For Freud, the instincts in us that are most animalistic don't operate in the realm of the unconscious. He distinguished between the instinct (*Instinkt*) and the drive (*Trieb*), a constant inner pressure for the expansion or dissolution of the self, and it was only the drive that he located in the realm of the unconscious. The lambs don't have an unconscious for Freud, but for Lawrence they do; for Lawrence this delighted, wriggly feeding is an unconscious act that we can learn from. He wanted us to be more like sheep. 'Don't you see,' he wrote in a late, grumpy essay called 'Aristocracy', 'you idiot and fool, that you have *lost* the ram out of your life entirely, and it is one great connection gone, one great life-flow broken? Don't you see you are so much the emptier, mutton-stuffed and wool-wadded, but lifeless, lifeless.'[10]

Watching the lambs, I wonder why I am so determined to stand by Lawrence in his thinking about the unconscious. His arguments with Freud were often childish and ill-conceived. And there is so much to repel us in his theories of blood-consciousness, especially when he gets into comparing the different levels of unconsciousness of different races. In that 1913 letter where he said that his religion was a belief in the blood, the flesh being wiser than the intellect, he went on to say that this was why he had decided to live in Italy. 'The people are so unconscious. They only feel and want: they don't know.' He wrote about the unconsciousness of the Italian 'peasants' in the essays collected in *Twilight in Italy*. There is the elderly spinning woman, looking at Lawrence with unchanging, unthinking eyes that he sees as resembling 'two flowers that are open in pure clear unconsciousness'. There are the men attending the theatre with 'dark, soft eyes, unconscious and vulnerable', their minds not alert enough to run with their 'quick, warm senses'. There is 'Il Duro', a man godlike in his animality, who crouches with his haunches doubled together 'in a complete animal unconsciousness'.

It was blood-consciousness he had in mind here, and he thought of blood not just as a substance coursing through our veins but as a substance separating one race from another. 'His blood of one race tells him one thing, his blood of another race tells him another,' says a rather unpleasantly didactic character called Toussaint in Lawrence's Mexican novel, *The Plumed Serpent*. He's talking about mixed-race Mexicans, and Lawrence's heroine Kate challenges him, saying that 'some people believe in the mixed blood'. But there's still an acceptance that blood is inflected by race here. Once Lawrence started to think about Italians being better at blood-consciousness than the English, who's to say that he couldn't have started to think that some bloodlines were preferable to others. Years later, Bertrand Russell would write in his autobiography that Lawrence's philosophy of the blood led 'straight to Auschwitz'. But in 1915, just when Lawrence was formulating his ideas of blood-consciousness, Russell was full of praise. 'He is amazing,' he told his lover, the society hostess Lady Ottoline Morrell in 1915, 'he sees through and through one ... he sees everything and is always right.' He continued to be receptive and enthusiastic when, in December, Lawrence wrote to say that he had been reading *The Golden Bough*, James Frazer's vast 1890 tour of religion and magic around the world, and as a result was more convinced that there was 'another seat of consciousness than the brain and the nerve system: there is a blood-consciousness which exists in us independently of the ordinary mental consciousness'. With friends thinking like Russell, it's hard to see how Lawrence could have avoided getting wrong-headed. Russell's 'he is infallible' reminds us of the dangerousness of Lawrence's persuasiveness. But Lawrence didn't go down the route that Russell feared he would, so perhaps he was never going to; perhaps he knew what he was doing, even when he took his thoughts too far, pushing them beyond the palatable, beyond the liveable.[11]

On one of our trips to see the lambs, P mentions that the male lambs are the ones more likely to be eaten, while the female ones will be saved to breed. H is horrified – it bothers him particularly that it's the males. We regret telling him, though we both think that as carnivores we have to face the reality of the processes that bring the meat to our tables and that not to do so is to separate ourselves even further from the natural world. We are mutton-stuffed, we are empty, we may well have lost the rams out of our lives. I have done my time in psychoanalysis, though it hasn't helped me to know whether I do or don't have an unconscious. For Lawrence, I was wasting my time; I was allowing the mind doctors to mechanise my mind and I would do better to learn how to live from the sheep. I'm inclined to agree with him. This is why I'm such a hungry reader of Lawrence, why I'm hungry for the particular mixture of critique and affirmation and imaginative transformation that he offers.

I think that we gain from his thought experiment of situating the unconscious in the stomach. It's true that there's something fatalistic about Freud's vision of who we are: people who might commit incest, people with phobias, people whose psychic and bodily lives are constantly liable to be thwarted by repressed fears and desires. Lawrence says that we can be better. He offers the possibility for imaginative transformation, for living instinctively, for feeling ourselves closer to animals. It's compelling: to take that first cry of the baby, that first feed, as a model for our lives, rather than to see it as a lost ideal that leaves us destined to sexual disappointment. It may be partly just a semantic shift, to redefine the unconscious as a different set of mind/body intersections. But it takes us away from any notion of a talking cure, takes us into a world where language might be profitably escaped altogether.

Looking back, it can feel as hard to know what to make of Freud now as what to make of Lawrence. For many of my friends, Freud is still the great authority on mental life, but does that make us Freudians? Is his work a literary achievement or a source of therapeutic cure or a scientific account of the nature of man? I can feel nostalgic for a time when this seemed clearer, which makes it helpful to be reminded that in fact that clarity was obfuscatory and embattled, and that there were plenty of people noisily disagreeing in 1921. Indeed, Freud disagreed with himself almost as much as Lawrence did. Dialectic and contradiction are internal to his presentation as well.

Lawrence's powers of affirmation came out of his contradictions. His mind, set to work, whizzed into the dialectical mode, but there was something so generative about the act of writing for him that the will to affirm seems always to have been a part of it. He was constantly constructing scenes that work, narratives that generate conviction, and this seems to have fuelled his confidence that the world could be imaginatively transformed. He was surrounded by people bemoaning the crisis of Western civilisation – he did his share of it too. People outdid each other with ideas of where things had gone wrong. T. S. Eliot saw Lawrence as a symptom of decline, and Lawrence saw Freud as one. But somehow out of this, out of all his own negating and assailing, Lawrence found a way to affirm experience and give value to life. It's not that Lawrence believed, any more than Whitman ultimately did, that we would remake ourselves in a new, thoughtless state, in a new and perfect world. It's not that he really believed that we had ever lived like that. But it adds lustre and possibility, churned through our lives in our postlapsarian, Freudian world. It gives us the visionary intensity of the novels and it gives us the possibility of a life lived more from the body than from the mind. And on this particular early evening in a field in West Oxfordshire, it makes us aware, as we turn away rather dejectedly from the male lambs we may one day find ourselves eating, how mutton-stuffed and wool-wadded we are.

# 2

# Will

Even while sucking milk from his mother's breast, Lawrence's imaginary baby discovers his own power: 'Its own new, separate *power*.' Startled, the baby draws back and takes it in. And then he screams, the first scream of the ego. 'The scream of asserted isolation. The scream of revolt from connection, the revolt from union.' For Lawrence, this first manifestation of temper is a moment of negation. The baby pulls away from the easy, unconscious union with the mother, asserting his independence, coming into himself as a separate being. This is the beginning of will.[1]

Will is such a crucial, charged term for Lawrence. He can seem to celebrate it as he does here. But he was always telling people – especially women he felt uncomfortably indebted towards – to be less wilful. There was Ottoline Morrell, who invited him repeatedly to her house, Garsington, and did much to connect him in the world of arts and letters when he was first becoming well known. 'Why must you always use your *will* so much,' he wrote in April 1915, blaming her for the suicide attempt of a friend she had tried to help, 'why can't you let things be, without always grasping and trying to know and to dominate.' And there was Mabel Dodge, who summoned him to live with her in New Mexico, in the colony she had set up among the Indigenous Americans, and then gifted Frieda a house there. Why did she always want to force things with her will, he asked in June 1924: 'You can't just let it be. Even you apply your *will* to your affection and your flow.' It can't have escaped his notice that he so often selected wilful people – especially wilful women – as his friends. He was drawn to people who wanted to shape the world according to their vision of it. He was also aware that he was always trying to do the same. He had the grace to add, 'I'm too much like this myself' in his letter to Ottoline Morrell, and he acknowledged that Mabel Dodge would respond that he wanted to exert his will too, though he pre-emptively corrected her, saying that in fact he wanted his will 'to be a servant to the "flow"'.[2]

Critics like Kate Millett have complained that Lawrence saw wilfulness as more acceptable in men than women. I don't know how true this is in his fiction – Gerald Crich in *Women in Love* is the ultimate wilful man. Gerald sets himself against nature, mechanising the mines to increase his profits in what Lawrence characterises as a battle between 'his will and the resistant Matter of the earth'. But it was definitely true in life, and Lawrence put the wilful women he knew, rather cruelly, into his fiction. Ottoline Morrell became Hermione in *Women in Love*, who makes her deathly blow to Birkin because she hates his separateness from her when he's reading and so, driven by 'the unfailing mechanism of her will', she brings the paperweight crashing down on his head. Originally, Lawrence was collaborating with Mabel Dodge to write a novel about her life called *The Wilful Woman*, but this was abandoned after Frieda put a stop to their research sessions (the first was conducted in Mabel's bedroom with her in her dressing gown) and Dodge became the woman in 'The Woman Who Rode Away', who rides wearily away from white civilisation and finally has her modern female will knocked out of her by the Indigenous Americans, who turn her into a human sacrifice.

This is one of the aspects of Lawrence that I'm finding hardest, reading him here, where all my resources of will have been called on. I have found this house, rented out ours, hired a tutor who specialises in autism to come and help us in the mornings, found ways to get the children up and down to London to see their father. These are all acts in which I have imposed my will on other people. Six people's lives have been shaped by my will. But, against so many odds, we seem to be thriving. Would Lawrence be critical? 'Why can't you let things be,' I can hear him telling me. It's a relief when I find the women he knew arguing with him. 'Your puppets do not always dance to your pipe,' the poet H.D. told him in her autobiographical novel *Bid Me to Live*, though there were years during the First World War when she, like many of his friends, was trying to live according to his precepts. I'm glad to come upon Rachel Cusk channelling a more defiant version of Mabel Dodge in *Second Place*, where M tries to get L to understand 'that this will of mine that he so objected to had survived numerous attempts to break it, and at this point could be credited with my own survival and that of my child'.[3]

I know all along that Lawrence's sense of the will is more complicated than it can seem when he's chastising wilful women. The will isn't always negative in his novels. There are scenes where it feels close to the unconscious for him – where the will has the power to save us from the excessive mentalisation he hated. Dancing together in *The Rainbow*, Ursula and Skrebensky find that their consciousnesses melt away and 'his will and her will locked in a trance of motion, two wills locked in one motion'. There's an extraordinary scene, long before Ursula's birth, when her parents Will and Anna are falling in love. They have kissed once previously, but have become awkward and distant with one another again. One evening, they go out into the moonlit fields on her parents' farm and come upon the corn sheaves lying on the ground where the reapers have left them. The moonlight spreads against their faces in the open field; they don't want to turn back, but are too 'separate, single' to carry on walking together. Anna suggests that they should gather the sheaves, so they start to carry them, two at a time, taking it in turns to put them down. The atmosphere is horribly charged with possibility; trees seem to be waiting like heralds; Anna feels that her heart is 'like a bell ringing' and is afraid the sound will be heard. Lawrence describes it all in great detail: Anna brings her sheaves, Skrebensky brings his; we can feel the heaviness and wetness of the bundles, can feel the crackle as their bodies almost touch as they pass each other.

> They worked together, coming and going, in a rhythm, which carried their feet and their bodies in tune. She stooped,

she lifted the burden of sheaves, she turned her face to the dimness where he was, and went with her burden over the stubble. She hesitated, set down her sheaves, there was a swish and hiss of mingling oats, he was drawing near, and she must turn again. And there was the flaring moon laying bare her bosom again, making her drift and ebb like a wave.

It's excessive, in a way, clumsy in its recording of every gesture, but the rhythm of the prose brings out the rhythm of the action and the feeling that gradually they are getting drawn into the drift and ebb of a set of forces that is larger than they are. It's in this state that the aptly named Will begins to feel his will pulsing, and it's clear that there's something triumphant about this – it isn't him imposing his will on the world, it's him thrillingly feeling his power and hers, against the background of the rhythm they have created between them. 'His will drummed persistently, darkly, it drowned everything else.' It's a will to union that pulses through 'the moving to and fro in the moonlight, engrossed, the swinging in the silence, that was marked only by the splash of sheaves, and silence, and a splash of sheaves'. Eventually they meet and face each other, sheaves in hand. They kiss, and he feels all the thrill of possession and of consummation: 'All the moonlight upon her, all the darkness within her! All the night in his arms, darkness and shine, he possessed of it all!' This is far from grasping and trying to dominate. It's an act of will that feels charged with an elemental inevitability.

In *Psychoanalysis and the Unconscious*, Lawrence makes explicit that there are two kinds of will, one that he celebrates and one that he derides. We're back here in the realm of his crankier, theosophically driven pseudoscience, and it can get difficult to follow, but I think it's just about worth bearing with him. There's the kind of will we see in that first scream of the baby. This is the lower will, and he situates it at the bottom of the spine in the lumbar ganglion and sees it as a companion to the unconscious (he calls them the two 'lower centres'). He describes the baby's little back stiffening as he demonstrates his power in that first scream. Crucially, this is where selfhood begins for him. The mother matches her baby's anger with a brief surge of anger of her own, there is a flash like lightning and then the storm subsides. The mother and baby can now see each other as separate – 'perfect' – individual selves. The baby's bodily life is grounded at once in the 'warm rosy abdomen, tender with chuckling unison' and the little back, strengthening itself. He relies on the mother's will to flash back at him, just as he relies on her to respond sympathetically to his needs. His will is strengthened by hers, and in the process she helps him to become himself, driven by his spontaneous, creative will and by the blind power of the unconscious. 'The soul bursts day by day into fresh impulses, fresh desire, fresh purposes, at these our polar centres.'

I can follow him this far. I have felt the little fingers of two babies squeezing my breast, and seen two little backs held rigid in sudden rage. I remember my son's outrage when he was first presented with a bottle of milk, instead of the breast, remember my daughter flinging food to the floor when I first suggested she should move beyond milk to solids. Did I see these as moments of self-formation? I don't think so; I was too resistant to conflict, too sleep-deprived, longing for peace and for the freedom that the first stages of weaning would bring.

It's an enticing thought to me now, though, that it's through our acts of will that we become ourselves. This is what Ursula discovers at her microscope in *The Rainbow*, when she rejects the materialism of her university botany tutor, who tells her that living creatures are no different from anything else in the universe. She sees the cell moving, sees 'the gleam of its nucleus, as it slid across the plane of light'. She sees that even this cell is driven by its will. 'What was the will which nodalised them and created the one thing she saw? What was its intention? To be itself?' This is the revelation: that simply being oneself can be an expression of will, and that in being ourselves we are connected to all the other wilful selves in the universe. 'It was a consummation, a being infinite. Self was a oneness with the infinite. To be oneself was a supreme, gleaming triumph of infinity.'

It's a revelation that will hold true for all of Lawrence's characters, even as he decries the will. It's in the background of his statement to his publisher Edward Garnett in 1914 that he should not look in *The Rainbow* for 'the old stable ego of character', because Lawrence is not interested in individual psychology but in 'the inhuman will, call it physiology or like Marinetti – physiology of matter'. Lawrence's whole philosophy is in the microscope scene, and it's a philosophy he got from the vitalist theories of Schopenhauer and Nietzsche. He'd read Schopenhauer in adolescence with Jessie Chambers – his copy of 'The Metaphysics of Love' is much underlined. From him he took his sense of the individuality of the self as a manifestation of a universal, cosmic will, a sense of an opposition between will and idea (and of the opposition between sensuous apperception and intellectual knowledge) and his sense of sexual polarity as driving our will. But Schopenhauer could only take him so far, largely because Lawrence wasn't convinced by his notion that the best people are those who manage to transcend the impulses of the will through their intellects. Schopenhauer's concept of a universal will, pulsing through everything, also didn't allow for Lawrence's conviction of the need for each individual being to differentiate themselves. It seems, he wrote in his study of Thomas Hardy, 'as though one of the conditions of life is that life shall continually and progressively differentiate itself, almost as though the differentiation were a Purpose'. It seemed to him essential that the individual should have 'nothing in common with any other individual'.[4]

This can appear confusingly as though he's advocating the kind of ego-driven differentiation of personality he spoke against in the letter to Garnett. Arguably there *are* people with personalities in his novels, but I don't think that's what he meant here – he meant that we are to see individuality as a deep state, operating below the level of the ego. This is in part what he got from Nietzsche, whose *Beyond Good and Evil* he read in Croydon in 1907, and whose larger philosophy he was getting partly though his subscription to A. R. Orage's radical socialist magazine *The New Age*. As a thinker, Nietzsche was such a good model for Lawrence: he was as impulsive, as aphoristic, as Lawrence was to become, and Nietzsche gave Lawrence a model of the kind of writing that grasps the reader, making us feel personally addressed, seducing and assailing us. And, however much Lawrence mocked the idea of the 'will to power' in his novels (as when Ursula chides Mino the cat for his '*Wille zur Macht* – so base, so petty'), he took it on in his thinking, deriving from Nietzsche his belief that we are formed by a competing selection of instinctual urges; that, as Nietzsche wrote in *Beyond Good and Evil*, 'a living thing seeks above all to *discharge* its strength'. He added to the understanding of the world he got from Nietzsche his own very particular passion for nature, and his delight, walking around, in feeling that each flower or tree or bird was striving to be fully itself. His statement that the final aim of every creature is its own full achievement of selfhood, in the Thomas Hardy essay, is an argument that our will urges us ultimately towards fullness of being and not self-preservation. 'The final aim is the flower, the fluttering singing nucleus which is a bird in spring, the magical spurt of being which is a hare all explosive with fulness of self, in the moonlight.'[5]

It's telling that he was secretive about his reading of Nietzsche. He didn't let on to Jessie that he was reading him, though she started to pick up on the new language he was using. Even in his novels, there's the sense that he's mocking Nietzsche, partly in order to disguise his indebtedness to him. This new phase of his development needed to be secretive as he became more himself, more the writer he knew himself to be, all explosive with fullness of self. Lawrence and Nietzsche were both fans of Emerson's essay 'Self-Reliance' (though Lawrence chided him in his *Studies in Classic American Literature* for being too much of a moralist), where Emerson writes that 'to believe your own thought, to believe that what is true for you in your private heart is true for all men, – that is genius'. He'd found that kind of genius in Nietzsche and knew that he was going to be that kind of genius as well. He was in the process of working out what was true for him in his private heart, assuming, like Emerson (this is the sometimes monstrously egotistical side of both of them), that this would be true for all men. 'One is not only a little individual, living a little individual life,' Lawrence wrote to his friend Gordon Campbell (an Irish, philosophy-loving barrister he met through his friend

John Middleton Murry) in March 1915, 'One is in oneself the whole of mankind.' And he wanted to achieve that, as Emerson advised, alone.[6]

So what of the second kind of will, the one that Lawrence didn't like? – Hermione with her paperweight, Gerald with his machines. This is the parodic version of Nietzsche's will to power that Ursula mocks. It's an over-conscious, mental kind of will (and Nietzsche was clear that the will he described was in fact largely unconscious). In *Psychoanalysis and the Unconscious* Lawrence goes on to describe a second circuit that comes quivering into consciousness: the two upper centres, above the diaphragm. Where the lower centres are subjective and instinctive, the upper centres create what Lawrence calls 'objective consciousness' – mental activity. Initially, he doesn't think that the mother and her baby have an objective idea of each other. But the baby's hands awaken as he sucks the breast. 'The little hands and arms wave, circulate, trying to touch, to grasp, to know.' Now the positive upper centre, the cardiac plexus, is activated, and the child becomes aware of his mother as a beloved. Love comes from this upper plexus. Hence, Lawrence says, we say that we love from the heart. Small infants, he observes, are often seen to be gazing at the mother with curiosity. This is the objective realisation of the beloved.

There is a negative upper centre, too, to complement the cardiac plexus. This is the thoracic ganglion, at the back of the shoulders. At best, this is the site of curiosity and exploration. The little hands exploring the mother's breast reach out into the world, finding things out. The thoracic ganglion is at the back of the diaphragm, activated when we breathe out. In Lawrence's formulation, it's the cardiac plexus that allows us to breathe in. 'When we breathe in we aspire, we yearn towards the heaven of air and light.' Then it's the thoracic ganglion that lets us breathe out, relinquishing the air back into the world. And as we send out our breath, we explore our surroundings. The thoracic ganglion is the centre of 'the delightful desire to pick things to pieces, and the desire to put them together again, the desire to "find out," and the desire to invent'.

Things start to go wrong when the thoracic ganglion becomes a vehicle for will. The will exerted by the lower centre is lively and spontaneous: this is the child who 'joyously *smashes*' as he goes about becoming himself. But in the over-cerebral Western world, Lawrence thought that the upper centres became too prominent, making our lives too conscious and not spontaneous enough. The centre of upper sympathy becomes 'abnormally, inflamedly excited' and the child becomes exaggeratedly sensitive. At the same time, the negative upper centre becomes overactive, and the child becomes consciously wilful. This kind of 'spiritual' will involves 'the deliberate forcing of sympathy, the play upon pity and tenderness, the plaintive bullying of love'. It's a cold, obstinate will, and there's worse to come, because the real danger emerges when the brain takes charge, applying its mechanical force to the living unconscious, 'subjecting everything spontaneous to certain machine-principles called ideals or ideas'. The will assists in this, becoming an instrument of the mind. Now the mind assumes control over the bodily circuits and 'the spontaneous flux is destroyed'. Humanity deranges itself, because 'what tyranny is so hideous as that of an automatically ideal humanity?' That's why he tells us to stop being wilful, why he was bent on destroying the wills of his friends. He thought we were living too much in our heads and that our wills had become the wills of the dictatorial, bullying mind.

Over the last year, before I came here, I felt that I had come to the end of will. I told P that I felt deracinated, uprooted, and somehow this was a question of will. I felt I had lost touch with life's more organic rhythms because I was always imposing my desires upon the world. I had willed my daughter into being, determinedly continuing with IVF even after her father and I had started talking about splitting up, and then willed our home into being, resolutely driving the pushchair through the snow every day to harangue the builders into finishing the work that was going to make our new flat habitable. I had willed through the divorce, when my ex-husband seemed to stall, chasing him day after day to sign the papers. I was shaping a new life for myself and it was so exhausting that even small acts of will became suddenly unbearable. It felt like everything, from my daughter learning to eat solid food to my son learning to swim, was an act imposed by my will; nothing happened on its own.

For a while, I tried not willing anything. After we got through weaning, I stopped pressurising G to attain new skills, enjoying the fact that she was a late walker, a late talker. Even now, we have not begun potty training and she will drink water only from a baby bottle. With my son, who matches my will with his in his frequent rages, I tried a form of parenting known as containment, telling myself that the way to make him feel loved was to 'love bomb' him, allowing him everything he wanted. Then there would be no more battles and he could in turn relinquish his will, losing his stubbornness. With P, I tried not to complain when plans didn't work out as I'd wanted, tried not to push him into hospital for the operation he needed or to make him come more often than was easy to London. I was trying not to bend our weekly lives into a shape willed into being by me. Sometimes I thought, hopefully, that now I had a life that worked, I would never need to be wilful again.

When I cried in exhaustion, defeated both by my own wilfulness and by my attempts to deny the will, P told me that it was wrong to try to eliminate the will altogether. Informed by some combination of Lacan, Nietzsche and the *Bhagavad Gita*, he told me that it was all right to strive, to fulfil your nature if you're a striving person, but that life is easier if you don't expect to get what you want. It was possible to be both wilful and accepting. I found this counterintuitive, but I tried it out. There is a side of me that is very obedient and always desperate to follow advice. It might have made me a receptive friend for Lawrence. I tried to be less stubbornly set on a single course of action and more open to the world, while still allowing for my own desires.

It's because of all this that Lawrence's asseverations against will hit me in so tender a place now. I find it peculiarly satisfying, reading his doggedly eccentric theories of the lumbar ganglion and the thoracic ganglion, and clarifying my sense that there are kinds of will he can condone – that he sees as essential to selfhood.

I like in particular his description of the will in his essay 'The Reality of Peace', which he wrote and published in Cornwall in 1917, in the middle of the First World War. Peace was a pressing question, and Lawrence worried about seeking peace without casting off 'the old habitual life' that he saw as resulting in the war. The will – both collective and individual – has, he says here, been divorced from 'the impulse of the unknown'. We need to find a new kind of will, one that emanates from those unconscious, primordial impulses that he'd read about in Nietzsche. If everyone can only listen to the 'inner silence as complete as death', then, after the pain of being destroyed 'in all our old securities that we used to call peace', a new life will come. The new peace will be like a river, where people can flow upon the tide towards an end they know nothing of. Their will can be a rudder steering them, strengthening them to keep adjusting to the current. 'We must lapse upon a current that carries us like response, and extinguishes in repose our self-insistence and self-will.' They must give up the indomitable will and yield to the 'current of the invisible', while still allowing the will to be a source of strength.[7]

It may sound like this is a more passive version of the lower will than the one he went on to describe driving the baby's rage in *Psychoanalysis and the Unconscious*. But the essay ends with a long disquisition on lions and lambs. We are caught, Lawrence says, between life and death. There is the life of the 'slug-like sheep', feeding on moist, fat grass till they are 'sodden mounds of scarcely kindled grey mould' (how do these connect, I wonder, to the rams Lawrence tells us to emulate in 'Aristocracy'?). There is the blazing fire of the lion, 'the golden lion of wrath'. Strength and peace, Lawrence declares, are found in allowing ourselves to be both the sheep and the lamb. We cannot be all one or the other. When we have the courage to be both, we become 'roses of pure and lovely being'. This is an idea connected to religion for Lawrence (the lion and lamb as God the Father and God the Son) and it relates also to Nietzsche's sense of our competing inner wills. In the middle of a bloody war it had a practical urgency. Everywhere, people were asking how to avoid a war of this kind again. Lawrence thought that peace could only be attained through acknowledging that the will to destroy and the will to preserve were related parts of the self. We could allow for these impulses while also relinquishing the determination to control the world.

It can feel like Lawrence's rejection of will is a rejection of modernity. So often, his most modern characters are his most wilful. But here – in a vision that, after all, is shaped by one of the key thinkers of the modern world – he's offering a model of wilfulness that's peculiarly well-suited to the flux and constant change of modernity. There is nothing static about Nietzsche's will or Lawrence's. The modern world may indeed require a modern will, albeit one drawing on our most primordial urges. Lawrence allows us to keep striving, even as he tells us to stop being so wilful. Is this the same as P telling me to strive without expecting to get what I want? It may be, but this time I hear it more clearly, energised by Lawrence's imagery. I stop worrying about stepping back from the world and from myself. I start experimenting with the golden lion of wrath. As I do so, I realise that H needs me to shout at him sometimes after all, to match his will with mine. It is possible that in saying yes too much, I am in danger of eroding the boundaries he needs, and of preventing the self-formation that the will enables. I begin to say no and to allow myself to express anger again, with both H and P. It sometimes feels like the blazing fire that Lawrence envisaged. 'You're not in charge of me,' H shouts, when I tell him to do his schoolwork, 'you're not in charge of anything.' 'I am in charge!' I shout back, feeling like a maniac whose power-lust has been exposed. It is hard to know, in the incandescence of the moment, whether you're in the grip of your indomitable, mental will or are satisfactorily channelling a larger current. We lie on his bed together, exhausted. He complains that I say yes to my daughter all the time. It's true, but she doesn't seem to ask for very much. I realise that I am still hoping that I can avoid a battle of wills with her, hoping that we will continue to gurgle at each other out of our unconsciousnesses forever. Wearily, I wonder when our battle of wills will have to start. Meanwhile, H suggests that we should play a game called 'Hard Labour' and that he will be king. We have to snap out of this. I stop feeding on moist, fat grass and tell him that I can't take any more of this, matching his will with mine.

Lawrence has a whole long section on child rearing and education in *Fantasia of the Unconscious*, his second, even crankier book on the unconscious. This might have been rather irritating to his friends with children, not least perhaps to his wife, whose motherhood he never quite acknowledged. But he was known to be unusually good with children – friends did ask for his suggestions on how to manage difficult sons in particular – and I find that his advice makes unexpected sense to me, in this phase of parenting. Lawrence tells us that we shouldn't be afraid to show our anger. The problems come not when we're angry but when we love our children with too demandingly adult a love. Children, he thinks, need simple sensual love, but instead we offer the 'higher' emotions of gentleness, pity, charity, using our 'spiritual love-will' to stimulate the child into an excessive mental consciousness, robbing him of spontaneity. He wants us to leave our children to it, leave them to develop their feelings unconsciously, without naming them or analysing them. (Nietzsche, incidentally, was as much against introspection as Lawrence – he thought that we were mistaken to give too much credit to our thoughts, which were self-deceiving misrepresentations of our unconscious wilful impulses.) As the child develops volition in his lower plane, becoming 'self-willed, independent, and masterful', he might become destructive and defiant, determined to have his own way. Lawrence thinks that parents should supply 'the roughness, and sternness which stiffens in the child the centres of resistance'. If the child is robust enough, then he can occasionally have his bottom 'soundly spanked' by either parent. But you must do this impulsively, with strong emotion. Don't bully, don't pervert the child with ideals or with the will. Don't say 'dear' or 'darling' when you're telling him off or telling him what to do. 'Why try coaxing and logic and tricks with children?'

I find it a surprising relief to discover that kindness can be briefly discarded, that I can inhabit the conflict between us as H does. 'Don't use your angry voice,' he used to say all the time, when I thought I was using my patient voice. It turns out that my angry voice is precisely what he needs to hear. Gradually we settle into a new rhythm, in which the conflicts become briefer and less frequent. There are moments of companionable and observant chatter on our walks through the local fields. He learns the route to the lambs and takes pride in directing me. We play cards and Cluedo. It reminds me that as a child I was convinced that I could throw whatever number I wanted with the dice. There were days when it really seemed to work, and I wonder now if my over-loving mother was strengthening my mental will when she made me feel this way. When we let H win, are we making him feel that he can power the world into being? One day, he decides that he wants to let P win for once and I relax, thinking that decision-making of this kind can be a form of generosity, though of course it's another wilful plan, another refusal to surrender to the current. He is excited all day before it happens.

I am coming to the realisation that this is a life that works better for us than our previous life and this makes me uneasy because I know that more wilfulness on my part will be required if we are going to stay here. Around me, friends talk about enjoying the lockdown, while sometimes acknowledging their guilt at enjoying a time that is so grim for people less supplied with incomes and gardens than they are. What they are appreciating is, it seems, partly the absence of will, the sense that this is a situation they have to respond to passively. Yet somehow, and characteristically, I have turned this into a wilful time. I grind back up through the gears of determination, recognising that soon I will try to bring a new version of our lives into being. I tell myself that this is acceptable because I am bending to circumstance rather than creating a plan out of nowhere. The original urge to move was sudden and unplanned, so perhaps Lawrence would count it as an act driven by the lower will rather than the higher, and might even see me as submitting to 'the current of the invisible', the flow. Right now, absurdly, it matters to me what he'd have thought of me, though I half know that he would have disapproved of me too much for it to matter. I am a modern woman with a modern will; the kind he designated as a cocksure hen.

Why do I care? Lawrence was more wilful than anyone, if abrupt decision-making counts as will. He wasn't floating easily along the current when he decided to leave Nottinghamshire for his first teaching post, to leave teaching to write, to tear Frieda away from her children because he was convinced that she was the woman for him. He was almost always the one deciding for them both that it was time to move, away from Britain and back again, to Ceylon, to America, always with a grand plan for how to live, always catching other people in his plans. He created new homes with as much energy as I have created mine, only to discard them, suddenly, as I have apparently done. The impulse to elaborate homemaking and the impulse to escape were both so strong in him. Were they part of the same impulse, or two competing impulses? It is hard to know. He was a superhero, a woman says on a group I join virtually, to talk about Lawrence and illness. He willed himself to be well, to be strong, even when he had collapsing lungs, driven by an ideal of health that again has parallels in the also sickly Nietzsche. It strikes me, more slowly than it should have done, that it's because he was so determinedly wilful himself that he was able to theorise the will. It strikes me also that it was simply because he couldn't make up his mind about the will that he needed to invent two forms of will, and situate them in different parts of the body. It was his own ambivalence that he was giving rather literal form to. I find, though, that I don't particularly mind the hypocrisy of his criticising his own faults in others, though I do mind that he found conscious wilfulness particularly unappealing in women. I don't mind the peculiar form he gave to his ambivalence – after all, it takes much richer form in the novels. Anyway, I seem to have made my decision. I write to the owners to ask if we can stay in the house for another year. This is the life we have been assigned by the unexpected twist of fate that is sending everyone around us into new gyrations.

One Saturday in late May, when the children are with their father, P and I drive to Eastwood to see Lawrence's houses. They are larger than I expected; even the smallest miners' cottages are bigger than the flats of lots of my friends in London. His second house, where he lived when he was the age of my daughter, reminds me of my marital home, a brick terraced house with a porch and a garden. Once, it had a view of the countryside, but that's now been blocked by the erection of a red-brick primary school and nursery, which he'd have considered himself lucky not to attend. He thought children were over-educated as well as over-parented. He wanted schooling to be as brief and light-touch as possible.

We walk out into the fields he saw from his house, and I find that I'm underwhelmed because the countryside here is very similar to the countryside I've just left. The hills undulate gently, the fields are covered with buttercups and cow parsley, the greens are richer than feels real. I'd hoped for something stranger, more extreme. I had also hoped to see bluebells in the woods between his house and Jessie Chambers's farm – I'd had his descriptions of them ready to call to mind – but there are just a few, past their peak, and it's hard to believe there have been as many this May as there were in Lawrence's day. Instead there are profusions of dark pink flowers that grow in high bushes, flowers that don't look wild, seen individually, but must be, given their multiplicity.

I settle into the landscape, coming to enjoy its familiarity, admiring the way that he created a whole mythological world out of a tiny, ordinary section of the Nottingham countryside, out of these hawthorn bushes, these fields, this reservoir. I'm glad of the animals we encounter along the way, animals that seem more easily, casually connected to the world of Lawrence's novels than the landscape does. Just by the woods that have been planted over the remains of the colliery where Arthur Lawrence once worked, there's a small field of cows, with two dead trees in it, too small to have been around when Lawrence was here. The cows are finely coloured in shades of brown and grey, no two the same. They would be boutique cows in the Cotswolds, carefully bred, but here I can just about believe them to be accidents of nature. They have young calves, and one is feeding from a proud-looking mother. Unusually, the bull is in the field with them. P guesses that he's a bull from his face, thicker set than the cows', and then we see the giant phallus with which he's presumably fathered all the calves in the field, hanging down heavily like the overfull udders of the females. What Lawrentian cows, we say, knowing we are not the first to say this, because everything round here has been marked out for us as Lawrentian. There are acts of homage everywhere: a blue Lawrence trail running through the streets, phoenix symbols carved into the pavements, the Lawrence vet, the Lady Chatterley pub.

These are the fields where his own early battles of wills played out, with his parents, with Jessie Chambers. It was here that he felt his own upper will taking over, in response to his mother's anxious love for him. 'No child should be induced to love too much,' he wrote in *Fantasia of the Unconscious*, 'it means derangement and death at last.' He was thinking of his own childhood, and when he condemned the upper will as 'spiritual', he was thinking of the long tussle with Jessie. The Eastwood countryside is the setting for the three novels, *Sons and Lovers*, *The Rainbow* and *Women in Love*, where he found a way to give shape to the struggle between spontaneity and wilfulness. 'Setting' isn't quite the right word here. The landscape in Lawrence's novels is more than a setting: it's a crucial part of the drama. How people respond to nature matters, but perhaps even more important is the feeling that the fields, trees, flowers and lakes offer a counterbalancing force to the human will. As he put it in the essay on Hardy, nature is 'a great background, vital and vivid, which matters more than the people who move upon it'. In Lawrence's Hardy, the 'primitive, primal earth, where the instinctive life heaves up' takes the form of something like Schopenhauer's universal will. People are born, some die, but the heath persists, a 'sombre, latent power'. This isn't quite true for Lawrence. Birkin may say that it would make no difference if humanity was wiped off the face of the earth, but there's the feeling that the earth has been changed by our occasional moments of perfect selfhood, by the direct expression of human will.[8]

The name that Lawrence gives to these moments, the moments when people act in perfect accordance with their unconscious will and become their full, 'gleaming' selves as a result, is 'utterance'. It's a word that I have in my head here, thinking about Lawrence's struggles in this landscape to become himself. Utterance. It's a word he didn't use at all in *Sons and Lovers* but becomes crucial in *The Rainbow* and *Women in Love*. Utterance isn't unconscious: the early generations of women in *The Rainbow* hear the lips and mind of the world 'speaking and giving utterance'. But it's not a product of pure mental consciousness either – Ursula, as a teacher, talking to her friend Maggie about life and ideas, feels that 'her fundamental, organic knowledge had as yet to take form and rise to utterance'. It's an expression of the deepest will, and so souls can give utterance and wombs can, as Anna's does when she has her child: 'If her soul had found no utterance, her womb had.' Art can be a form of utterance. After twenty years as a draughtsman, Will Brangwen turns back to his sculptures because 'he wanted again to carve things that were utterances of himself'.

For Birkin in *Women in Love*, utterance takes human communication beyond speech. He doesn't care about the content of Gerald's words, which he knows to be foolish; instead he loves the 'brilliant warm utterance' of his friend. In the crucial conversation with Ursula where he tells her that he wants love to be a free expression of their individual wills, Birkin finds speech confusing but knows that there can be a new kind of speech: 'to know, to give utterance, was to break a way through the walls of the prison as the infant in labour strives through the walls of the womb'. It's because utterance transcends speech that Birkin thinks it may be able to transcend human life altogether and take the form of earthly utterance of the kind that Lawrence had found in Hardy. 'Let mankind pass away – time it did. The creative utterances will not cease, they will only be there. Humanity doesn't embody the utterance of the incomprehensible any more.'

Perhaps we could think of Lawrence's writing as utterance, in this sense. Often, the content of the individual words matters less than their rhythms. Think of that passage with Will and Anna and the corn.

> She stooped, she lifted the burden of sheaves, she turned her face to the dimness where he was, and went with her burden over the stubble. She hesitated, set down her sheaves, there

was a swish and hiss of mingling oats, he was drawing near, and she must turn again.

We don't need to know who is bringing which sheaf and placing it where, but Lawrence uses the actions to build up the sense of the rhythm that is carrying their bodies along together. At his best he found ways to make content and utterance work alongside each other, giving a sense of something unwilled while also finding a way to write out of a kind of Nietzschean, unconscious will. It may have been partly because of this that he had such a peculiar relationship to will. He willed his books into being – he was always writing, always trying to get his writing published, though he also resisted it – but he also genuinely felt the words arrived on the page without being consciously willed into being by him. And what he described were often acts of will: it's will that creates narrative, so he relied on his characters being capable of wilfulness.

We don't get as close to Jessie's farmhouse as we would like to – it is private land. In the fields in front of it there are horses galloping, too large and too fast for the landscape here. It is starting to rain and, with all cafés still shut because of the lockdown, we stop for takeaway teas at a grocery store and sip them on a bench next to a row of modern houses that Lawrence would have seen as signs of the ever-encroaching man-made ugliness he hated. I find a phone message saying that we can stay in our cottage for another year. It's a relief and I settle into the thought of it, wondering how I'll make it more ours, which pictures I'll bring from our old flat. There will be months of negotiations and arrangements ahead, working out how our lives will be run, but right now I feel glad most of all that we will continue to watch the seasons change alongside Lawrence, in the countryside that turns out to be very like his, and that my children will grow up with a stronger sense of these rhythms than I did.

Looking at some lambs leaping surprisingly high as we walk down the slope back to Eastwood, I say that it's the first time that I've felt the things I'm noticing day by day to be so similar to those noticed by a long-dead writer I'm living alongside. The lambs, the cows, the cow parsley, the hawthorn trees. It is peculiar how much of rural England is unchanged. It's taking us longer to walk to Eastwood than we expected and I'm aware of the drive that awaits us before dinner. I've had back problems recently, and am worried about getting stiff again. I find it remarkable that Lawrence, with all his bronchial and lung troubles, did this walk to Jessie's farm every day without making much of it. P says that his weakness was part of his strength – part of what powered him on to do more than everyone else.

Then, just as we walk down the hill that Lawrence used to look out to from his childhood bedroom window, a rainbow appears. First only half is visible, pushing its way through the clouds, then the whole arc can be seen, stretching its way right across the horizon. This is our utterance, I tell myself. We stand beneath it, framed by it, grateful to have the day given to us suddenly whole, grateful that our life together has come, over these months, to make sense. I am desperate to pee and there are no woods around, so I crouch down, exposed, on the path.

The rainbow in Lawrence's novel comes gradually into focus. There's a metaphorical one that Anna glimpses on the distant horizon. Contented after the birth of Ursula, she still has an expectant feeling, a reluctant sense that she may have further to travel. She sees 'a rainbow like an archway', a long way off, and hopes that she can trust that the Cossethay dawn and sunset are 'the feet of the rainbow that spanned the day' and that she doesn't need to travel further. Then the rainbow comes into view, in all its gleaming, flickering actuality, for Ursula in the final chapter. The sequence begins with her discovery that she's pregnant, and her decision to submit to Skrebensky in order to give herself and her child a home. Waiting to hear from him, she goes out for a walk in the autumnal rain and shelters in the woods that P and I walked through by the lake. On the way back she has the terrifying, self-defining encounter with the horses that Lawrence conceived as an encounter in which she loses her will. They follow her and block her way; she eludes them, only to feel caught by them again as they thunder upon her, their flanks crinkling, their hooves flashing bright. Her 'will alone' carries her, set against the collective will of the horses, as she manages to climb an oak tree and clamber into the next field. She collapses, 'as if unconscious upon the bed of the stream', walks home and is deliriously ill with a fever for several weeks.

Eventually she starts to feel regenerated. The horses, that giant mass of power, have taken her will from her and enabled her to throw off Skrebensky and to re-emerge like the 'naked, clean kernel' of an acorn, free of the old decaying husk. She realises that she is no longer pregnant, receives word that Skrebensky is already married, and, like a newborn, experiments with her will once more, determined to find her way to utterance, to 'find the creation of the living God, instead of the old, hard, barren form of living'. From her window, that same window from which the young Lawrence used to look out over the hills where we stood looking at our rainbow, she watches the colliers walking past, seeing them as an image of living death, their 'stiffened bodies' already enclosed in a coffin. And then she sees a rainbow forming itself, 'a band of faint iridescence colouring in faint colours a portion of the hill'. The arc bends and strengthens till it arches 'indomitable', making great architecture of light and colour and the space of heaven. She knows that 'the sordid people who crept hard-scaled and separate on the face of the world's corruption' are living still, however dead they seem, and that the rainbow is arched in their blood and will quiver to life in their spirit, issuing a new world, 'built up in a living fabric of Truth, fitting to the over-arching heaven'.

This is the rainbow as God's offering to Noah after the flood. He has made a covenant that 'the waters shall no more become a flood to destroy all flesh'. Why a rainbow? It joins together earth and sky, exposing the coherence of the world, offering the promise of a universal will, connecting things, but offering also luminousness and evanescence. For Ursula, the rainbow brings the promise of life, the promise that the world can never be destroyed. But she has moved out of the Old Testament world of her ancestors, so the rainbow brings questions about the kind of life that will be. How can real life emerge from living death? How can she find the living kernel of the modern world she is fitted for and destined to live in? This is the beginning of the second phase in her struggle to live according to her unconscious will and bring her 'supreme, gleaming' self into being.

# 3

# Sex

Choose any particular sex passage in Lawrence's novels and it is likely to read awkwardly to us, whether it's the blazing mysticism of *Women in Love* or the cunts and arses of *Lady Chatterley's Lover.* There are some wonderful kisses. There are the playful kisses that Ursula and Skrebensky exchange in their 'delicious, exciting game', where he 'gently, with his hand wrapped round with hair behind her head, gradually brought her face nearer to his, whilst she laughed breathless with challenge, and his eyes gleamed with answer, with enjoyment of the game'; the kisses that make Ursula glow, kisses she drinks and that leave her 'filled as if she had drunk strong, glowing sunshine'; those 'soft, blind' kisses that Birkin bestows on Ursula, giving her the unsettling feeling that there are 'strange moths, very soft and silent, settling on her from the darkness of her soul'.

But what, out of context, can we make of this, the description of the first time Ursula and Birkin have sex, on an early autumn night in Sherwood Forest, a few hours after the fight with the hurled rings:

He extinguished the lamps at once, and it was pure night, with shadows of trees like realities of other, nightly being. He threw a rug on to the bracken, and they sat in stillness and mindless silence. There were faint sounds from the wood, but no disturbance, no possible disturbance, the world was under a strange ban, a new mystery had supervened. They threw off their clothes, and he gathered her to him, and found her, found the pure lambent reality of her forever invisible flesh. Quenched, inhuman, his fingers upon her unrevealed nudity were the fingers of silence upon silence, the body of mysterious night upon the body of mysterious night, the night masculine and feminine, never to be seen with the eye, or known with the mind, only known as a palpable revelation of living otherness.

She had her desire of him, she touched, she received the maximum of unspeakable communication in touch, dark, subtle, positively silent, a magnificent gift and give again, a perfect acceptance and yielding, a mystery, the reality of that which can never be known, vital, sensual reality that can never be transmuted into mind content, but remains outside, living body of darkness and silence and subtlety, the mystic body of reality. She had her desire fulfilled. He had his desire fulfilled. For she was to him what he was to her, the immemorial magnificence of mystic, palpable, real otherness.

This isn't what you would expect from Lawrence if you'd followed the proceedings of the Chatterley trial. We don't hear about any particular parts of their bodies or have a sense of what they are actually doing sexually. It is all about the inner experience of bodily contact. What I like here again is the combination of the prosaic – 'they threw off their clothes' – with the transcendent. The laying out of the rug, the undressing, his gathering of her to him (the careful delicacy of gathering reminds us that this is sex that comes out of the tenderness with which they ended their fight in the afternoon), is followed by the transfiguration of their bodies in the darkness.

As in the passage with the sheaves in *The Rainbow*, it's the night itself that they are touching, along with each other – 'the body of mysterious night upon the body of mysterious night'. His fingers, as they touch her, are 'quenched, inhuman'. They have been on fire but now the flames have died down and they have lost their living, human quality, becoming part of the silent darkness that surrounds them. They are silent fingers on a silent body, confronting the 'living otherness' of his night-time lover. Within a single sentence, they pass from being ordinary, speaking and undressing people to being gathered collectively within the larger forces of the night. And the reader too, gathered in by the rhythms, contorted by the shifts within the sentence, is left in a new place alongside them.

The second paragraph hones in on desire. 'She had her desire of him.' It's a modest locution, a phrase that has meaning in common parlance, but by placing it here, Lawrence brings out its odd, billowing suggestiveness, using it to intimate that desire itself is a palpable entity that you can be given by someone else. Then the sentence becomes more sinuous as the words, simple in themselves, build up – 'touch, dark, subtle, positively silent' – culminating in that great, ungrammatical 'a magnificent gift and give again', where we see that the lovers have lost any sense of who is giving and who receiving; they are together in the 'living body of darkness and silence and subtlety'. The sentence is played out at last, phrase layered on phrase as touch layers upon touch in sex, the syntax loose and adventurous but the phrases within it tight and unassuming. And then Lawrence gives us two simple sentences, one after another, turn-taking sentences rather like the accounts of turn-taking with the sheaves in *The Rainbow*: 'She had her desire fulfilled. He had his desire fulfilled.' We hear what they have become to each other within the space of these two paragraphs: 'the immemorial magnificence of mystic, palpable, real otherness'. Palpable is a good word here; we are back to bodies that we can feel and touch. They have confronted each other's otherness – this is going to be their task for the rest of the novel – and they are confronting it foremost in bodily form.

So this is, I think, a powerful, seductive scene, emerging out of the vagueness of the darkness and the magnificence. Arguably, describing sex calls for precisely this mixture of originality and insistent unoriginality. But perhaps the pleasure of reading Lawrence on sex, the sense of feeling that you're taking part in the scene, comes not from any individual sex scene, but from the speed with which he allows his characters to spill between emotional landscapes, at one moment feeling together, at the next reaching for each other across a great distance. Ursula and Birkin, at this point, are perfectly fulfilled. This, fifty years earlier, would have been the happily-ever-after at the end of the novel. Here, though, the perfection comes from a recognition of otherness, and it is not therefore going to last; it's precisely that otherness that will continue to disturb them. A few hours earlier, she was shouting at him, telling him that 'it *stinks*, your truth and your purity. It stinks of the offal you feed on, you scavenger dog, you eater of corpses. You are foul, *foul* – and you must know it.' This new tenderness, this feeling of release, comes out of that rage, and we know that they will rage again.

Immediately afterwards, Lawrence tells us that they hide away from their knowledge of the experience. The next time we see them, they are buying a chair, which they then give away because they are frightened of domestic life. There can be no happy ever after for them because they have submitted to a life of conflict and flux in which they are at the mercy of the unconscious impulses driving their separate wills. The world into which they are marrying feels unknown. They cannot trust in the kind of marriage, the kind of domestic life, that their parents and grandparents had. They want a new kind of coupledom, which neither looks back to the past nor takes its place in the domestic life of the present. This is a modernity that has yet to be born.

I've said already that my enthusiasm for Lawrence began with his sex writing. It did for so many of us. Think of Doris Lessing, roaming across the African bush, learning about sex from *The Rainbow*, thinking that 'no one ever knew so much about women'. There was a generation of readers (men as well as women) in 1950s and 1960s Britain who got their bearings on sex from reading Lawrence at school and university. It's probably right that Lawrence's reputation should be foremost as a writer of sex. Yet all his reputations are false. The smutty pornographer, determined to pollute the literary canon by infesting it with graphic descriptions of the phallus and with four-letter words; the puritan who disapproved of promiscuity; the homosexual who was far more enthusiastic about male bodies than female bodies; the lascivious womaniser who risked everything by writing audaciously about ecstatic heterosexual sex; the impotent invalid who got through his wife's affairs by writing about the potency of men.[1]

Each of these fails to capture Lawrence as a man or a writer – all the more so because they are all partially true. The problem is partly that Lawrence's reputation was calcified by the 1960 court hearing, when the country decided it wanted to put sex itself on trial. It was inevitable that when the book was declared innocent, it was seen as a victory for sexual permissiveness and that Lawrence emerged as a warrior, fighting for honesty about sex.

But sex was so far from straightforward for Lawrence. Powering all his novels is a basic question about what sex is: is it a source of life or of death, an opportunity for the will to go into overdrive or a source of mutual self-formation? It's all of these, and even when, as for Constance Chatterley and for Ursula, sex is a source of freedom and power, it also brings defeats and insights that belie any notion of sexual liberation. If sex is an experience so powerful that it destroys us, allowing us to remake ourselves, then of course this process is going to be fraught and dangerous. And in the mix were all of Lawrence's own personal hang-ups and prejudices: his homophobia, his increasing commitment to phallus-worship, his apparent dislike of the clitoris. It was right that the feminists should tear down his reputation as a life-giving freedom fighter, but it's still worth remembering that it wasn't a reputation that he had straightforwardly sought.

Sex was caught up with will for Lawrence. In *Fantasia of the Unconscious*, Lawrence describes it (in terms taken from Schopenhauer) as a 'dynamic polarity' between two people, flowing from all four centres of consciousness. 'In the act of coition, the two seas of blood in the two individuals, rocking and surging towards contact, as near as possible, clash into a oneness,' he goes on. Afterwards, the two individuals separate, but they are not as before. 'The air is as it were new, fresh, tingling with newness.' From the upper centres, in the back and the heart, 'new impulses, new vision, new being' arise. This is sex as a culmination of Nietzschean will and as a force that makes the striving and shape-shifting of will possible.

All this was going to take the form of the agonising struggle between men and women – in which sex was just one element of the fight. That's why sex scenes are rarely pleasurable, in any straightforward way, in his novels. And I find it compelling as a vision of the world, partly because he is so good on the way that sex amplifies moods, and the gyration of moods that can surround it. One of the most remarkable things about sex, I find, is that any mood can be incorporated into it, giving a distinctive feel to that encounter, and at the same time sex itself is always mood-altering.

This was the ideal for him – a struggle between a man and a woman that drives them towards death and then back towards life. And so he disapproved, rather anxiously, of people who approached sex differently: the promiscuous, the homosexual, the wilful, the pornographic (his erotic writing wasn't, he insisted, smutty, however much he used the word 'cunt' and in however much detail he described the phallus). After a 'false coition', he goes on in *Fantasia of the Unconscious*, 'like prostitution, there is not newness but a certain disintegration'. In *Women in Love*, Gertrude and Gerald destroy each other because they impose their will through sex, and are unable to allow each other continued separateness. When they first kiss, under the bridge, Gerald's embrace is 'powerful and terrible'. Gudrun swoons and melts into him and he is 'perfected' – this has all the possibilities of perfection for Lawrence – yet she is kissing him as 'an unutterable enemy', wanting to annihilate him by possessing him, because she fears that he will annihilate her. 'She wanted to touch him and touch him and touch him, till she had him all in her hands, till she had strained him into her knowledge.' When Gerald dies in the snow at the end, it's because of the intensity of the electric sparks that have met between them. Sexual conflict can lead to death.

It's because of his belief in sex as an act of remaking enabled by the encounter with otherness that he was peculiarly disturbed by homosexuality. Lawrence is at his worst when writing about homosexuality, as he is when thinking about racial consciousness and strong leaders. What kind of man was it who, after inviting E. M. Forster to stay in 1915 and finding him wanting, complained to Bertrand Russell that Forster needed to save himself by having sex with a woman? 'Love is,' Lawrence explained, 'that I go to a woman to know myself and knowing myself to go further, to explore in to the unknown, which is a woman, venture in upon the coasts of the unknown, and open my discovery to all humanity.' It's a tortuous sentence – a kind of parody of his novelistic repetitions – but we get the idea that women are the great unknown to men. Lawrence was finding creative fulfilment with a woman and wanted everyone else to do so too, dismissing homosexual sex as masturbation. He believed at this point (though he did become more open-minded later on) that if sex was an encounter with otherness, then the genitalia had to be different as well. There is no getting round it, except to point out how strong his feelings about homosexuality were. These weren't easy prejudices: they were frightened, passionate thoughts in motion.[2]

He wrote up his ideas about sex many times over the course of his life, but perhaps the most extreme statement, the one that has most alienated his female readers, is the one in 'A Propos of *Lady Chatterley's Lover*'. Here he describes the problems of contemporary 1920s marriage, where real feeling has given way to counterfeit, and draws on the ancient religions (he was thinking most of all about the traditions in Mexico) to say that 'marriage is no marriage that is not basically and permanently phallic, and that is not linked up with the sun and the earth'. He goes back to blood-consciousness here in defining what sex is. He says that marriage is a union of two blood-consciousnesses but the problem is that the blood of the man and of the woman are 'two eternally different streams, that can never be mingled'. Luckily there's the phallus, which is 'a column of blood that fills the valley of blood of a woman'. Blood joins blood to blood. Simone de Beauvoir pointed out that because it's the phallus that enables the mingling, 'man is not only one of the terms of the couple, but also their relationship; he is their surpassing'. This is true, but luckily Lawrence didn't live out these ideas in his life or his fiction in more than a vague, metaphorical way. What he did insist on was that sex was a means of smashing up the self and forming it again alongside your lover, with some combination of mutuality and antagonism.[3]

All this was worked out alongside Frieda. I think it's worth telling their story once again because it provided the template of all his imaginative visions, however comically terrible their relationship subsequently became. In later years, it became hard to take them seriously as Wagnerian lovers, but we need to, because their first years together were fundamental in shaping his vision and because in his imagination they lived on in this incarnation, right up until his death.

So, picture a Nottingham upper-middle-class drawing room in March 1912: there would be polished dark-wood tables, spindly legged, cushioned chairs, substantial rugs – all the furniture that Birkin and Ursula reject. This is where Lawrence, aged twenty-seven, a coal miner's son, the still unknown author of two novels, met Frieda Weekley, aged thirty-three, a German aristocrat, the wife of a Nottingham professor whose evening classes Lawrence had attended ('I have got a genius in my evening class,' Ernest Weekley had reported to his wife) and who Lawrence had come to ask for advice about getting a teaching position in Germany (he wanted to escape Britain, escape the women he had failed to liberate from nun-hood, and find a new setting for self-formation).[4]

Before lunch, Lawrence and Frieda talked alone for half an hour. The conversation turned to Oedipus, and he discovered that she knew a lot about psychoanalysis; this was a woman, he felt, from another world, and he knew immediately that it was a world he needed to take on. She was a blonde German beauty, with pale skin and a regal nose, slim-waisted and full-hipped. He later described her at this point as 'full-bosomed, and full of life, gleaming with life, like a flower in the sun, and like a cat that looks round in the sunshine and finds it good'. What did she see in him? In photographs from this time he is thin, neat and energetic-looking, with his reddish-brown hair slickly flattened and with a fairly full moustache. He was an awkward, clever young man, surer of his own genius than of his physical attractiveness; a man open in needing her.[5]

The miracle of this encounter is not the overpowering sexual attraction, though it's there in Lawrence's early letters to her. It's that Frieda came along just when he needed her, just when he had finally freed himself from his dependency on his now-dead mother, and when he was recognising his own claustrophobia in a world that, however free-thinking, made, as Paul tells Miriam, dirtiness out of purity. Lawrence's achievement was both to see so clearly that he needed her and to convince her of her need for him. 'You are the most wonderful woman in all England,' he wrote to her a week later. It was a kind of command – certainly an act of will. He was courting her, while knowing that he wouldn't be taken all that seriously by the settled mother of three children, even if he knew (did he?) that she believed in free love and had recently had two affairs in the freer world of her family in Germany. And so, just that – a compliment that was also a claim. And she responded by mocking him. 'You don't know many women in England, how do you know?' Was she frightened? Did she guess what was about to happen? Within six months she would be living with him in Italy, separated from her children. They would be surviving on his precarious income and she would be shaking up everything he thought as he rewrote one of the great novels of their century.[6]

Before this, Lawrence's ideas about bodily freedom had been left out of his fiction as well as his life. His early novels believe in freely expressed sensuality but don't quite have the courage of their convictions. Cyril, the Lawrence-like narrator of *The White Peacock*, seems to be a virgin, detached from the sexual to-and-fro of his cohort, and towards the end he admits the loneliness that results. 'In my heart of hearts, I longed for someone to nestle against, someone who would come between me and the coldness and wetness of the surroundings.' Lawrence's second novel, *The Trespasser*, is about a passionate adulterous affair, modelled on a real affair he'd been told about by Helen Corke, a fellow teacher he'd had an erotic liaison with in his early twenties. There's plenty of ecstatic sex here, but we don't really see the lovers as embodied people except when they're communing with nature, as when Siegmund feels the sand 'warm to his breast, and his belly and his arms' at the seaside. And then he met Frieda, and turned the women in the novel he was writing into full, embodied women, and Paul's desire for Clara into intense sensual desire.

There were a couple of months of clandestine meetings. Although he would quickly become ruthless about making her choose between her children and him, Lawrence won her over by playing with her daughters during an early excursion, making paper boats to sail in a brook and setting them alight. She was unhappily married. As an older Englishman, an intellectual and a sportsman, Weekley had seemed enticingly exotic when she met him and swiftly got engaged to him at nineteen, partly needing to escape her parents' unhappy marriage – 'I had been reading Tennyson, and I thought Ernest was Lancelot,' she said later. But it had become immediately clear on their wedding night that this was not going to be a sexually fulfilling marriage, and she was increasingly enervated by the weekly routine in Nottingham with its laundry, shopping and bourgeois social calls, desperately in need of stimulation and sensuality.[7]

She and Lawrence seem to have gone to bed together within the first few weeks. They managed to arrange a simultaneous trip to Germany, for Frieda to visit her parents and Lawrence some cousins. They went first to Frieda's family in Metz, a neat, cathedralled garrison town, filled with soldiers, which had been passed between the Germans and the French for thousands of years. The world that Lawrence saw here was a world on the edge of war and he may have been aware that his choice of a German woman had an odd, prophetic aspect to it, given his commitment to conflict. Frieda told her free-thinking sisters and parents that he was a lover, but publicly he was meant to be a friend, so they hardly saw each other alone. He was angry and frustrated, writing away in his attic room in a 'semi-religious kind of family hotel', hating keeping their love affair a secret.

Questions came from England, and when Frieda hesitated about telling her husband, Lawrence wrote to him on her behalf, informing him that 'all women in their natures are like giantesses' who will break through everything to live. It's a shocking act, unless we think, as I more than half do, that she was allowing him to do it, wanting him to take responsibility for the ruction.

In the process, he made it less likely that she'd get custody of her children, but he didn't care – he felt he needed to live openly, and Frieda was coming to accept this. By the time that Lawrence had gone off to stay with his cousin in Waldbröl in mid-May, it was Frieda who was hurrying him, and Lawrence who was saying that this was his marriage, 'a great thing in my life – it is *my life*' and he wanted time to get used to it before they came together. It's understandable that Frieda found this irritating. He'd written to Weekley, only to abandon her to her husband's fury and go off and flirt with his adoring cousin.[8]

By the beginning of June, they were living together in Icking, in a small, olde-worlde Bavarian flat looking out over the Isar, owned by the sociologist Alfred Weber, who was Frieda's sister Else's lover. They were within reach of the Sternberger See, the huge lake where Bavarians hiked and holidayed. Lawrence sat writing on the balcony, looking out at the mountains and the river while Frieda looked on, delighted to witness the process of creation, and almost immediately the fights began. 'And because you love me / think you you do not hate me?' Lawrence asks, in a poem called 'Both Sides of the Medal', written at this time. 'Ha, since you love me / to ecstasy / it follows you hate me to ecstasy.' Frieda accused Lawrence of separating her from her children and treating her as his skivvy. There are accounts of thrown crockery and public taunts. 'You needn't think we spend all our time billing and cooing, and nibbling grapes and white sugar,' Lawrence told his publisher Edward Garnett at the end of the month. 'Oh no – the great war is waged in this little flat on the Isarthal, just as much as anywhere else. In fact, I don't think the *real* tragedy is in dying … the real tragedy is in the inner war which is waged between people who love each other.'[9]

Lawrence and Frieda both told themselves that they had met their match, and that the conflict was part of the process of mutual regeneration and transformation that he was already formulating as his life philosophy. Out of the war came knowledge and a new kind of living. 'As a matter of fact,' Lawrence told Garnett from the Tirol as they journeyed across the Alps towards Italy, 'we are fearfully fond of one another, all the more, perhaps, when it doesn't show. We want remarkably the same thing in life – sort of freedom, nakedness of intimacy, free breathing-space between us.'[10]

The walk through the Alps was a symbolic journey in search of regeneration, as it is in *Women in Love*. It was a journey through space that was also a journey further inside each other. 'Let every man find, keep on trying till he finds, the woman who can take him and whose love he can take,' Lawrence wrote home to his old Eastwood friend Sallie Hopkin (the wife of his early mentor Willie Hopkin) from Mayrhofen in the Tirol on 19 August. It's appropriate that it was on this journey that Lawrence confronted all he had taken on, in choosing a woman like Frieda, who was determined to live as she chose. They were joined in Mayrhofen by Garnett's son, Bunny, and his friend Harold Hobson, walking with them over the Pfitscherjoch pass and sleeping in a hut beyond Ginzling. One evening when Lawrence and Garnett had gone off to look for mountain flowers, Frieda and Harold Hobson made love in a hay hut. She told Lawrence about it after Hobson had gone, while walking perilously over the 2,000-metre high Jaufenpass. They lost the path and ended up on an even steeper route than they needed to be on. Then, in the darkness, as they were wearily making the final ascent, 'the night', as Lawrence reported it to Bunny Garnett, 'rolling up filthy and black from out of a Hell of a gulf below us, a wind like a razor, cold as ice', Frieda told Lawrence about sex with Hobson.[11]

As always, we can turn to his fiction to see what he made of it. He was someone who lived his life through his fiction and his fiction through his life – with the art shaping the life at least as much as the life shaped the art. Repeatedly, I find myself gravitating towards his fiction to explain what was going on in his life and then being thrown back from his fiction into his life. And according to the account Lawrence gave of this scene in his later comic novel *Mr Noon*, he forgave her, while feeling furious and resentful. At first here, Gilbert doesn't know if he feels anything at all, then he tells her that 'we do things we don't know we are doing', kissing her 'in a sudden passion of self-annihilation'. Johanna feels humiliated by his forgiveness, while he feels exalted by it. But then he begins to feel more enraged, experiencing 'a pang of hate and contempt' for her lover; his soul goes 'acid and hard'.

Looking back at them, alone in the wind on that dark night, this feels to me like the moment when Lawrence faced what his choice to spend his life with Frieda meant. In a sense, he had written her into being in his early fiction, before he met her, and that must have been part of his appeal to her as well. 'If I were a man,' says Lettie in *The White Peacock*, 'I would go out west and be free. I should love it.' He knew already that he wanted to write about a new kind of womanhood. He wasn't the only male novelist of his generation (think of the end of Joyce's *Ulysses* or of Musil's *The Man Without Qualities*) to follow Tolstoy and Flaubert in seeing that the imaginative investigation of women's lives could be the source of the novel's power. And he saw that Frieda would teach him how to do this. We can see her spirit in Clara in *Sons and Lovers* and more directly in Ursula. 'She wanted so many things,' Lawrence writes of Ursula in *The Rainbow*. 'She wanted to read great, beautiful books, and be rich with them; she wanted to see beautiful things, and have the joy of them for ever; she wanted to know big, free people; and there remained always the want she could put no name to.' By the time of *Women in Love*, Ursula believes herself to be too modern to get married. Lawrence meant it when he wrote to Sallie Hopkins from Italy that he wanted to 'do my work for women, better than the suffrage', and this is what he was doing in making Ursula and Gudrun a new kind of woman. In another letter he described 'the woman question' as '*the* problem of the day, the establishment of a new relation, or the re-adjustment of the old one, between men and women'. He knew that in taking on Frieda he was taking on a woman who'd been described by her previous lover Otto Gross (whose letters to her Frieda had made him read) as 'the woman of the future'. But at the same time, he loathed many of the modern women he met; he hated the idea of women having the vote because he hated the idea of voting altogether, wanting to do away with organised politics. And he was coming to hate promiscuity – his vision of sex was now too serious for casual encounters – and hated it most of all when Frieda was unfaithful. It seemed possible that modern women made the self-formation of sex harder, because they didn't take it seriously enough, even if they made it easier by being less prudish, and more willing to give more of themselves.[12]

Yet he forgave her. He knew that he needed her not in spite of but because of her capacity to enrage and disturb him. It was out of this openness to disturbance that he wrote Will and Anna, and Ursula and Birkin, and Constance Chatterley and Mellors. Love in these novels is the feeling of suffering another person as much as delighting in them. If Lawrence got from Nietzsche a sense that we are constantly developing and changing in response to our various impulses of will, then this brought the inevitability of conflict. For Nietzsche we are drawn into sexual relationships because we recognise the capacity of our lovers to enable our own growth and change. Inevitably, there will be failures of understanding and clashes because we are not in control of our own fluctuations of sympathy and recoil. We see this in slow motion in the early weeks of Will and Anna's marriage in *The Rainbow*.

They spend their honeymoon in their cottage, in bed all day, lost 'at the heart of eternity' while the world carries on elsewhere. She scatters his previous beliefs like an expert skittle-player but then she announces that she wants to re-enter the world. She will host a tea party. She starts to do housework, moving furniture around energetically, and it frightens him; he feels she is destroying the world they have made together in their bedroom. She tells him to go out, to leave her in peace – isn't there some job he needs to do? – but he stays at home and 'his hovering near her, wanting her to be with him, the futility of him, the way his hands hung, irritated her beyond bearing'. She turns on him with blind, destructive rage and he becomes 'a mad creature, black and electric with fury'. Fearful of rejection, he retreats into 'his own tense, black will'. She is hurt by his departure; he returns, 'beat up in flames', holding her 'in sinews of fire'. He doesn't understand what is happening but is coming to learn that these are not rhythms that can be understood cerebrally. 'Here could be only acquiescence and submission, and tremulous wonder of consummation.' I like the way that an argument about housework becomes an elemental struggle here. We could accuse Lawrence of making too much of what is, after all, a minor fracas about sweeping the floor. But what he reveals so well is that the words spoken are only the surface manifestation of deeper 'electric' undercurrents, way below speech or even conscious thought, as the lovers are buffeted by their wills, pulled between action and inaction and between intimacy and separation.

Living with Frieda, Lawrence opened himself to this kind of constant movement between joy and suffering. And he was living out his own ambivalence about female freedom at the same time as he thought through the 'woman question' in his fiction. Years later, in 1928, he would write an essay called 'Cocksure Women and Hensure Men', riffing on his dislike of modern women. The up-to-date woman, he complains here, is cocksure. 'She doesn't have a doubt or a qualm. She is the modern type.' He prefers hensure women, like the hen who marches off to lay her eggs, securing 'obstinately the nest she wants', stepping forth again 'with prancing confidence'. The problem comes when there are cocks cackling and pretending to lay eggs, and hens crowing and pretending to call the sun out of bed.[13]

He doesn't talk explicitly about his wife in this largely unpleasant but occasionally amusing essay, but surely Frieda's genius was to be both. She was at once the old-fashioned hen and the modern cock. She kept him unsure of himself, racing between visions of womanhood. It's this that gives his novels the uncertainty about modern womanhood that makes them so much more powerful and sympathetic than an essay like this one. There's a page in Lawrence's notebook where, furious after an argument, Frieda annotated a poem he'd written about his mother before he met her. 'I hate it,' she notes in the margins next to his description of his mother as 'a doorway to me'. 'Good God,' she exclaims when he portrays his mother 'blooding' him twice, 'Once with your blood at birth-time / Once with your misery.' Frieda did this to his writing and his thinking every day, and it's to his credit that he knew he needed to be unsettled, that without this he would become a mere crank, incapable of communicating with others or of laughing at himself. We have her to thank for preventing this, and she was doing this, wittingly or unwittingly, that evening on the Alps when she lay in the hay hut with Harold Hobson.[14]

Soon they were in Italy in another upstairs flat looking out over water, this time Lake Garda. They were in a village called Villa di Gargnano, a couple of miles along from Garda. Frieda wrote Garnett a letter that showed her observing her own ideas through Lawrence's prism, as she expected him to do with her. She wrote that they were '*really* happy; though we fight like blazes, we shall bring it off. Yes, my theories have sadly altered; there are two sides to human love, one that wants to be faithful, the other wants to run; my running one was uppermost, but it's going to be faithful now. I used to think I should never have enough love, now I think I have got as much as I can swallow.'[15]

I have been to their flat in Villa di Gargnano, sequestered away from the main town. I have swum in the lake where they swam, just below their building, and I have swum, too, in the Sternberger See, where the water, even on the hottest summer days, shocks you with the cold when you enter, as it does here in Oxfordshire. The day I visited their flat in Icking, and persuaded the owner to let me up to look over the balcony, it was raining, as it is in 'On the Balcony', where Lawrence describes the thunder separating them from the 'sombre mountains' where there's 'a faint, lost ribbon of a rainbow', and from the labourers in the green wheat below them. I thought of the poem as I stood there, thought of Frieda standing next to him on the balcony. 'You are near to me,' he writes, 'and your naked feet in their sandals / And through the scent of the balcony's naked timber / I distinguish the scent of your hair.'

It was July – a couple of months after my trip to see Kate Millett. I was six months pregnant with my daughter, still living with my husband while we worked out how to live apart. I had decided that I needed this trip, two weeks away in search of Lawrence, driving from Germany to Italy with an older artist whose own marriage had recently ended and who had stepped into my life, sure that what I needed was fine food and time in the sun. He was right. This was a necessary breathing space while I took stock of the end of my marriage; an interlude of the erotic life that was otherwise on hold for me for now. So there we were, me and my more flamboyantly hedonistic lover, following Lawrence and Frieda on their journey, though I was the only one who had read Lawrence. Our hire car had been upgraded to a Ford Mustang, an outrageous open-top phallus-turned-car that I didn't have the confidence to drive but told myself was good for me in its excess. I thought, vaguely, that I was being Lawrentian, I was defying convention, I was living as fully as I could.

I became irritable in Germany and more so by the time we got to Italy. I didn't like long lunches, I wanted to be left to write, though I didn't think the novel I was writing was going particularly well. I kept my irritation to myself; it didn't seem worth arguing when this wasn't going to last. I lashed out only once, about lunchtime drinking, I think, but really about a feeling of lostness within the trip, a feeling that my real life must now consist in finding the baby, who would be born three months later, a place to live. I was in the process of realising that I was neither Lawrence, with his ruthless work ethic and determined abstemiousness, nor Frieda, with her proud hedonism and wastefulness. In my marriage I had been the extravagant one but also the one who hated wasting time. Now I had become the disapproving one, less gripped by carnality than I liked to think of myself as being, happy only when I was swimming makeshift lengths of front crawl in the lake, my goggles on, liking especially the way that I could see my hands, legs and protruding belly below the surface of the clear water.

I worried, as we drove between green, empty lakes and hearty hill towns in our absurdly flashy car, that I was too cautious to live up to Lawrence's standards, that I was thinking about sex less than he would want me to be. Reading him again – I read the poems he wrote to Frieda, I read *Lady Chatterley's Lover* – didn't make me think about sex more; it made me alienated and made me want to be reading women. But I can see now that for Lawrence, my encounter with the artist, if it had any merit, would have been all about the clash of polarities – the bringing together of two very different people and the necessary sundering. I could have just seen us as acting on the impulses of inhuman will and worried less about the intricacies of our differences. I could have seen any alienation I felt within sex as an integral part of the experience. For Lawrence, sex is never satisfying as an end in itself – it's a way into enhanced selfhood. Birkin, attracted to Ursula, feels exhausted at the prospect of 'further sensual experience', but then she wears him down with her rage, making him face his own tenderness. 'This was release at last,' she feels. 'She had had lovers, she had known passion. But this was neither love nor passion. It was the daughters of men coming back to the sons of God, the strange inhuman sons of God who are in the beginning.'

Part of why Lawrence confuses and frustrates is that he offers such a narrowly patriarchal and heterosexual vision of desire in his essays and then in his fiction offers something much stranger and more diffuse. This may be why Kate Millett got so cross with him for not writing lasciviously enough about the female body in *Lady Chatterley's Lover*. He wasn't doing what he'd said he was doing! That Easter, sitting in the rain looking out onto her American lake, I had said to Kate Millett that what I liked about *Sexual Politics* was that she was in two minds about Lawrence. She loved him as well as hating him. 'Yes, I loved him,' she repeated back to me. 'You minded that he didn't love women enough,' I suggested. She laughed, and repeated it. 'He didn't love women enough.' She was clearer in the book itself. 'There is,' she writes, 'apart from the word cunt, no reference to or description of the female genitals: they are hidden, shameful and subject.' In fact I don't think they are shameful, even if they're sometimes hidden; perhaps Millett herself was frightened at that point that they might be shameful. Lawrence brings out this kind of confusion in his readers, and perhaps this was part of the problem for me as well, driving around in that phallus. I was hoping to have this heterosexual adventure affirmed by Lawrence but instead got something more complicated from him. I was too imprisoned in myself to be seduced by the full complexity of desire that we find in Lawrence.[16]

This is a male writer, a stupidly homophobic male writer, enraptured by the male body. We know that he was in life. There's his letter to Henry Savage (a reviewer of *The White Peacock* who became a friend) written not long after he left Lake Garda, where he said that he wanted to know 'why nearly every man that approaches greatness tends to homosexuality, whether he admits it or not: so that he loves the *body* of a man better than the body of a woman'. He goes on to say that he himself is kept by tradition and instinct from loving men because it results in the 'extinction of all the purposive influences', because it's with a woman that a man can be reborn, reconstructed and sent back into the world.[17]

We know that he was enraptured by the male body in his narrative persona too. This was one of the things that he used language to do, to describe the sinuous flesh of a man, in his early books and in his late books. Usually they are seen from the perspective of women. There are all the miners, black with dirt, stripteasing back to their naked flesh when they wash. Think of Alfred, whose back Louisa finds herself washing in the 1911 story 'The Daughters of the Vicar'. She finds it 'all so common, like herding' at first, but then is fascinated by the 'beautifully white and unblemished' skin and she finds that she has 'reached some goal in this beautiful, clear male body'. There are the miners who Gudrun and Ursula glimpse in the back yards of dwellings in Beldover, one 'naked down to the loins, his great trousers of moleskin slipping almost away', enveloping the daydreaming Gudrun in 'a labourer's caress', with a 'glamorous thickness of labour and maleness' surcharging the air. There's Mellors, also seen washing, his 'clumsy breeches slipping down over the pure, delicate, white loins, the bones showing a little'. Sometimes they are seen from the male perspective, as in the wrestling scene where the two men undress and Birkin surveys Gerald with his rounded limbs, his contours 'beautifully and fully moulded'. This has all the elements of a sex scene, and fulfils the criteria of good sex for Lawrence: the escape from conscious thought, the merging followed by separation. They wrestle 'swiftly, rapturously, intent and mindless at last, two essential white figures working into a tighter closer oneness of struggle, with a strange, octopus-like knotting and flashing of limbs'. They end almost unconscious, with Birkin lying prostrate on Gerald, and then they clasp each other's hands. Birkin tells Gerald that he is beautiful.

Originally, Lawrence wrote an opening chapter for *Women in Love* where Birkin's desire for Gerald was made more explicitly sexual. This was a scene showing the development of Birkin and Gerald's friendship on a mountain holiday with two other men. Here Birkin recognises that

> although he was always drawn to women, feeling more at home with a woman than with a man, yet it was for men that he felt the hot, flushing, roused attraction which a man is supposed to feel for the other sex … the male physique had a fascination for him, and for the female physique he felt only a fondness, a sort of sacred love, as for a sister.

He cut it in 1916 and I think this was the right thing to do. Without it, the novel is more open. Without it, we are plunged instantly into the world of the two women that is the imaginative heart of the book, even if it's in the male bodies that the erotic force is gathered. We're left with a Birkin who does also desire Ursula, and not only with a sacred fondness, like Paul's feelings for Miriam.[18]

I don't think Lawrence was self-censoring when he removed that chapter, or only partly. He wanted to leave it more open because it wasn't the final word on Birkin, any more than it was the final word on Lawrence. It's important not to forget that there was such clamorous desire in Lawrence's early letters to and about Frieda, expressed in some of the poems he wrote during their first year together and in *Mr Noon*, where he interrupts the light comedy for a moment of grandiose seriousness when he describes their desire. Gilbert sees Johanna lift her eyelids 'with a strange flare of invitation', a 'bright, roused' look on her face, and experiences a 'storm of desire'. 'Oh thunder-god,' the narrator apostrophises, 'who sends the white passion of pure, sensual desire upon us, breaking into the sensual rottenness of our old blood like jagged lightning … god of the dangerous bolts.' This isn't Lawrence at his best, but the desire is just about convincing enough to believe in it, though perhaps Lawrence was trying too hard to impress his readers with his own virile heterosexuality when he described his hero as having sex with Johanna three times in a quarter of an hour.

I am finding it easier, now, to respond to the shape-shifting of desire that Lawrence offers. The possibilities of desire are endless in writing and in reading. Lawrence understood this – understood that desire and its proliferations can be available to you in greater amplitude because your life contains writing and reading – and knew how to make the most of the possibilities for desire to metamorphose within the novel. It's part of what Angela Carter was getting at, describing him as a 'drag queen', celebrating his fetishistic love of stockings. Ursula desires Birkin who desires Gerald but turns this effectively (after his bout of wrestling with Gerald) into desire for Ursula. Constance Chatterley desires Mellors who desires no one because desire is dead in him, but the narrator desires Mellors too and eventually all this is turned effectively into Mellors being able to desire Constance Chatterley. When Lawrence wasn't telling us what sex was, he was so open to the strangeness and fluidity of desire. I talk about this with P, who advises me, again, to read Lacan, in search of a more fluctile sense of the phallus than Lawrence's. Lacan designates the phallus (as opposed to the penis) as a symbolic organ. In a heterosexual couple, both the man and the woman seek the elusive phallus in each other and outside the couple. Desire, by its nature unsatisfiable, is ultimately a restless search for the phallus.

Reading Lacan, reading about what he calls 'the paradoxical, deviant, erratic, eccentric, and even scandalous nature of desire', I find that this is a better description of what is happening in Lawrence's writing than his own manifestos are. In his essays, Lawrence is too determined to oppose body and mind-consciousness. In his novels and poems, he knows that you can't ever reach a point of mute materiality and that bodies are made of consciousness (of life and desire and motion in the world). His characters have living, perceptually enriched mind-bodies and body-minds, and desire floats freely, outside their bodies. No one in a couple is consistently ascendant. I like Lawrence's poem 'Wedlock', from *Look! We Have Come Through!*. There's a constant exchange here between the lovers, as both bodies are enclosed by each other. Here is the first section:

> Come, my little one, closer up against me,
> Creep right up, with your round head pushed in my breast.
>
> How I love all of you! Do you feel me wrap you
> Up with myself and my warmth, like a flame round the wick?
>
> And how I am not at all, except a flame that mounts off
>     you.
> Where I touch you, I flame into being;—but is it me, or you?
>
> That round head pushed in my chest, like a nut in its socket,
> And I the swift bracts that sheathe it: those breasts, those
>     thighs and knees,
>
> Those shoulders so warm and smooth: I feel that I
> Am a sunlight upon them, that shines them into
>     being.
>
> But how lovely to be you! Creep closer in, that I am more.
> I spread over you! How lovely, your round head, your arms,
>
> Your breasts, your knees and feet! I feel that we
> Are a bonfire of oneness, me flame flung leaping round you,
> You the core of the fire, crept into me.

Lawrence reminds us here how many ways there are for bodies to enclose each other, her head enclosed by him, like a nut in the socket, like the core of the fire creeping into him. We are far from the phallus as a bridge of blood here, entering the emptiness of the woman. His characters pass the phallus up and down. This is what happens during all the fighting as couples shift the power between them. It's why love wasn't enough for Lawrence. 'The stupid woman keeps on saying love, love, love,' he complained to his mother-in-law in 1923, 'to the devil with love! Give me strength, battle-strength, weapon-strength, fighting, strength, give me this, you woman!'[19]

I have always been too frightened of anger to live like Lawrence, relishing the smashing of plates and the taunts, riding the waves of another person's moods as they come and go. In sexual relationships, I have hated being shouted at, hated being found fault with. When men have shouted at me, I have shut my eyes, wishing it would stop. P doesn't shout, but when I first experienced his anger, I inwardly crumpled. Even moments of irritation made me run upstairs and hide in bed, as my son does sometimes if he feels he's been told off. I felt myself losing faith in all we had begun to build. Reading Lawrence, though, I have started to wonder if I am the unusual one. I have always blamed the men for initiating the conflict. But perhaps they can blame me for not meeting them in their anger, as Frieda met Lawrence. Perhaps I need to have more faith in my ability to survive confrontation in a couple; more of a sense that this is our unconscious wills living out their freedom, allowing us to be changed and rearranged.

This spring we are having light, irritable arguments about the dust in P's house or the noise of his radio or his insistence on having days when we don't go anywhere. I make my case more strongly than I would have done in the past; I even have moments of rage. He holds his ground, arguing back, and we face each other, both tetchily sure of our own right to be ourselves in the world of the other person. I ask myself if conflict is possible after all, if I have been wrong to say that arguing is a sign that you respect your sexual partner less than you respect your friends. Perhaps, in fact, we need to allow ourselves to argue with our friends as well, as children do at school. I am wondering, now, why I needed Lawrence to show me this, why it didn't occur to me before.

I have always found that conflict makes me want to have sex. This was never possible in marriage. Our arguments took us too far away from our more tender selves. He was rarely prepared even to speak until the next day. P doesn't relish argumentative sex like I do, but he's more prepared to let conflict go quickly, and move into another mood, so it's possible to have sex that still has the tension in the background. I ask myself why I like this so much. Is it just the itch of irritation, needing physical release? At its best, it feels more than that. It is harder to think of yourself as a civilised person when you argue. You let some of that go. And it's exhausting, fighting for yourself, fighting for a self that counts as a self, rolling yourself up into selfhood. Then you give up, you expand, you stop insisting on your right to work in silence or to sleep without dust, and you find a release in letting go of an idea of yourself as a person at all. There's an expansiveness in that, which can lend itself to the expansiveness of sex, where you cease to be yourself and merge with the other person, or both just accept the larger currents driving your bodies from outside. Or perhaps that's wrong. Because there are times when it feels in sex as though you are both supremely, absolutely yourselves. Those are moments when it feels that it's two complete, separate bodies merging, when the feeling of touching the rib, buttock, ear of the other person is the feeling of coming up against their absolute otherness, the absolute separation between your buttock and theirs. Lawrence understood all this. He understood that sex can be many different forms of union, from merging to agonistic struggle.

I think that this is part of why Lawrence liked writing, why I like writing: the feeling that you are both yourself and are no one. One Sunday morning I come back to my house from P's after breakfast with the cat, to have time to write before the children return in the evening. There's a heaviness in me and I decide to write in bed. Quite quickly, I fall asleep, and wake up feeling contentedly weightless. I have slept myself out of selfhood. After a week of being myself with the children and with P, I seem to need these hours where I can be no one. I write, enjoying the sensation that I am writing out of this nothingness. And then I cycle to the river and swim, alone, taking an abstract pleasure in the heat of my limbs plunging into cold water. We had sex that morning, before I left, as he emerged out of sleep. As I swim, I think that the sex was an act of unmaking that sent me back into the nothingness. If Lawrence thought, as Emerson did, that he was not just himself, he was everyone, then the obverse was true too: he was no one. We can discover this through being alone after intense togetherness.

Sex, as part of my life, is calmer than it has been for me for years. Writing to Frieda across Germany, after they had written to tell her husband that they wanted to be together, but before they were living alongside each other, Lawrence wrote that she had him all to herself, and he didn't flirt any more. 'It's a funny thing, to feel one's passion – sex desire – no longer a sort of wandering thing, but steady, and calm. I think, when one loves, one's very sex passion becomes calm, a steady sort of force, instead of a storm.' He was trying to reassure her – this was when she was impatient, and he was telling her she needed to wait. But it was true for him. After all, he only had one affair during their long marriage, in Italy for a few weeks in 1920. This feeling of steadiness worried me when I was married; resisting the calmness, I sought the eyes of other men. Now, as I argue with my ex-husband about how our life here is going to work, as I concentrate all my energy on holding together my children in their moods, as I read in the news about the people who are dying in their thousands every day, I think I have no need of storms.[20]

As we settle into monogamy, it bothers me a little to think that so many of the female writers I admire have been promiscuous throughout their lives. It's part of what I love about Doris Lessing, Martha Gellhorn, Mary McCarthy, Simone de Beauvoir; their impatience, their energy for new adventure. I could use this as a chance to stop living devotedly alongside writers from the past, but I don't. I list the others, the calmly married writers. Virginia Woolf, Elizabeth Bowen, who loved Charles Ritchie single-mindedly enough for thirty years for it to count as a marriage, George Eliot. Monogamy has been made more extreme by lockdown. Sexual fidelity is now emotional fidelity; it's hard even to have a wandering eye because we do not see people to be attracted to and the world loses its erotic colour and fades to grey.

Walking up a hill, late one hot Saturday afternoon, as the heat settles into gentle warmth, P asks me, suddenly, if I think that one day I'll leave him for a 28-year-old. I ask him where the thought came from, and he says it came from looking at my bottom while he was walking behind me. I say that perhaps I'll have an affair with a 28-year-old when I'm fifty, that I might want by then to try out sex with a younger man, but that I probably won't leave him for the new lover. I say that he mustn't feel licensed to do the same, because it would be too seedy, in an aging man. It's the kind of answer, I think afterwards, that I imagine Frieda making to Lawrence, and it's certainly how she lived, rejoicing in her own sexual freedom while fiercely guarding her husband's. But the truth is, that at the moment I am more identified with Lawrence. I like his steadiness; I like the marriedness of his lovers: Anna and Will, Ursula and Birkin, Constance Chatterley and Mellors, who he manages to make seem unusually married to each other, though they are actually wedded to other people. They seek freedom and lightness, they project themselves off, to the end of the rainbow. But they have Lawrence's calmness in love, his sense, announced to Frieda that 'I know in my heart "here's my marriage"'. If they are Frieda, then they are Frieda as he wished her to be, even as he needed her carelessness and her lightness. Lawrence marries his characters off and at the same time reminds us that marriage can itself be a great adventure, a vast imaginative terrain. His own marriage provided the emotional extremes for book after book for him; provided the homes in which he could write them, aided by the noise, the challenge, the leaping moods and the flying crockery.[21]

It is strange, in this locked-down, silent world, walking now in a valley where the hill in front of us reaches high enough to suggest there may be nothing beyond, to contemplate a life of action in the future, a life where I might go out into the world and touch the body of a new person. It's strange, also, during this lull of togetherness with P, which is so complete, in its way, that it feels as though it might go on for ever, to think about having sex with another man. But when the trees start rustling in the evening wind, they seem to speak of the future, reminding me that this peacefulness coexists with conflict, that if we suffer each other in love, then we also have the power to destroy each other, as Gudrun and Gerald do, that if sex gives us new impulses and new visions, then these are impulses that take us away, back into the storm to chase the rainbow.

# 4

# Parenthood

At last, as you stood, your white gown falling from your
    breasts,
You looked into my eyes, and said: 'But this is joy!'
I acquiesced again.
But the shadow of lying was in your eyes,
The mother in you, fierce as a murderess, glaring to England,
Yearning towards England, towards your young children,
Insisting upon your motherhood, devastating.

All spring I have been angry with Lawrence for denying Frieda's
motherhood. 'The mother in you, fierce as a murderess.' How
could he write that? He saw her as murdering their love for the
sake of her children. But why couldn't she be a mother and a
lover? Eventually, her ex-husband would stop alternating between
sentimentality and vindictiveness and shore himself up with old,
heavy British laws, preventing her from seeing the children who
until recently had earthed and centred her life. But now, while
they were still in Germany, she looked towards England because
she couldn't believe she'd be stopped from seeing them, however
publicly she lived as Lawrence's lover.

    Lawrence may have been so frustrated with her partly because
he knew they were already lost. He accepted that the law was
on Weekley's side before she did, and didn't want to put wasted
energy and humiliation into resisting the unfairness of a legal
system that tended to deprive adulterous mothers but not
adulterous fathers of custody (despite the law officially changing

in 1873 to give mothers rights over their children and to make questions of child welfare supersede questions of adultery). 'No man felt the sting of humiliation more keenly than he, or resented it more deeply and lastingly,' Lawrence writes of his alter ego Gilbert Noon. Surely, though, it wouldn't have hurt to complain more, to wail alongside her as she wanted him to. He thought that wailing was false when she had made her choice with her eyes open. But I'm not sure she had. She allowed Lawrence to write that note to Weekley because she had come to feel with and through him, and understood that he couldn't bear the secrecy any longer. I think she had confidence in Lawrence's confidence and assumed that it would be all right, that they'd find some way of making a life that included her children, even if she rejected her parents' (probably sensible) advice to separate from Weekley first without mention of Lawrence, and secure herself a new life in which Lawrence could then play a gradually less discreet part.

This poem, called 'She Looks Back', goes on to describe the joy they feel, together in their room in Bavaria with frogs leaping in a pool outside their window, and how it is stronger than the sorrow that nonetheless eclipses it, the 'white sharp brine' of sorrow, worse than tears. He has seen that sorrow, he writes, felt it in his mouth, 'Burning of powerful salt, burning, eating through / my defenceless nakedness.' He has been enveloped by the pillar of salty sorrow and has learnt to curse her motherhood. 'I have cursed motherhood because of you, / Accursed, base motherhood.' He tries to remember that 'it is also well between us', that she looks over her shoulder but never quite turns around, but he still feels inside him the curse against all mothers 'who fortify themselves in motherhood, devastating the vision'.

There's the suggestion here that motherhood itself is a false feeling, a false fortification, and that Lawrence is therefore right to scourge and curse it. One of the many ways he told himself that he'd done the right thing in separating Frieda from her children was to think that he had rescued her from a form of motherhood as corrosive as his own mother's. Frieda was the one who had told him about the Oedipus complex, as he rewrote *Sons and Lovers*. If the account of their first meeting in that oddly slight, half satirical *Mr Noon* is to be believed, she told him that 'Mothers are awful things nowadays' and that mother love is 'the most awful self-swallowing thing'. Now he wrote to his publisher in England explaining that the guiding principle for *Sons and Lovers* was to write a book about the 'tragedy of thousands of young men in England' who were selected by their mothers as lovers, '*urged into life by their reciprocal love of their mother*' and couldn't love as a result. This was how he viewed his own mother now, and he convinced himself that if Frieda were to leave him and return to Weekley, she'd become the kind of frustrated mother who lived through her children, turning them into mini-suitors, forcing an idea of love on them that suffocated their capacity for unconscious life. 'If Frieda and the children could live happily together, I should say "Go",' Lawrence wrote in December 1912 to Frieda's sister Else, who had written pleading with him to send Frieda home.

> But if she would only be sacrificing her life, I would not let her go if I could keep her. Because if she brings to the children sacrifice, that is a curse to them ... if Frieda gave up all to go and live with them, that would sap their strength because they would have to support her life as they grew up.[1]

More disturbingly, Lawrence developed the theory that children who came out of bad, unloving marriages were somehow corrupted irredeemably by their beginnings. In *Fantasia of the Unconscious*, he sees 'dissatisfied' lovers as 'perverting the miserable little creatures' they bring into the world. This is the puritan in Lawrence, believing in a kind of psychoanalytically inflected predestination, and I don't think it's a theory he consistently stood by. In many moods, his vision of the world was more complex and more life-affirming, allowing us second chances. But it must have been disturbing for Frieda to hear him saying these things while knowing that her own marriage had been sexually unsatisfactory. There may have been moments when she half believed him, and what then was she to think about her three children – twelve-year-old Monty, ten-year-old Elsa and eight-year-old Barby. Were they all, for Lawrence, irredeemably lost, perverted souls?

This bothers me partly because I find some of his theories of parenthood helpfully bracing. I have got a lot out of them this spring, learning to redefine boundaries with my son. I don't want to think that they come out of his jealousy of Frieda's mother love, his absurd sense that her sorrow made her a murderess. I am not angry with Lawrence for his ideas about sex. I can just about tolerate even his most clumsy enthusiasm for the phallus. But I am angry about his ideas of motherhood, and more particularly his refusal to honour Frieda as a mother.

Frieda had been a very involved mother before Lawrence came into the picture; though she always had a nurse to help with the children, she was more immersed in their daily lives than many women of her class. She describes in her memoirs her joy at having the three children in bed with her in the mornings, infuriating the nurse by letting them ride and tumble on her raised knees. Lawrence might not have approved of her pleasure in her children's love of her ('it touches me, as he thinks me a little god,' she wrote about Monty, describing how he ran into rooms in search of her if he hadn't seen her for a while, 'I wish it could so remain') but her love is palpable, and it's notable that she usually took her children with her on the trips she made to Germany in search of the sexual and intellectual fulfilment she couldn't find in Nottingham. This made it all the more frustrating that Weekley now denied her the children he had always explicitly left to her care (he had often not seen them for days or weeks at a time). Weekley does seem to have been a loving father. His letters to Frieda's mother about the birth of their first daughter, Elsa, can read rather touchingly if you don't read them in the light of what was to come. 'The child is, as was after all to be expected, a fine specimen,' he wrote a few days after the birth. 'Immediately on its arrival it said, "My name is Frieda Elsa Agnes, and I despise Nottingham." At least I got that impression from the long-lasting and powerful exercise of her voice ... We so much wanted a girl and it seems entirely natural to us that it is a girl.' But he would have felt nothing like Frieda's grief at their absence if they'd been with her, and he was fully aware how much they missed their mother, using this to try to blackmail her into coming back. It was becoming clear how callous he was beneath his sentimentality – rather than allow the children to be with their mother, he dispatched them to his relatives in London and only visited a couple of times a week.[2]

In her memoirs, Frieda asked herself why Lawrence was so tormented and angry about her sadness over her children. While in Icking, Frieda told her sister that she got up sometimes in the night and went out into the garden, 'because I can't bear the pain'. Yet Lawrence merely went on cursing her mother love, and fell ill himself, as though rivalrously seeking her sympathy. 'No man can understand it,' he told her when she begged him to see what motherhood meant to her. She wondered later if 'he, who had loved his mother so much felt, somewhere, it was almost impossible for a mother to leave her children'. The problem was partly his fear of being abandoned by Frieda. Weekley had turned it into a choice between Lawrence and her children, so for Lawrence to inhabit the pain of her mother love too fully would be to accept that she should leave him.[3]

When they were back in England, Frieda had to talk about her children out of Lawrence's earshot, because he got angry when she described her unhappiness. It was her lost children who formed the basis of Frieda's friendship with the modernist short-story writer Katherine Mansfield, who they met after Mansfield wrote to ask Lawrence for a story for the magazine *Rhythm* in 1913. Mansfield sympathised with Frieda and offered to help, taking secret messages to her son by waiting outside his school at the end of the day. Although Lawrence joined Frieda in one of these expeditions, he hated the subterfuge and hated the implication that he wasn't enough for her.

It seems possible that Lawrence didn't want Frieda to win custody of her children. He talked about wanting to have children with her himself, writing in May 1912 that he had never expected to have so definite a desire to have a baby and that they would 'stir ourselves to provide for it' if an infant came. I think he meant this. But if he wrote here that he believed it was 'wicked' for people who loved each other to prevent procreation, then he also believed his own, again convenient theory that children born of a loveless marriage are polluted by this. And, though he liked the idea of filling Frieda's womb with his progeny, he also liked the way they were living at present, with him earning only enough to live for a few months at a time, moving on when places became disagreeable or he had visions of a new way of life he wanted to pursue. This wouldn't be possible with Frieda's children in tow. If we believe in Lawrence's writing, then perhaps we need to believe that he was right to make decisions at every stage that would stop him needing to earn more money than he could do by writing what he wanted to write. Frieda did believe in him, and was prepared to live without the servants and large houses she'd been accustomed to, even if she couldn't accept a life without her children. I wonder if it made it easier or harder for her that Lawrence put such care, thought and tenderness into portraying children in his writing.[4]

Lawrence is so wise on children in his novels: their little bodies, their intensity of affection. *Sons and Lovers* is powered by the feeling that Paul grows up claustrophobically confined within his mother's consciousness, but there are moving scenes between them nonetheless, scenes where we feel his childish pleasure in her accomplishments. I like the one where she buys a cornflower-patterned dish at the market and comes home, delighted with her prize but anxious that she has forced the seller down to too low a price. She and Paul stand 'gloating' over the dish. 'I love cornflowers on things,' he says. Then she tells him it was only fivepence, they agree it wasn't enough, and Paul consoles her that the man wasn't forced to sell it. 'The two comforted each other from the fear of having robbed the pot man.' I love the way we feel the companionship in this, but also feel the new separateness that's emerging between them. Paul is starting to have his own views, though they are closely related to hers, to be a separate person with the ability to comfort her.

It's in *The Rainbow* where Lawrence is at his best on children. The first child we meet is Anna, who Tom encounters while he's courting her mother. Initially the child is hostile to him, anxiously jealous of her mother. 'When are we going home, mother?' she asks, demanding that Tom should leave her mother's bed. Then he shows her the chickens, and helps her overcome her wrath at the geese, who she thinks are behaving rudely. 'I live here, because Mr Brangwen's my father now,' she tells the birds, self-importantly. When Lydia gives birth to a new baby, Tom and Anna have to wait together while she screams in pain in her bedroom. Tom undresses the child and puts on her nightie while she cries in abandoned rage, a 'wet, sobbing, inarticulate noise' coming out of her stiff, unyielding body. He carries her outside to feed the cows, and the cold night air calms her. Her body shakes with a spasm, 'eddying from the bygone storm of sobbing', and then she is still as he methodically distributes the hay and the food to one cow after another. 'Will the cows go to sleep now?' she asks when he's finished. They sit quietly in the barn, listening to the snuffling and breathing of the animals. He holds her close and gradually her eyelids sink over her dark, watchful eyes. From this point the man and the girl are allies, sharing nursery rhymes and jokes and caring for the animals together.

It's the attention to detail that makes this scene so moving: the snuffling of the cows and the shakes of Anna's body. That spasm, echoing from the bygone crying, is perfectly observed, reminding us how much crying in children is a physical rather than a mental act. Anna's little body feels tenderly present. She herself then becomes a mother, and Will's relationship with their daughter has echoes of Tom's relationship with Anna, though it's especially powerful because it begins in Ursula's babyhood:

> He learned to know the little hands and feet, the strange, unseeing, golden-brown eyes, the mouth that opened only to cry, or to suck, or to show a queer, toothless laugh. He could almost understand even the dangling legs, which at first had created in him a feeling of aversion. They could kick in their queer little way, they had their own softness.

As she gets older, and as Anna becomes preoccupied with her second baby, Ursula comes to belong to Will, becoming 'the child of her father's heart'. He teaches her 'all the funny little things' and she answers him with her 'extravagant infant's laughter'. Toddling, she is a 'busy child', amusing herself easily. At the end of the day, Anna sends her across the fields to meet her father. Will, at the bottom of the hill, sees 'a tiny, tottering, windblown little mite with a dark head' running towards him down the steep hill, 'running in tiny, wild, windmill fashion, lifting her arms up and down to him' until he catches her.

How did these scenes feel for Frieda, reading them? He was writing them at a time when she hadn't seen her children for months and didn't know when she would see them again. Were they a gift, offering her an alternative world in which Lawrence tended to her children? When she read the description of Ursula's tiny, tottering body, or of Anna's desperate sobs as she cries for her mother, I can only imagine her finding it horribly painful. Lawrence knew what love between a parent and a child could be, he knew what she had cut herself off from, yet he refused to suffer with her, and felt abandoned by her when she looked towards England. Instead he gave her this, Tom's life with little Anna, the life he could have had with Frieda's children, if only they'd lived in a world where her husband was dead like Lydia's, or in the more open modern world his writing was going to bring about.

Reading these scenes must have been rather like watching Lawrence play with other people's children. Friends commented, again and again, how good he was with children; good at pottering alongside them in a childlike way. Frieda had seen it in those early encounters where he played with her children, and she'd see it repeatedly throughout their life together. Yet he wouldn't have the chance to engage with her children till they were eighteen, and instead he wrote into being these tender scenes of parental love that seem to make a lie of his theories of parental indifference.

Arguably, when it came to children, Frieda gave Lawrence a lot more than he could give her. This was a time when idealised children cavorted through the culture at large (*Peter Pan* had been published as a novel in 1911, having previously been a play) but Lawrence's major literary contemporaries weren't generally writing about childhood, though Proust, Woolf and Joyce were all experimenting with finding language to give voice to the sensory experiences of the child. Lawrence's style was calling out for children to describe. They are ordinary, they are like us, but they are also wholly distinct, and given to intensities of mood far beyond our own. For a writer who wanted to describe people in constant motion, children are ideal because they are always changing, always ready to assert a new will. Frieda seems to have shown him that children could be one of his subjects, and to make available for him his unidealised, rich perspective on them. And if we have Frieda to thank for Lawrence's portrayals of children, then surely this is all the more the case because her children were lost to her. Lawrence is compelled by the intensity of feeling – the mutual engrossment – between parents and children, and, as with the engrossment between lovers, it maps on to the intense intimacy of his address to us as readers. He is reaching out to us, lifting his arms up and down towards us as Ursula does running down to Will.

If we can hold Frieda responsible for the violent tenderness with which Lawrence portrays children in his fiction, then she was probably responsible for his madder ideas about child rearing as well. 'Oh, parents, see that your children get their dinners and clean sheets, but don't love them,' he exhorts us in his 'Litany of Exhortations' in *Fantasia of the Unconscious*; 'leave them alone, to find their own way out.' He may have needed to believe this in order to survive what he had done to Frieda. And surely the same is true of his suggestion that children are better off in their father's care.

It matters that it's through the eyes of men that we see the small Anna and the toddling Ursula. Lawrence was more open to the love of fathers than the love of mothers in his writing. Simone de Beauvoir wrote that Lawrence revered motherhood: 'mothers appear in his work as magnificent examples of real femininity; they are pure renunciation, absolute generosity, and all their human warmth is devoted to their children'. I don't think this is quite true. Beauvoir complains that motherhood is crucial to a woman's fulfilment in Lawrence's fiction. Certainly Constance

Chatterley's empty womb is partly responsible for her sorrow, and when she has sex with Mellors it's her womb that goes 'open and soft, and softly clamouring', in preparation for the baby that she's pregnant with by the end of the novel. But it's more complicated than this, because the most satisfying Lawrentian heroines, Ursula and Gudrun, don't become mothers by the end of *Women in Love*, and it may be a tribute to Lawrence's preparedness to imagine a new kind of womanhood that it's very possible to believe that they never will have babies yet will manage fully to realise themselves nonetheless. It's more complicated too, because motherhood is not in fact a straightforwardly ideal state, even for the more old-fashionedly womanly of Lawrence's women.[5]

So much selfhood is lost for Lawrence's women when they become mothers, which is seen as more dangerous both for the mother and the child than Beauvoir acknowledges. This was true even before Lawrence met Frieda. Meg in *The White Peacock* is 'secure in her high maternity', 'mistress and sole authority', ignoring and humiliating her husband George, who complains that 'Meg never found any such pleasure in me as she does in the kids.' There's a sense that George's fecklessness and drunkenness are somehow the result of Meg's pristine motherhood, and the Lawrence-like narrator, Cyril, finds that it's 'with some perplexity, some anger and bitterness' that he watches the Jessie-Chambers-inspired Emily 'moved almost to ecstasy by the baby's small, innocuous person'. He longs for a time when babies 'would be obsolete, and young, arrogant, impervious mothers might be a forgotten tradition'. After meeting Frieda, Lawrence gave these ideas more frighteningly nihilistic expression. We barely see any children in his 1922 novel *Aaron's Rod*, but hear lots about how pernicious they are from Aaron, who has abandoned his wife and children in search of selfhood. 'When a woman's got her children, by God, she's a bitch in the manger,' Aaron says to his friend Rawdon Lilly, two avatars of Lawrence in conversation together. 'You can starve while she sits on the hay.' Lilly couldn't agree more. 'Men have got to stand up to the fact that manhood is more than childhood – and then force women to admit it,' he says in one of his especially charmless and openly envious pronouncements. And something of this is felt already in *The Rainbow*. 'To Anna,' Lawrence writes, 'the baby was a complete bliss and fulfilment. Her desires sank into abeyance, her soul was in bliss over the baby.' By the time of her third baby, Anna is in a 'violent trance of motherhood, always busy, often harassed, but always contained in her trance of motherhood. She seemed to exist in her own violent fruitfulness.'

This is Beauvoir's renunciation, but it's neither untroubled nor peaceful, and it's almost as though Will has to step in to rescue both mother and baby from this helpless bond. These ideas become starker in *Fantasia of the Unconscious*, where Lawrence writes that when there is too much maternal sympathy, the child doesn't learn to resist enough. 'The father by instinct supplies the roughness, the sternness which stiffens in the child the centres of resistance and independence,' but, from this distance, can also support and nourish the child so that 'it is ultimately on the remote but powerful father-love that the infant rests, in a rest which is beyond mother-love'. What does this mean? Lawrence goes on to say that if mothers are too sympathetic, children will be too gentle, and the father must provide the rougher, cruder play they need, as well as the occasional spank. If, on the other hand, mothers are too hard and indifferent, then fathers can provide 'delicate sympathy'. The father corrects the defects of the mother and therefore becomes the parent the child grows into and is sustained by. So fathers come out better than mothers in Lawrence's account. There is obvious need in this on his part – we can feel him finding a way to assuage his guilt about the father he had reviled during his period of intense union with his mother. But however necessary it was for him as a theory, there is something unpleasantly and unacknowledgedly patriarchal about it. And there's also an element of cruelty in it, given Frieda's circumstances. Reading this, she may have felt that Lawrence was saying that her children didn't need her anyway: they were better off with the father, who could provide that nourishing rest beyond mother love. Certainly I think it's what he was telling himself about the children he had foisted, willingly or unwillingly, on Ernest Weekley.

I wonder, intermittently, if I'm being a bad feminist by caring so much about motherhood. Lawrence's carelessness about Frieda's children, his pronouncements about motherhood, don't come into the attacks on him by Kate Millett. Simone de Beauvoir, as we've seen, doesn't seem to notice the violence of Lawrence's antipathy towards mothers. None of this has presented a problem to most of his female admirers either: there's no mention of motherhood in the writing on Lawrence by Anaïs Nin, Doris Lessing or Angela Carter. For those mid-century generations of women, it wasn't the role of feminism to defend women's right to be mothers. Instead, the opposite was true. Because motherhood had been turned into a cult by men, feminism has needed to demystify it, describing maternal ambivalence as Adrienne Rich did so beautifully and suggestively in her 1976 *Of Woman Born*, as Lessing did in many of her novels.

Earlier generations of activists fighting for the rights of women were concerned with the rights of mothers. It was a woman, Caroline Norton, who was responsible for getting the first Custody of Infants Act passed in 1839; before then married men had automatic rights over their offspring. But as maternal rights became more assured and as hundreds of writers (mainly men) stepped in to urge women to devote themselves ever more fully to the care of their children, it was the ideal of motherhood that feminists found themselves needing to challenge. In recent years, I've been stimulated by Meghan Daum's 2015 collection of essays by writers choosing not to have children (*Selfish, Shallow and Self-Absorbed*) and by Sheila Heti's more ambivalent, philosophically driven *Motherhood*, a quest to assure herself that there are significant forms of creativity and love and care that don't involve raising a small human being. It seems necessary to me, as it does to most feminists, to honour the women who have never been pregnant, the women who have aborted foetuses or miscarried them, the women who have been primarily absent from the home or have left their children behind.

I came up against this writing about Doris Lessing, who left behind two small children when she left her first husband at the age of twenty-three. For several years, when I told people I was writing about Lessing, I found that I needed to explain why I empathised with her decision and didn't judge her for it. In Frieda's case, we can feel something of the same; we can feel the need to defend her for making a decision that took her away from her children because there was something else – her unhappiness living with her husband, her love for Lawrence – that seemed to her more essential. But it feels to me now that in defending Frieda's right to leave her children we are telling the wrong story. When she went to Germany with Lawrence, she did not think that she was leaving her children behind for good. So instead I want to defend her right to retain her children, and want to feel that this too can be feminist. I want to think that as feminists we can honour both a woman's right to leave her children and her right to have her children with her when she leaves her husband – which is also the children's right to their mother. A wrong was done to Frieda and to her children when the law prevented this and it's thanks to feminism that within a few decades it became normal for adulterous women to have rights over their children.

It feels to me like it's feminist anger that makes me so angry with Lawrence. It's anger that feels fuelled by larger feminist causes and that fuels a search for the structures underpinning wrongdoing or injustice. But I worry that this is simply that, rightly or wrongly, whenever I feel angry towards men for failing to recognise female suffering, my anger acquires extra force from the feeling that there are centuries of suffering women and centuries of callous men behind them.

Arguably, Lawrence was in fact a feminist himself when it came to motherhood. If he was indeed doing what he described as his bit for the cause of women, then he was doing this when he undermined the cult of motherhood. The world he was writing into was one that had for decades been dominated by childcare manuals exhorting women to love their children. 'Love is the element God designed them to move in,' wrote the otherwise rather dour Scottish Chartist Samuel Smiles in his 1838 *Physical*

*Education: Or, the Nurture and Management of Children.* The American poet Lydia Sigourney went further in her absurdly popular *Letters to Mothers*, published the same year. Here she described how the mother's gentleness and love acted on the young child's soul 'like sunshine on a rosebud'. 'What a loss, had we passed through the world without tasting the purest, most exquisite fount of love.' Lawrence had seen his mother and the other women of Nottinghamshire losing their identities to motherhood. Many mothers in Lawrence's time wanted the freedom to leave their children alone, and might have been grateful to have been told to do so by a man.[6]

Lawrence wasn't the only man of his generation to tell women to stop smothering their children with love. The American behaviourist psychologist John B. Watson warned parents of the danger lurking in the mother's kiss in his influential 1928 childcare bible *Psychological Care of Infant and Child*, describing spoiling as an infectious disease that could maim a child for life. By this point the New Zealand healthcare reformer Truby King's 1913 *Feeding and Care of Baby* had gone into many editions, convincing many mothers (including Doris Lessing) to ignore their children's demands for food and cuddles and stick to a regimented schedule in order to create the self-denying empire builders of the next generation. We can see how Lawrence's ideas came out of the same moment as King's and Watson's, though it's only Lawrence who insists on freedom, going back to something more like Rousseau's theory that children should be left to grow up in accordance with the dictates of nature (though Rousseau was keener on maternal indulgence than Lawrence was), wanting to leave children free to become themselves.

Nonetheless, it's as a feminist that I feel angry with Lawrence for suggesting that there was something false, or convenient, or unconvincingly excessive, about Frieda's sorrow. My anger with Weekley feels like feminist anger too. He used the children to punish her and failed in the process to think through their experience or needs. It makes me angry when he justifies this by saying that they will forget her, and learn to see his sister as a new mother, and that it's better for them not to have the confusion of her coming and going. And it makes me even more angry when he begs her to come home, or gets the wife of one of his close friends to write to her saying, 'the children you brought into the world can't be cast off like this', while Weekley is the one forcing her to cast them off. I hate the feeling of these men seizing control of Frieda's motherhood. It's almost as though Lawrence and Weekley collaborated in making her no longer a mother. The patriarchy over-valorises mothering, sets us impossible standards, and then takes it away from us. I don't think the feminists who have taken on Lawrence have made enough of his cruelty on these questions. A wrong was done, and it feels to me like a black hole within Frieda's marriage to Lawrence that this wasn't a cause for shared suffering, and that he wasn't prepared to fight harder to prevent it. Without this, they may not have ended up quite as jaggedly combative as they did, quite so caught up within the burlesque dance of comedy and thundering that came out of unacknowledged wounds.[7]

It can be bracing, thrilling even, feeling angry with Lawrence – it can feel part of the excitement of reading him. But it feels different when I am angry with him for the way he lived rather than the way he wrote; it feels more alienating. This leaves me wondering what I should make of Lawrence's theories of parenting and education. Can I still see so much good in them if I believe that they emerged in part from his fear of Frieda as a mother? I have been rereading that section in *Fantasia of the Unconscious* where he tells us that a sound spank is fine, but we should avoid lovingly bullying our children when we tell them off. It is two months now since I stopped lovingly pleading when I told off my son. When he asks repeatedly for something he can't have, and complains when I say no, I explain less than I used to, inhabiting my authority in this relationship as someone with the right to say no briskly. It still feels as though this is improving things, as though the shouting in the house dies down more quickly and more completely. But after the shouts comes the need for love. We cuddle his teddies, I make them talk, telling him that they feel better. We take them down to my bed and huddle under the duvet together to watch TV. I am far from obeying Lawrence's polemical demand to leave your children alone. 'Oh, parents,' Lawrence pleads, 'see that your children get their dinners and clean sheets, but don't love them ... don't even hate them or dislike them.'

I'm not going to follow Lawrence this far, so I could reject him as my unwitting childcare advisor altogether. But, as always, the polemic is a play between extremes. This is the same book where Lawrence describes the baby's small fingers meeting the mother in wondering ecstasy: 'bliss, bliss, bliss, it meets the wonder in mid-air and in mid-space it finds the loveliness of the mother's face'. Lawrence, in his essays as in his novels, requires a new way of reading, one where we can know that there are two strong opinions in the air simultaneously exerting a powerful attraction, giving the life of the mind charge and intensity. It's precisely because our communion with our children can be so easy and so blissful that it's hard to accept that there are moments when we have to leave them alone, moments when we have to see that our feelings are unhelpful to them, because they need a break from feeling. For Lawrence, whose ideas were extraordinarily joined up, despite their jaggedness, it was once again all about avoiding self-consciousness. Unconscious mutual bliss is fine, but we should avoid forcing 'a personal, conscious recognition' into the eyes of our children, he wrote in his 1918 'Education of the People' essay, where he advises that 'babies should invariably be taken away from their modern mothers and given ... to rather stupid fat women who can't be bothered with them'. There's enough truth in the thought that we need to avoid smothering our children with love that it feels helpful for him to push it to its comic extreme. It feels true to me that the parents who demand an emotional response all the time, turning every argument into an emotional struggle, deprive their children of privacy, deprive them of the blank curiosity about the world they need if they're going to feel their way into it as independent beings.[8]

I have never found it difficult to leave my children alone. I have too much of my own need for mental space not to seek this when I can. But there is a new pleasure in doing it now, when we are so much together, hardly spending time in different places. When I say no when they ask me to play with them, when I hear H upstairs conducting his own games with his Lego figures or watch G doing her puzzles next to me on the sofa while I read, I hear Lawrence telling me to leave my children in darkness, to avoid tangling them up in the 'intimate mesh of love, love-bullying, and understanding'.

Part of what is appealing about Lawrence as a writer is that, however polemical he is being, I don't feel that he is bullying me. There's a curious take it or leave it aspect to his hectoring. He's laughing at himself when he calls that chapter 'Litany of Exhortations'. He's not cajoling us or wheedling or trying to persuade us that he's sympathetic. Instead he offers us his comically excessive polemics and leaves us to it. I think it's this aspect of his writing that makes his parenting theories convincing to me, or at least more helpful than theories I'm more convinced by. He is able to offer advice but then leave us alone, and as a reader I can appreciate the appeal of being left to my own devices. This makes me think, now, that my anger towards him has been too simplistic a response, or rather that I shouldn't feel so complacent in that anger. He wants to provoke a strong reaction. He reminds us of how exciting it is to be angry and disturbed by someone you really admire – he knew what this was like from reading Nietzsche. The challenge is to allow the admiration and the anger to be part of the same feeling, and for his part, he's up for that. Why should writers want to be liked, any more than parents?

There's a wonderful, amiable account of a parent who succeeds in leaving her offspring alone in Lawrence's 'Tortoise Family Connections', part of the series of tortoise poems written in Italy in 1920 that ends with the ecstatic agony of 'Tortoise Shout'. Lawrence wrote these poems while staying near Rosalind Baynes in Italy. Her house, the thirteenth-century Villa Canovaia in San Gervasio, had been destroyed by an explosion at an ammunition dump, and she lent it to him, all eleven windowless rooms and a large garden with a fountain on the hillside, open to the sunlight, while she and her three little daughters decamped to a house in nearby Fiesole. Each evening, he climbed up the steep track through olive groves, walking under the remains of Fiesole's Etruscan walls, to have supper with Rosalind and her children. She began as a friend, who appreciated, as many women did,

LOOK! WE HAVE COME THROUGH!

his insight into her situation during a difficult time – she was
getting divorced from her philandering husband. Then, after a
supper of mortadella and marsala, they walked out beyond the
cypress woods onto the hillside and he asked her how she felt
without sex in her life. They agreed that it was (as Lawrence put
it in her account of the conversation) 'no good just making love;
there must be more to it than a few pretty words and then off
to bed', and then they said goodbye, kissing their promise, until
he came to lunch a few days later and they made love after her
children had gone to bed that night. Out of their days together
came the sexiness of his fruit poems ('I love to suck you out from
your skins,' he writes in 'Medlars and Sorb-Apples', going on to
describe 'A kiss, and a spasm of farewell, a moment's orgasm of
rupture') and the happy lightness of his tortoise poems.[9]

He liked spending time with Rosalind's daughters – she described
him playing with her two-year-old, Nan, and understanding her
'as he did with children – with delicate, amused perception'.
There were tortoises in the grounds of his villa, tortoises that he
watched mating and wandering and doing their tortoise version
of family life. Out of her girls, and the tortoises, and his new
happiness, came a new, lighter account of his ideal relationship
between parents and children. Here's the beginning of the poem:

> On he goes, the little one,
> Bud of the universe,
> Pediment of life.
>
> Setting off somewhere, apparently.
> Whither away, brisk egg?
>
> His mother deposited him on the soil as if he were no more
>     than droppings,
> And now he scuffles tinily past her as if she were an old
>     rusty tin.

This is the baby tortoise going off into the world, at once ornament
and origin of the world, yet a mere brisk egg. He is purposeful,

ready to leave his parents behind. The poet watches the tortoise and his parents wandering around the garden, each apparently unaware of each other. It's no use his telling him, Lawrence goes on, 'This is your Mother, she laid you when you were an egg.' He just looks the other way, and his mother does the same. 'As for papa', he merely snaps when the poet offers him his offspring, an irascible tortoise devoid of fatherliness.[10]

Tortoises don't look for companions because they don't know they are alone. 'Isolation is his birthright, / This atom.' They don't respond to sentimentality, and they emerge as all the more robust and fully themselves.

> To be a tortoise!
> Think of it, in a garden of inert clods
> A brisk, brindled little tortoise, all to himself –
> Adam!

This tortoise, like the red poppy, fully inhabits his own tortoisehood and is as self-sufficient, as lordly, as Adam as a result. This is possible because he hasn't been weighed down by ideas or ideals, he hasn't been claimed by the clammy bonds of parenthood. Here he is, 'wandering in the slow triumph of his own existence', biting the frail grass arrogantly.

It's impossible to be angry with the author of the tortoise poems, however angry I feel with Lawrence on behalf of Frieda, who must have found Lawrence's relationship with Rosalind's daughters more painful than she found the knowledge of the sex. It's unfair that Lawrence should have expected Frieda to live like a tortoise, absurd to hope that she and her children could become pebbles scattered in a garden, 'not knowing each other from bits of earth or old tins'. But there's such charm in that brisk, brindled little tortoise, going off on his own, such ease in this as an alternative mode of family life. Why not, it leaves me thinking, why not just wander at will around the house and garden, biting the grass when we feel like it. I think it's the most generous case for neglect I've ever heard, though that may also make it the most hazardous.

*

As one week of lockdown follows another, my Sundays can feel lived in a half-light of need. Saturdays are joyful days, filled with relief at being able to work without interruption, and with the pleasure of being able to go off and walk or cycle with P, moving and talking at an adult pace. It is June now and the fields are unexpectedly full of poppies, which make me think of Eastwood, and Lawrence's delight in the red of the flower. Occasionally I pick them and bring them home, forgetting each time that they are too delicate to pick, that the petals will fall as I pick them, thinking of Lawrence who once wrote in an essay about his childhood that it was always the women who wanted to pick flowers, though in *Sons and Lovers* it's Paul who picks them and Miriam who disapproves. Lawrence thought that we loved poppies the most on our holidays, dismissing them as weeds the rest of the time, and therefore that every day should be treated as a holiday, chasing the phoenix as it 'gads off into flame'. Being outside here always has that holiday feeling for me, and perhaps always will. I pull up on my bicycle and pause to look at the flowers, or to watch the lambs, who are so big now that they've almost lost their sweetness; they are less light on their feet, some soon to become mothers themselves.

Then on Sundays, alongside the pleasure at free time, there is a feeling of blankness that I escape as soon as I see the children getting off the train at the station and feel G's little arms clinging to my neck. 'Mummy,' she says repeatedly, that onomatopoeic word that can feel as aggressive as it can feel tender, before she falls asleep in the car. One Sunday she cries in the car. 'I want milk,' she says, and then something that H and I think must be 'I want a cuddle.' It feels too much, the rush of love that I feel, there is too much wanting in it. I don't think Lawrence would like it.

The debates start with my ex-husband about where the children will spend the school nights if I carry on living here. I had assumed, wrongly, that he'd agree that they should continue to be with me. My children, I think, fiercely, and I hear Frieda, and a century of women since, behind me. 'Can they undo the fact that those children are mine, that I bore them, that they are flesh of my flesh?' Frieda has a semi-fictionalised alter ego ask, rather histrionically, in a story she wrote about her life. Many of us have felt this. Here is the violence of motherhood that Lawrence angers me by observing in *The Rainbow*. It's true, that there's something in the trance of pregnancy and the early months of motherhood that gives us this sense of our inalienable fleshy bond. I was alone with G in those months; for the first three months we shared my double bed at night, our bodies finding each other like lovers, semiconscious in the night for those dreamlike feeds. These are memories that can surface, unbidden, with a fierceness whose latent savagery Lawrence was perhaps right to fear. My children. That refrain, that cry of ownership as absurd in its way, but also as necessary as G's when she clings to her lion, saying, 'My Linus.' Sometimes we leave Linus in the window, waiting for us, when we go to places where I think he'll get dirty or lost. She finds it hard, but possible, trusting in me to bring her back to him, as my former husband and I must trust each other to return our children each week.[11]

Because of Frieda, and because perhaps of my sense that my life here is becoming more permanent, and will bring a rupture, one way or another, from the life that preceded it, the loss of my children each weekend starts to bring fear, a fear that they will not come back. Yet we are meant to lose our children; that's part of what Lawrence was getting at in reminding us not to treat them as lovers. He was telling us that their relationship with us will not be their primary relationship for ever. This toddler, carefully putting red squares on her magnetic picture, pushing her little barrow around the garden, I will lose her soon; she will grow into a different child and I will be left with these memories while she discards them. There's a lot of pain in this thought, as I watch her unloading her dinosaurs from her barrow one by one and hiding them all behind the hedge, talking to herself in a language half ours and half hers as she does so. Estrangement of the kind that Frieda suffered makes the normal feelings of loss more terrifying, just as the feelings of loss make the estrangement feel more frighteningly irreparable. By harshly telling us not to love our children in order to set them free, Lawrence reminds us that loss is built into parenting, that our role is to bring our children into the world and then to allow them to leave us. I tell myself that the fear and blankness I feel on Sundays is as sentimental as my fear of losing G's little toddler form. This is a child who needs to become more fully herself, and this will involve shedding the skin that I see her in now. Lawrence, however ruthlessly, is helping me to see this.

Sometimes I wonder if it makes no difference. Frieda got her children back, in a reduced form, adults flashing in and out of her life. Her daughter Barby in particular became a regular visitor to Frieda and Lawrence in adulthood, coming to stay in Italy, sitting painting alongside Lawrence. It's no less than most of us can expect, no less than my own mother has, though there was no moment of rupture, just the gradual pulling away that parents are meant to prepare for. What is the particular gain of knowing that I will see my children during these years, the years that Frieda didn't see hers? It is everything – it's the possibility of a living relationship, the possibility of a childhood without trauma. But it's also nothing, because the outcomes are, in some sense, the same.

On Sundays, when the children are both in bed, and P and I sit having supper together downstairs, I am sometimes frightened by my own need, now that I feel it assuaged. Over the last year, before we came here, the separateness of my two lives was starting to feel unbearable. Either I missed P or I missed my children. Now it feels, tentatively, as though it might be possible to weave my lives together. During the week, day after day, we tend to the children together, talking to them and about them. At supper, P tells me his views of the story he has just read to G: the naughty goat is mocked too harshly, too much is made of the jeopardy of the mummy owl's departure. It moves me. This is a man who has chosen not to have children, who guards his working time fiercely, as I do, but who I watch playing hide-and-seek with G, or helping H with magic tricks, and who suffers the screams of lockdown meltdowns alongside me.

Would this have been Lawrence, a century later? I think that it would, in spite of all his tirades about motherhood, and am grateful that so much has changed, while angry that he didn't, in all his manifestos for a new world, make more of the need for this particular change. When I observe P's ease and patience with children in general, it reminds me of Lawrence's reputed ease with children. Playing with H, I wonder what he would have made of Lawrence. Would Lawrence have had new magic tricks to teach him? Would he have done better than we have in teaching him the names of trees?

There are moments, especially when it feels like nothing I do is working and that my reading of Lawrence is making my child rearing worse, when it's tempting to dismiss Lawrence's theories on the grounds that he, a childless man, can't be expected to know how to bring up children, and that his theories of child rearing were more reliant than they should have been on his experiences as a son. Yet my daily life with H is guided by the wisdom of P, another childless, opinionated man. Together we mentally chart H's moods and try out different approaches to them. I listen, however reluctantly, when he tells me I am saying no too much, that I should look for things I can say yes to. It feels as though I am coming to understand my own children better through having P alongside me, which makes me regret all the more that Frieda didn't have the chance to do this with Lawrence. That afternoon of sailing boats in the brook must have become a memory more painful than happy as the months away from her children wore on.

One of my favourite poems in *Look! We Have Come Through!* is 'Frohnleichnam', named after Corpus Christi day in Germany and meaning 'Body of the Lord'. 'You have come your way, I have come my way', this begins.

> You have stepped across your people, carelessly, hurting
>    them all;
> I have stepped across my people, and hurt them in spite of
>    my care.

Steadily they have come their separate ways to togetherness, and met in that upper room with the balcony in Bavaria, looking out over the wheat and the river and the pinewoods to the blue mountains, flashing with snow. This is a sex poem:

I have done; a quiver of exultation goes through me, like
   the first
Breeze of the morning through a narrow white birch.
You glow at last like the mountain tops when they catch
Day and make magic in heaven.

As a sex poem, it is also about will: about two people smashing
themselves up and remaking themselves together. At last they
can meet 'unsheathed and naked', throwing immortality off,
glistening with 'all the moment'. They can dance 'in triumph of
being together',

Two white ones, sharp, vindicated,
Shining and touching,
Is heaven of our own, sheer with repudiation.

To assert themselves is to repudiate who they once were.
   This is a poem that I hear often this June, unfolding inside my
head. 'Shameless and callous I love you.' 'You have come your
way, I have come my way.' I think, more than almost anything he
wrote about their marriage, this gets across the sense of the beauty
that emerges from the trampling, without diminishing the peril of
the trampling. It's partly from Whitman that Lawrence got this
rather miraculous combination of conversational intimacy and
biblical orotundity. It does feel like we're within the dialogue of a
marriage and that these are real things being said. But there's such
largeness of poetic register, such feeling for how grand sentences
can become. I can't think of many writers who manage to be so
casually realistic and so stylistically dexterous at the same time,
and it's this combination that gives the lines their intensity of
feeling.
   Sometimes I worry that he seems to blame Frieda in that
'carelessly' in the second line, but I think we are meant to read
the second and third lines as interchangeable; to feel that people
get hurt whether we are careless or careful, that life brings
casualties as its price of care. This is the poem in this volume
where Lawrence acknowledges most generously the pain he has

caused not only to Frieda but to her children. And it's a poem that leaves me tentatively hoping that whatever trampling I have done, my children can come through alongside me. This doesn't feel, a century later, too much to ask.

# 5

# Community

I have made so many homes in the last decade. There were the two marital homes, the rented London flat where my daughter spent her first months, three different rented flats in Berlin, a cottage in Suffolk, the London flat I own. They have always been homes, never just places to live – I have painted the walls even in the places I have rented. Not long before I had my son, I rented an unfurnished room in a Berlin flat and, rather than just buy some things from IKEA, I bought a selection of grand, rather monstrous nineteenth-century furniture from a man in the countryside whose grandmother had recently died, and had to locate two men and a van to drive it across the country.

It somehow reassures me, spending this time with Lawrence, to find him doing this too. Wherever they went, Frieda hired or bought a piano and had it transported at often considerable effort and expense. After they returned from Italy at the start of the First World War, they moved from Berkshire to Sussex to London to Cornwall, and at every stage Lawrence put elaborate care into homemaking, despite not expecting any new address to be permanent. He painted walls, he made furniture, he gardened and repaired. When he wasn't teaching aristocratic women to wash their floors, he was cooking and cleaning and washing up. In his 'Education of the People' essay, he goes into a brief rhapsody about the 'pleasure in performing our own personal service, every man making his own room, making his own bed, washing his own dishes'. Dishwashing, he says, teaches you about the quick, light touch of china and earthenware, 'the feel of it, the weight and roll and poise of it'.[1]

To have a home or not to have a home, to have friends or not to have friends, to live with other people or in isolation, to be part of a society, a democracy, a nation, or just live as a singular being in the cosmos – all of these were such urgent, undecided questions for Lawrence. He was always worrying away about how to reorganise both the lives of his friends and society as a whole; his vision for his novels was often a societal one and his hopes for world-making were often interchangeable with his hopes for novel-making because both involved nothing less than a total rethinking of the world. It is not yet clear to me what this all amounted to, but I do know that it always came back to his frenetic ambivalence towards the idea of home.

He knew himself well enough to know that he was going to leave, even as he settled in so fully. In April 1915 he wrote to Ottoline Morrell, who was preparing yet another cottage for them to stay in, that he knew he should be restless all his life:

> If I had a house and home, I should become wicked. I hate any thought of possessions sticking on to me like barnacles, at once I feel destructive. And wherever I am, after a while I begin to ail me to go away.

Perhaps this began early, with all the house moves in Eastwood. It can seem as though Lawrence and his family were very rooted, given that he spent his whole childhood in one small district, given that his sisters stayed nearby for the rest of their lives, given that he set book after book in that small patch of ground. But his family moved so often in Eastwood when he was a child, and between four houses that were within a single square mile, that I wonder if he inherited his fear of settledness from his mother. Was she fleeing the life she had made, as well as seeking a new life, even if she didn't have the courage to go more than a few streets away? Was it for both of them somehow the same impulse that led them to make homes and to abandon them? They both needed to locate themselves but to do so lightly and to leave quickly.[2]

Think of that scene in *Women in Love* where Ursula and Birkin buy a chair, only to give it away immediately. It's powerful because Lawrence makes both impulses seem so overwhelming and so right. It's an eighteenth-century wooden armchair of such 'fine delicacy of grace' that it 'almost brought tears to the eyes'. Birkin is cross about the wooden seat, which lacks the lightness and unity of the original cane, but he buys it nonetheless, finding that its beautiful purity 'almost breaks my heart' and reminds him that their 'beloved country' still had something to express when it made that chair. At this point Ursula scorns the past, deciding suddenly that she doesn't want the old chair, she doesn't want old things, and he goes further, declaring that the thought of a house and furniture of his own is hateful to him. 'As soon as you get a room, and it is *complete*, you want to run from it.' So Ursula takes the chair and gives it to a pregnant woman and her fiancé. She finds herself fantasising about this working-class man, imagining the 'still, mindless creature' as 'a dreadful, but wonderful lover to a woman'. As a result, she comes across as odd and patronising, gushing too much, smiling too dazzlingly. Birkin steps in and convinces them that there's nothing wrong with it and that they've simply changed their mind about wanting to have a home at all. 'It's all right for some folks,' the pregnant woman says, noting the middle-class nature of their problems. And then, in a kind of parodic version of the double couplings in the book, the four of them discuss their plans for marriage. 'Don't break your neck to get there,' the woman says, ''Slike when you're dead – you're long time married.' They part on good terms, with Ursula compliant in trying out the chair one last time before they go. As they walk on, Birkin tells Ursula that these are the people who will inherit the earth, leaving them the chinks to live in, and both seem relieved at the prospect – they don't want to inherit anything, they want to be free to wander, dispossessed.

As soon as you get a room and it is complete, you want to run from it. This is a privileged problem if there ever was one! – but the feeling is real. P avoids it at his house by never making rooms feel complete; he has so little furniture, so few pictures, that there's a provisionality to many of his rooms. I, on the other hand, do all I can to complete each room, as Lawrence did, though at some level I know that one day I may need to run. I relish the transience even as I defy it, as in that Berlin flat where my poor flatmate had to live with that dark old German wardrobe in her room for months after I left because I couldn't find any Berliners who wanted to buy it – unsurprisingly, they had less enthusiasm for the past than I did.

Oddly, until now, I have never thought of myself as particularly restless, or as hating to have a house or a home. For years, my urge to homemake elsewhere was driven by always being on the verge of doing building work at home. My ex-husband, an architect, was drawing up ever-more extravagant plans for turning our small Victorian house into a light and spacious masterpiece, and in the meantime most of the lights in the house had stopped working, because there was no point getting them fixed, and the crazy paving on the sitting-room walls was making its way inside my head. I yearned to strip them, to paint them, but couldn't, and it left me with a frantic urge to homemake that I assuaged elsewhere. But perhaps, in retrospect, he was delaying it partly because he sensed my restlessness, sensed that once the rooms were complete I would want to move on, either with him or without him.

Frieda committed to this process with Lawrence. She must have known after a few years that she would never have a settled home while she was with him. So she let him paint walls pink or white; she lazed in the sun or in bed as he did so. There was no point her joining in when she was soon to be uprooted. When they married in 1914, marriage itself had to provide a home for both of them. 'It's one way of getting rid of everything,' Ursula says, 'to get married.' 'And one way of accepting the whole world,' Birkin responds.

It wasn't only marriage that homed Lawrence, it was his writing, and it was an act of imaginative generosity on Frieda's part to find a home in his writing as well, offering him her memories of her own girlhood to write into his novels. His books had much in common with the dwellings he made: there were similar combinations of effortfulness and casualness in his prose and his rooms, a similar readiness to let go of a draft of a novel and a newly finished home. In a way, his whole impetus to write was a response to his childhood in Eastwood, where he was so immersed in his home community that he was in danger of drowning, so had to get away even as he was drawn back. By describing Eastwood in his early stories and novels, he found a way both to be from there and to escape it, offering his writing to the world and in doing so writing his way out of the place he was describing. He was abandoning his home at the same time as he immortalised it, and in the process he was forging himself a new home through his prose.

Meanwhile, here we are in Oxfordshire, settling into the house whose fireplace reminds me of Lawrence's childhood homes, putting up pictures, installing a new desk. Now that we know we're going to stay, I go back to our London flat in search of some of our things: Lego for H, summer clothes for G. It is a horribly hot June day. The grass in the fields along the motorway is already dry and in the city the summer already feels burdensome, the parks overcrowded, the bins overfull, discarded ice creams melting on the yellowing grass. The playgrounds, off limits because of lockdown rules, taunt the children with their cheerless red and yellow slides. I am glad that I haven't brought my children, that I can sit quietly and sip my car-warmed water, an interloper to the life I was living only three months ago.

The flat itself is close and sticky, the kitchen floor is more chipped than it was when I was last here, but otherwise everything is unchanged, the unfamiliar duvet covers and towels the only real sign that a new family is living here. I just need to go through the storage cupboards in my son's attic bedroom, but I go from room to room, taking a book from my bedroom, a DVD of *Women in Love* from the sitting room, curious about my relationship with this other life that, if it wasn't for the virus, I would probably still be living. There is so much care on display, so much commitment to building a life. There is the Victorian glass lampshade I carried home on the back of the pushchair from the antique shop; the wing-backed armchair, one of the few bits of furniture I took from the marital home and which I had to persuade the movers to scrape along the walls to fit down my narrow hallway; the window seat I had made, with the William Morris fabric on the cushion that I spent days choosing. Everywhere, from the arsenic-green walls of G's little bedroom to the blackish-green gloss of the hallway, there are signs of a life planned, of a vision of myself with my children and friends that found a focus in these choices. And now I have left it all behind. Even the pictures, a portrait of my father, a drawing of me with H as a baby, have not really been missed. Maybe I wouldn't mind never seeing any of it again. I hurry through my tasks and leave quickly, returning the flat to its new inhabitants.

Back in Oxfordshire, it is a peculiar relief to feel that for now I am expressed by someone else's blank taste. The beige walls and sofas remind me that we are only the caretakers of a house whose coal-stained, hooded grate came into being centuries before my birth and will long outlive us. Perhaps this will eventually become too much for me. 'Any particular locality, any house which has been lived in has a vibration, a transferred vitality of its own,' Lawrence writes in *Fantasia of the Unconscious*, going on to say that old houses are saturated with human presence 'to a degree of indecency, unbearable'. Did he flee his houses because they became too alive? Was my flat in London becoming indecently saturated with human presence? Perhaps. By cutting loose, by starting again, we can cut the ties with the past that Ursula and Birkin find claustrophobic, and expose ourselves once more to the world in the present.

If you can't decide whether to have a home or not, it is hard to know whether you can be part of a community. Lawrence's ambivalence towards community-forming was intellectual. We rely on houses, on villages or suburbs, to allow us to be part of communal life. At the same time, it may be that having a house makes genuine community difficult. My flat. My house. We become possessive and territorial. That's why Lawrence wanted to abolish property ownership – it's an opinion he retained throughout his life. He thought that if we were less attached to houses, we could be more open, more porous to each other. He wanted communal life to be defined by people rather than property.

His ambivalence had a more chaotic, less-thought-through side as well. He could never decide if he wanted to settle, to commit to a particular group of people and live among them, or was just a visitor, diving in. He was a good visitor – he brought excitement and fun and a new set of ideas and ideals, and he was very good at playing charades. But being such a good visitor is exhausting because there's so much artifice and simulation involved in being a guest, creating a version of yourself that's right for the people and place. Visiting often left him needing to be alone, to transfer his efforts at simulation into writing. And during his stays, he could ask too much – he wanted everyone to change their lives, having heard the truth of his teachings. He was too forthright, too demanding, and his visits could leave his hosts frazzled and even repulsed.

The visit that left the most bitter taste for his hosts was to Greatham in Sussex, in 1915, as a guest of the Meynell family. He put the whole family into his story 'England, My England', making one of the Meynell daughters' husbands, Percy Lucas, responsible for the wound to his daughter's leg that had left her disabled. Part of him knew that he was wrong to publish it, but I think there was a side of him that thought this was an act of friendship. He was celebrating their closeness as a family by capturing it in print; he was writing his way into the family. At any rate, it was an act of truth-telling, even if some of the facts had been changed, and he convinced himself that it was better for everyone to know and face the truth about their lives. It may also simply have been that the efforts of visiting got too much for him and he needed to take control of the ménage, becoming the narrator and therefore in some grand sense the host, in control of the family's movements.

Part of the problem was that he often didn't know he was just visiting. At every stage, he was picturing utopian new lives for himself and his friends. He was imagining either staying on at their houses and turning them into communities or whisking his friends off and forming a community elsewhere. 'I want to gather together about twenty souls and sail away from this world of war and squalor and found a little colony where there shall be no money but a sort of communism as far as necessaries of life go, and some real decency,' he wrote to his Eastwood friend Willie Hopkin in 1915. He was proposing this to all his close friends. 'I want you to form the nucleus of a new community which shall start a new life amongst us – a life in which the only riches is integrity of character,' he told Ottoline Morrell, and wondered about forming it at her house, Garsington, before settling on Florida. He called his imagined community Rananim after the Hebrew version of Psalm 33:1, 'Rejoice in the Lord, O ye righteous: for praise is comely for the upright.' He wanted not just collective living but a new way of being, which would enable people to assume the best in each other and live free, sexually open lives. 'It is communism based, not on poverty but on riches, not on humility but on pride, not on sacrifice but upon complete fulfilment in the flesh of all strong desire, not in Heaven but in earth.' At this stage, this was in part a political project. He hated party politics, advising Ottoline's lover Bertrand Russell to 'drop all your democracy', but he wanted to 'form a revolutionary party', wishing to 'create an idea of a new, freer life where men and women can really meet on natural terms'. In some moods, he saw this as part of a larger political overhaul. 'There must be a revolution in the state,' he told Russell in February 1915, proposing grand nationalisations and the abolition of private ownership. 'Then a man shall have his wages whether he is sick or well or old.'[3]

It's not surprising that Russell demurred. This was a time when the Labour Party was on the rise, coming to power for the first time in 1924 (and Russell stood as a candidate for them in 1922 and 1923) – there were many more practically inclined visions of socialist life on offer. There were also many other attempts at artistic, often bohemian communal living, some with similarly idealistic aims. It was in 1916 that the painters Vanessa Bell and Duncan Grant moved with Vanessa's children and an entourage of lovers and relations to Charleston Farmhouse in Sussex, achieving something rather like Lawrence's Rananim but motivated at first by practical needs. They had to find farming work for Duncan and his lover, David ('Bunny') Garnett (the son of Lawrence's publisher, who had recently visited Lawrence and

Frieda in Germany), in order to avoid conscription. The house was chilly and there was no piped water or electricity; the garden was overgrown with weeds, but they began to paint murals or decorations on every available surface, turning it into a collective work of art.

Lawrence was disdainful of the Bloomsbury Group. In part, he was protective of Bunny Garnett, with whom he seems to have felt something of the blood-brotherhood he celebrates in *Women in Love*, and was upset by feeling that Garnett was becoming part of Bloomsbury. He worried that Garnett was getting sucked in by intellectualism and that he was becoming part of too homosexual a world (Virginia Woolf's term for this side of Bloomsbury was 'Bloomsbuggery'). He was peculiarly sickened when he went to Cambridge in 1915 and Maynard Keynes (soon to be an inhabitant at Charleston) opened the door to him in his underpants at eleven in the morning. 'Leave this set and stop this blasphemy against love,' he urged Bunny Garnett in April 1915, describing his new friends as 'beetles'.[4]

What did sicken him so much in Keynes's rooms? Some biographers have suggested that he saw a man coming up behind Keynes, making his homosexuality too carelessly explicit. But it may be simply that there was a kind of mannered casualness in Keynes's deportment that Lawrence found unsettling. There's a sense in which Lawrence wanted everyone to be free to wander the streets naked, and certainly to open doors in their underwear. Yet here was Keynes, seizing that freedom with a self-consciousness that repelled Lawrence, making him feel that this world was in fact less free because so much less natural than the world he had left behind in Nottinghamshire. He didn't belong here, and this made him frightened he could belong nowhere, frightened that the Cambridge aesthetes were taking charge of sexual freedom and sullying it in the process, which made freedom of the kind Lawrence himself wanted seem perilously out of reach.

This may have been especially frustrating because he knew that Bloomsbury was his most likely hope for communal living, as he recognised in selecting Ottoline Morrell and Bertrand Russell, both loose members of Bloomsbury, as the key candidates for

Rananim. Ottoline Morrell's set-up at Garsington was not dissimilar to Charleston, though conducted on a grander and better-heated scale. She too took on conscientious objectors as farm labourers during the war. The problem for Lawrence was that Rananim was, in a sense, already going strong, in houses like Garsington and Charleston, but Lawrence found it all too mannered and bourgeois and homosexual and he didn't like joining pre-existing groups. If he was going to manage group life, then he needed to be in charge and he wanted something less makeshift and more grandly intentional.

Lawrence had older models to look back to. It's telling that his thoughts of Rananim often led in the direction of America. He was an ambivalent enthusiast of Emerson and Thoreau, whose New England transcendentalist movement spawned Brook Farm in 1841. Believing, as Lawrence did, that people are at their best when self-reliant and that true communities can be formed only by real individualists, the transcendentalist George Ripley founded the farm in Massachusetts, hoping for 'industry without drudgery, and true equality without its vulgarity'. This sounds more like Rananim than the Bloomsbury experiments do, and Ripley's ambitions were as grand as Lawrence's. 'If wisely executed, it will be a light over this country and this age. If not the sunrise, it will be the morning star.' There were thirty-two farmers engaged there (including, briefly, Nathaniel Hawthorne), doing a mixture of farming and writing. It wasn't viable financially, and soon there was no meat, coffee, tea or butter on offer at the table. One of the (uninsured) farm buildings caught fire and in 1846 Ripley gave up, auctioning his book collection to begin to pay off his debts. Lawrence was at once fascinated and repelled by Brook Farm. In *Studies in Classic American Literature* he dismissed it as a haven of over-conscious intellectuals who over-idealised nature. Describing Hawthorne's *Blithedale Romance* here, he writes:

> This novel is a sort of picture of the notorious Brook Farm experiment. There the famous idealists and transcendentalists of America met to till the soil and hew the timber in the sweat of their own brows, thinking high thoughts the while,

and breathing an atmosphere of communal love, and tingling in tune with the Oversoul, like so many strings of a super-celestial harp.

Of course they fell out like cats and dogs, he goes on; the only music they made was their quarrelling, they 'left off brookfarming, and took to bookfarming'. But he writes more than he needs to about this experiment; you can feel him being drawn to it, unable to let it go as a lost ideal. He must have known that this was exactly the kind of criticism that people would have made of his Rananim, if he had got any further with it. It's telling that his descriptions of freedom in this book sound rather like the set-up at Brook Farm: 'Men are free when they belong to a living, organic, believing community, active in fulfilling some unfulfilled, perhaps unrealised purpose.' This was his ideal, however much he criticised it in others. And in complaining that hard work was beyond the intellectuals pretending to farm, he must have wondered if it was beyond him too. He may have grown up among the workers and farmers in Eastwood, but even Duncan Grant had ended up doing more farming than Lawrence ever had.[5]

P and I have our version of all this: a fantasy farm in Cornwall, in which we allocate imaginary roles to our friends – she can be the shepherdess, she can be the shearer. P is happy for it to remain a fantasy, but occasionally I get restless; I ask where we can find cheap land, how we will actually make enough to live. It turns out that farmers spend a lot of their time filling in grant applications, and I have too many of those already at the university I teach at. We may need to find some other way to live among our friends.

Sometimes I wonder if I need these fantasy friendships, this vision of a utopian community, because I find actual friendships and community hard. I ask too much from my friends; I overwhelm new friends with my desire for our lives to intertwine. It puts them off, or they get drawn in and then I panic and feel the need to escape. I've started to speculate about how I'd get on being friends with Lawrence, who was even more extreme than me in these ways. Being a devoted reader may always be an act of friendship, but for readers of Lawrence this possibility feels unusually strong, because his writing invites such strong responses.

Being friends with Lawrence, like reading Lawrence, was an unusually demanding experience. There would be the initial excitement, the delight in the joined-up-ness of his ideas, his curiosity about the world, his insight into you, if you were one of the people he really focused on. There would be walks, talks, meals, games, the occasional collective sing-song, an energetic sense of all you could accomplish together, of all that was wrong in the world and how you could change it. But the games of charades could start to feel too much. You be the Tree of Life, I'll be Gawd-a-mighty, as he said to H.D. The mischief could turn to aggression, making you think that he was more satyr than fawn, making it feel maddening that he couldn't just settle into conversation; he wanted to be with you without really being with you, proliferating options. And he'd start asking for so much, he'd want you to uproot to whatever new destination he'd decided on. He'd have chosen the colour of your walls and the nature of your diet. He'd tell you not to have children, or tell you how to educate the children you already had. Eventually you'd say no, it's too much. And then he'd chide you, as he chided Ottoline Morrell, for not committing as deeply, as selflessly as he had. He burned through friends as he burned through houses, always restless, always seeking to be left with nothing even as he sought to build new worlds.

As with Lawrence, there's a side of me that, fearing all this, doesn't want to socialise at all. When I was married, I thought of myself as someone who resisted coupledom, and always wanted to be part of a larger group. With P, though, it's usually been me who has resisted the pressure of the outside world. In London, I was hurt when he wanted to go to parties; I didn't really want to have people round. I thought often of that scene in *The Rainbow* where Anna leaves the comfort of their bedroom and starts cleaning. The point is that she wants to have friends over, she's decided to have a tea party. Will hates the idea. 'He was anxious with a deep desire and anxiety that she should stay with him where they were in the timeless universe of free, perfect limbs and immortal breast, affirming that the old outward order was finished.' But she wants the old world again, she wants to have her friends to tea. She throws herself into housework and he resists her until she sobs, 'like a curled up, oblivious creature', fearing not only his sudden separateness but the world she has invited in to spoil her bliss.

It's a debate that Lawrence and Frieda had continually. They couldn't decide if the couple was the beginning or ending of social life. She wanted to be left alone with him; he felt the need for more – more people, more purpose, more of a life beyond the home. Their moods changed and their roles alternated. During the lockdown, I have felt my mood changing too. The lockdown has made the combination of my urge to combine and my urge to isolate feel particularly charged. I am frightened by the government forcing everyone back into family units; it makes me yearn for more creative forms of togetherness. I suggest to at least three friends, self-protectively framing it as a half-joke, that they should move here alongside us. As the rules loosen, I invite people to stay. One friend says that she fears coming to stay with us because she fears that she will want to move. I risk a little more urging. Lawrence seems to permit my wayward needs of others. He seems to cheer me on as I ask too much of my friends, convinced now that we need each other as much as we need our families. 'We are so few,' I can hear myself saying, as Lawrence said to his friends, 'and the world is so many, it is absurd that we are scattered. Let us be really happy and industrious together.'[6]

Lawrence did make one small attempt at Rananim, in Cornwall in 1916, but it only lasted for a couple of months. Too much can be made of this, given it was so brief, and ultimately a failure. In essence, this was a peculiar whim in the midst of war and political and financial disaster that had less of a vision of collective life than even Bloomsbury's attempts at it – far removed from the money-free paradisal colony he proposed a year earlier. But it did offer a kind of small-scale test case for homemaking and community-forming, and, more importantly, it did become an inspiration for

*Women in Love*, a grander and ultimately more successful attempt to bring community into being.

The move to Cornwall began as a move to escape other people and the world at large. It followed a series of bleak months at the end of 1915. Lawrence had attempted to start a new magazine, *The Signature*, in October, which was a fiasco – there were only thirty subscribers for the first issue, and it foundered after three issues, at the same time as *The Rainbow* (published in late September) started to attract negative reviews (*The Daily News* called it 'a monotonous wilderness of phallicism'). 'My Soul is torn out of me now,' he wrote to his friend the translator S. S. Koteliansky (known as Kot) at this point, 'I can't stop here any longer and acquiesce in this which is the spirit now: I would rather die.' His friends, many of whose loved ones had recently been killed in the war, were not as sympathetic as he would have wished. Then, on 5 November, the police seized all unsold copies of *The Rainbow* under the Obscene Publications Act and Lawrence's publisher, Methuen, voluntarily recalled copies from bookshops. They failed to communicate with Lawrence and did nothing to defend the book at its hearing at Bow Streets Magistrate Court on 13 November – his publisher merely apologised and claimed not to have read the book. Shockingly, following the hearing, the remaining unsold 1,011 copies of the book were burned.[7]

It wasn't clear to Lawrence exactly why the book was banned, but it seems to have been some combination of its sexual explicitness (especially the lesbian sex between Ursula and Winifred Inger) and its lack of patriotism in relation to the war. 'We aren't the nation,' Ursula says to her ill-chosen lover Anton Skrebensky, when he's talking about the need to fight. He worries that if everybody said this, there would be no nation. 'There wouldn't be a nation,' she affirms, 'but I should still be myself.' If Lawrence believed in community at this stage, then it wasn't a national form of community – this war in which his and Frieda's families were fighting against each other made no sense to him. This was clear to the authorities, and their disapproval of him would harden his beliefs. 'All this war, this talk of nationality, to me is false,' he wrote in the summer of 1916. 'I *feel* no nationality, not fundamentally.'[8]

Lawrence could have done with the support of the Bloomsbury Group at this point, though this probably wasn't enough to make him regret alienating them. Ottoline Morrell did invite him to Garsington to recover and attempted to get some MPs interested in his case, and Vanessa Bell's absent husband Clive Bell tried to persuade the literary editor of the *New Statesman* to protest, but the efforts came to nothing and no well-known writers stood up for *The Rainbow* in public. At this stage, Lawrence planned to go to America within a few weeks. 'It is the end of my writing for England,' he had told his literary agent, J. B. Pinker, after the police raid. 'I will try to change my public.' But then the Committee of the Society of Authors took up his cause (ultimately with little effect) and he decided to delay his visit, bolstered by the support of some younger writers, who joined him at Garsington for some especially elaborate games of charades. By the time he was ready to go, the rules on military conscription had been tightened and he was told that he couldn't leave the country. A few days before the end of 1915, he and Frieda retreated to Cornwall, borrowing a house near Padstow from the novelist J. D. Beresford, who had been a supporter of *The Rainbow*.[9]

Immediately, he felt 'a good peace and a good silence' in Cornwall, which brought 'a freedom to love and to create a new life'. His new tranquillity brought two desires. There was the desire to renounce people altogether, which was increased by becoming severely ill with bronchial troubles that don't seem at this stage to have been TB. 'I am willing to believe there isn't any Florida ... I am willing to give up people altogether,' he told Kot, announcing that the world of others had to be 'all blown out to extinction' because there was another world that he preferred – 'a world with thin, clean air and untouched skies'. He no longer saw himself as leading his nation. He was an outlaw now, as he told Russell in February 1916, 'not a teacher or a preacher. One must retire out of the herd & then fire bombs into it.' But concurrently, there was the desire to make this new life communal. He wrote to a handful of friends – among them Ottoline Morrell, Koteliansky,

Katherine Mansfield and her lover John Middleton Murry – asking them to come. This wasn't any longer a desire to form a commune and change the world. He wanted to be alone, but he wanted a few trusted friends with him, and increasingly he pined most of all for Mansfield and Murry. 'My dear Katherine, I've done bothering about the world and people – I've finished,' he wrote to Mansfield. 'You and Jack will come if you like – when you feel like it: and we'll all be happy together – no more questioning and quibbling and trying to do anything with the world. The world is gone, extinguished, like the lights of last night's Café Royal – gone for ever.' Everyone had now become Judas, he complained to Murry a couple of days later.[10]

The two unmarried couples had been close since they met in the summer of 1913, and instantly embarked on a life of shared plans and projects and friends. Mansfield and Murry were themselves also a fairly newly formed couple at this stage. She'd had a rackety upbringing in New Zealand and an education in London; she had known since childhood she wanted to be a writer and that she valued experience over happiness. The result had been a series of intense, abrupt love affairs (including one with a woman), a pregnancy with one man that ended in a stillbirth just after she had married another man, and a dose of gonorrhoea that had left her a chronic invalid, because the gonococci had spread into her bloodstream. Like Lawrence, Murry came from a working-class background, though he was more determined to deny it – at Oxford he had declared himself an orphan and sought new families to adopt him, plotting his own life as a man of letters. By the time Lawrence met them, Mansfield was helping Murry in his work as editor of a literary magazine, *Rhythm*, and he was helping her develop as a writer of coolly precise short stories in which she skewered moments of tragedy and revelation within ordinary lives. She was often prevented from writing by a mixture of writer's block and ill health, but in early 1916, when Lawrence wrote his letters summoning them both to Cornwall, she and Murry were in Bandol in France, and she was writing well and happily. 'No more quarrels and quibbles,' Lawrence wrote to them in March, 'Let it be agreed for ever. I am Blutbruder: a Blutbruderschaft between us all.'[11]

Lawrence and Frieda had now moved further into Cornwall, to Zennor, close to Land's End, and rented two cottages looking out over the cliffs at Higher Tregerthen. Lawrence wrote to Mansfield and Murry that it was a splendid place 'just under the moors, on the edge of the few rough stony fields that go to the sea' and did them a little diagram of the houses and their rooms – '*such* a lovely place: our Rananim'. He insisted that this was going to be 'a union in the unconsciousness, not in the consciousness', based less on personal affinity than on instinctive warmth. Frieda wrote describing Lawrence's alterations – he'd made a dresser and painted the shelves blue and the walls pink, and had sewn buttercup-yellow curtains with green blobs on them. The Murrys (as Lawrence referred to them) agreed to come in April. They were a little reluctant because they were happy in Bandol, but this was a friendship they were as committed to as Lawrence and Frieda were. Mansfield was more affectionate than most of Lawrence's friends were towards Frieda – hence her efforts with Frieda's children. Lawrence and Murry were full of rivalrous admiration for each other, and had collaborated on *The Signature*; though Lawrence had been disappointed by Murry's lack of support for *The Rainbow* (Murry was repelled by its 'warm, close, heavy promiscuity of flesh' and Mansfield found it 'too female', though she may most have minded that she'd confided about her lesbian encounters to Frieda and felt that Lawrence had made use of them in the novel). And Lawrence and Mansfield recognised in each other kindred spirits. They had so much in common, probably more than they realised. Like Lawrence, Mansfield was ambivalent about England and about the class (in her case a kind of bourgeois monied colonial class) she'd been born to; like Lawrence she was ill with an illness she couldn't quite accept or acknowledge; like Lawrence she went into friendships with too much expectation and too much at stake, and tended as a result to polarise people between love and hate; like Lawrence she was an enthusiastic performer, and a woman of many names and none – born Kathleen Beauchamp, she had been Kass, Käthe, Yekaterina, Katya and even Sally before settling on the name of Katherine Mansfield.[12]

Even as they committed to the venture, the Murrys hedged their bets. 'We are going to stay with the Lawrences for ever and ever as perhaps you know,' Murry wrote to Ottoline Morrell (hoping in part that she might eventually invite him to Garsington), 'I daresay eternity will last the whole of the summer.' What came to pass was, in miniature, all the violence and ecstasy that Lawrence was capable of, rolled out on the cliff edge as the bluebells and primroses and sea pinks came into flower and the Atlantic waves crashed beneath it all. 'We are as yet rather strange and unaccustomed to each other,' Lawrence wrote to Kot shortly after their arrival, adding that it was 'so difficult to re-establish an old footing, after a lapse during which we have all endured a good deal of misery'. If this was a union of the unconscious, then it was the explosive conjunction of four unconsciousnesses in Nietzschean interplay. The Murrys were drawn into the Lawrences' fights and there were violent clashes.[13]

On 11 May Mansfield wrote an account of what she laughingly termed 'the COMMUNITY' to Kot. Here she describes Lawrence's continual oscillations between gentle lovingness and rage, detailing how in the worst moments he pulls out Frieda's hair and says, 'I'll cut your bloody throat, you bitch,' leaving her to run up and down the road, screaming for Jack to save her. The rage she reports is directed at the Murrys too. Lawrence hates being contradicted, so he gets into a frenzy when this happens. 'It is like sitting on a railway station with Lawrence's temper like a big black engine puffing and snorting.' By the end of the letter she describes herself as furiously angry and as hating Lawrence and Frieda for their degrading fights. 'I am very much alone here. It is not a really nice place.'[14]

Perhaps they were doomed from the outset by the war that battered relentlessly on in the background. Lawrence hated the war not because he hated violence, which he saw as a vital part of life, but because he thought that this was a war fought for false ideals by men who fought self-consciously and insincerely. A few years later, in an essay called 'On Being a Man', he would complain that the men fought not as 'the old Adam of red earth' but 'as heroes, as martyrs, as saviours saving Belgian babies from the bayonet'. They were fighting for democracy (always a hated ideal for Lawrence) and to make the world safe 'for the cowardice of modern men', pushing them irredeemably into the age of machine civilisation. Practically, at this point Lawrence was particularly frightened by the threat of conscription. It was very likely that both he and Murry would be consigned to office work once full mobilisation came in, and he'd be pushed into working in service of the ideals he scorned. A policeman arrived to check Murry's papers, suggesting that his rejection certificate from the Officers' Training Corps may not be enough to get him off. In this atmosphere, to make plans for new magazines and literary projects was, as Lawrence reported, 'like people contemplating schemes who are rolling on board a rotten ship in a storm'.[15]

Tempers frayed further as fears mounted, and by June Murry and Mansfield had had enough. They told Lawrence that the landscape was too rocky and bleak for them, they needed to move somewhere prettier. 'They should have a soft valley with leaves and the ring-dove cooing,' Lawrence told Ottoline Morrell. He wrote to everyone he knew, describing their departure. Reading his letters, you can feel him trying to make sense of this failure, which became for him a larger failure of connection and community. He had experienced the first year of war as a kind of death, but then he had risen from the dead to make one final, heroic attempt at friendship and it had failed. 'Murry and I are not really associates,' he wrote to their mutual friend the Scottish writer Catherine Carswell. 'How I deceive myself. I am a liar to myself, about people ... I give up having intimate friends at all. It is a self-deception.'[16]

After their departure, Lawrence found other ways to enjoy Cornish life. He had always loved spending time among farmers and he now became a regular visitor to the Hocking farm at Higher Tregerthen, becoming particularly close to the eldest son, William Henry, and showing the Hockings how sheaves were tied in the Midlands (think, as he probably did, of that scene in *The Rainbow*). But the stay in Cornwall ended abruptly in October 1917 when the Lawrences were served a notice to leave Cornwall by the military. The friendship with Murry and Mansfield would trundle on for years, with low-key visits and meetings and occasional forays into new collaborations. None of the four was at their best in the quartet now. It was one of Lawrence's most shameful acts to write to Mansfield as she lay horribly ill, alone and emaciated in a nursing home on the French Riviera in February 1920, that she disgusted him, 'stewing in your consumption'. There are other letters to read alongside this, though, letters where he wrote that he believed in 'sworn, pledged, eternal friendship' as deep as the marriage bond. It can feel, reading Murry's mean-spirited reviews of Lawrence's novels and his later memoir, that he went out of his way to betray his friend – at one stage Murry even went to bed with Frieda. But something came out of this wartime moment of experimental togetherness, and that is *Women in Love*, begun at the end of April, living alongside the Murrys.[17]

There was a sense for Lawrence, when his friends arrived, that his best self was somehow in hiding. He wrote to Catherine Carswell in April that he felt as though 'both I and my friends have ceased to be, and there is another country, where there are no people, and even I myself am unknown, to myself as well'. It seems to have been out of this unknown self that the novel emerged. 'One has a certain order inviolable in one's soul,' he told his friend the aristocratic writer Lady Cynthia Asquith, in a letter describing beginning his novel. He didn't quite know what it was that he was making, and didn't quite acknowledge to himself the extent that he was borrowing characters from his friends.[18]

Gudrun Brangwen had been conceived long before the trip to Cornwall, but with Mansfield in the mix she took on more of her characteristics, from her dark hair and fine features ('so infinitely charming, in her softness and her fine, exquisite richness of texture and delicacy of line') and boldly stylish clothes to her playful, sardonic wit, her bohemianism, her dashes of feminism, her resentful fascination with male power. She is there not just in Gudrun's character but in Lawrence's prose style. The narrator notices things that Mansfield would notice in her stories, as when Gudrun wakes Gerald up, asking him to 'convince me of the perfect moments' and is filled with delight, seeing her own mocking, enigmatic smile reflected on his face, making him smile unconsciously and making her remember 'that was how a baby smiled'. And, though Gerald is never a portrait of Murry, the friendship between Birkin and Gerald, with its violence and its yearning for *Blutbrüderschaft*, took on the disappointed intensity of the Cornish summer.

The whole structure of the novel became about the search for community of four difficult, determinedly individual people, all differently committed to living fully embodied, modern lives. Ursula and Birkin, having given away their chair and given up on domestic life, decide to marry and go abroad. They suggest that Gerald and Gudrun should join them, partly because Birkin, like Lawrence, is a great believer in male friendship, and to make his love for Ursula complete, he wants 'a real, ultimate relationship with Gerald ... a relationship in the ultimate of me and him'. At this stage Gerald and Gudrun are less secure as a couple, there is no suggestion of marriage, no peace in the rhythms of intimacy and distance. Lawrence is working out what being in a couple is through holding the two couples to the light beside each other at every turn. By throwing them closely into each other's space, he brings out the violence between and outside them, which they have somehow to learn to channel into a force more on the side of life than of death. It is such a daring move for the two couples to leave England together and try out collective life on this peculiar holiday that is meant to feel harder work than the working lives they have left behind, because becoming fully yourself is an arduous, danger-ridden process. There is so much creativity, so much hope put into the attempt. But here, as in Cornwall, we feel that there are too many feelings, too many desperate impulses of love and hate in the mix, and that someone is sure to be destroyed. In a way, it's an accident that it ends up being Gerald – it could have been any of them. But it's also inevitable, if only for the sake of readerly satisfaction, that it's Gerald, with his overreaching wilfulness, who should end up dying in the snow.

In the background of the quartet, in life and in the novel, was Ottoline Morrell, a devoted, wilfully divisive correspondent of both Lawrence and Mansfield, who seems to have been determined to create rifts both within and between the couples, partly in order to recentre their base for communal life in Garsington. It isn't surprising that Lawrence looked to her as a model for Hermione, his wilful, spirit-sucking anti-heroine, though it's more surprising that he managed to avoid acknowledging to himself how much she would hate it (in September he was even half planning to go to Garsington to finish the novel). In part, he hoped that his writing was a communal act that they would all willingly be a part of. He was no longer writing for the public at large. From the beginning, he knew the novel was likely to be unpublishable, and in some moods he relished this. 'It is beyond all possibility even to offer it to a world, a putrescent mankind like ours,' he complained to his friend the psychoanalyst Barbara Low in May, adding that he felt he could not '*touch* humanity, even in thought, it is abhorrent to me'. He had come a long way from his confidence, when he began these Brangwen books, that he had been sent to save the English from their vices and repressions. Instead, he was left writing for his friends, getting it typed so he could circulate the typescript among them as well as sending it to his agent. So it may have seemed to him appropriate that his friends should wander into his books – not just Ottoline and Katherine, but his old Eastwood friends Alan Chambers and George Neville, who are in the mix for Gerald, and his young composer friend Philip Heseltine, who is there as Halliday – their secret selves brought to life in secret by his secret self. He may have thought that he could create in his book the Rananim that he was failing to create in his life.[19]

The problem is that writing is solitary: only one member of the group has agency. For a few months, writing about his friends had given Lawrence the feeling that he was surrounded by his friends, flooded by the people he was half yearning for and half needing to escape, unsure whether he was with them or not with them because characters in novels take on lives of their own. Now, emerging and circulating the book, he wanted to be admired by his friends as much as he wanted not to care what people thought; he wanted to give himself back to his friends through the book and wanted to give his friends to the world. But as communal acts go, it was so incendiary. Mansfield loved the book – it's hard to see Gudrun as anything other than an act of homage – but

Ottoline Morrell was furious. The rift between Lawrence and Ottoline was to be permanent and it was to exclude him from the house where he had most successfully experienced communal life (perhaps even this occasional home had become too much, and he'd felt compelled to write himself away from being welcome there). No other openings were forthcoming. By January 1917 all the major publishers had rejected the novel. These books about the Brangwen sisters had been all about forming a readerly community; he had been determined to write into being a new way of living in the modern world, which could become a model for his generation. Something was lost when they failed to do so. He would never again believe in collective living or in collective politics. Yet his urges to create homes and to destroy them, to live among people and to retreat, continued to beat as conflictedly within him.

Our summer unfolds, rather like the one in which Lawrence wrote *Women in Love* – the sun and grass as absurdly luxurious as the sun he found in Cornwall. Here too the news that rumbles on in the background is deranging; here too there is death in the air and we are at the mercy of a mean-spirited government which makes us wonder, as Lawrence did, if it does or doesn't represent the people. The economy is collapsing; the homeless have been evicted from the hotels they were hidden away in for the lockdown and are back on the streets, reminding us that to stay at home, as the government advises us, is to have a home in the first place, and that it is a luxury to discard houses at will, as Lawrence and I have, knowing that you will still be homed. The isolation of lockdown is interrupted by Black Lives Matter protests, following the death of George Floyd in the US and his haunting final words, suffocated by the police – 'I can't breathe', repeated more than twenty times. P goes to a protest in Oxford aimed at removing the statue of the Victorian imperialist Cecil Rhodes. A week later, we hear that the college has agreed to take it down. There is the hope, for a while, that this can be the other face of lockdown, that the vision of Black Lives Matter is one that takes seriously the vulnerability of bodies that lockdown has been intended to honour. Those who have feared for their lives during the pandemic have known that lives matter, that breath is a fragile thing to sustain. This may be where politics can start again, with the bleak openness of bodily experience to destruction.

In the end, none of our friends have answered our determinedly wilful summons to move alongside us. So, seeking sociability again, I turn to the people who are already local. I start to swim regularly with my aunt, who begins to read *The Rainbow*, having not read Lawrence since she read *Sons and Lovers* for A level. She finds that it's too intense – she has to pause for breath in the middle of Anna and Will's marriage. We get to know our next-door neighbours, and G becomes friends with their daughter, trying out friendship for the first time. 'My friend,' she says proudly, when she goes to play in their paddling pool. I find a new female friend with whom to embark on the fizzy rush of intimacy, and it strikes me that Lawrence was partly humouring Birkin when he makes him seek 'a relationship in the ultimate of me and him', half-amused by his own tendency to be so much more religious, so much more high-minded about friendship than everyone else was.

My new friend, an Oxford don a little younger than me, tells me that she loved *Lady Chatterley* in adolescence, that she read it seeking knowledge about sex, and that it was thanks to Lawrence that she spent her twenties faking orgasms, attempting to emulate Constance Chatterley in her ease of soulful sexual response. I find this bizarre, but this is a woman almost as determined in her self-making as Lawrence and Mansfield, propelled into the maelstrom of competitive careerism by Turkish parents in New York, embracing it by tattooing the Library of Congress call numbers of her books below her breast, as I discover when we swim together, first accompanied by our children and then alone. She is half a character in a book to me, and I find that I relish the combinations of intimate involvement and cool appraisal that this enables, and feel less panicky than I usually do in new friendships. Also, I know now that I can take refuge in friendlessness if I need to. I have discovered, as Birkin does even as he resists it, that the couple can be enough.

Lawrence never attempted communal life as idealistically again after he dropped the idea of Rananim. His novels became, until *Lady Chatterley's Lover*, more solipsistic. This is especially the case with *Kangaroo*, drafted during his peculiar foray into Australia in 1922 and written out of his wartime disillusionment. The central character, Richard Somers, has arrived in Australia, having recently lived out a version of Lawrence's life in Cornwall. He hates both his Australian bungalow and the sinister Australian bush ('it might have reached out a long black arm and gripped him') and is pining for England or Europe in spring, longing for bluebells – 'he felt he would have given anything on earth to be in England' – though when in Europe, he had declared it 'moribund and stale and finished'. It's a book written in the jauntily comic mode of *Mr Noon*, mocking both Somers and his Frieda-ish wife, Harriet: 'Well, if a man wants to make a fool of himself, it is as well to let him.' What's most odd about the novel is that Lawrence, having given up on using his friends as characters, having given up on establishing Rananim through the written word, presents his reader with a series of characters modelled on himself and sets them all off, arguing with each other.

Somers has written a series of articles against democracy. These, we can assume, are essays very like Lawrence's own essays on democracy published in the magazine *The Word* in 1919 and revised as 'Democracy' in *Reflections on the Death of a Porcupine and Other Essays* in 1925. Here Lawrence criticises democracy because it assumes the existence of an average man. He suggests that our needs are identical but our selves are too distinct to be seen grouped within a nation. He takes issue with Whitman for his belief in democracy, because his principle of individualism is an intellectual ideal and as such 'a horrible nullification of true identity and being', though Lawrence does hope that there can be a new form of democracy, born of an acceptance of otherness and a disinterest in property ('sometime, somewhere, man will wake up and realise that property is only there to be used, not to be possessed') that will allow for the dismantling of the state.[20]

Perhaps Somers's articles also contain some of the rants against herd-thinking that Lawrence had included in that wartime essay about wilfulness 'The Reality of Peace'. Here, after decrying wilfulness in general, he says that we have to fear most not the overweening individual but 'the consenting together of a vast host of null ones': 'worse than the fixed and obscene will of the isolated individual is the will of the obscene herd ... They are a nauseous herd together, keeping up a steady heat in the whole.' At any rate, because of his book, Somers is invited to join a kind of proto-fascist movement comprised mainly of disillusioned soldiers and led by a man known as Kangaroo – another Lawrence figure. Also in the mix are Somers's neighbour Jack (a man with whom he attempts a rather sloppily half-hearted version of *Blutbrüderschaft*) and Jack's brother-in-law William James. For Somers, who tells Harriet that he intends 'to move with men and get men to move with me before I die', part of the appeal of these men is that they are working men, who see the working man in him. Sometimes he finds this frightening, he misses the physical reserve of the English upper classes. Collectively, the men are attempting to topple democracy ('We jolly well know you can't keep a country going on the vote-catching system,' says Jack) and to achieve power by gradual insinuation. Kangaroo wants to 'collect together all the fire in all the burning hearts in Australia'. He will wait for one political party or another to start a revolution, and then leap in to take over, offering something more loving.[21]

When I first read the novel, on a trip to Australia when H was two, soon after that near-miss of a Lawrentian job interview, I found this very alienating – this wasn't the Lawrence I had signed up to. Now, though, I'm more aware of Lawrence grappling with these sides of himself. It seems like a peculiar stroke of genius to take himself on in this way, at a time when he was as disillusioned by himself as by everyone else. Kangaroo's cult is much more childish than I recalled it as being. The narrator mocks everything from Kangaroo's own marsupial physique to the 'digger' clubs he runs, where the men do games and athletics with the occasional lecture thrown in, wearing white felt hats with white feathers on top.

Kangaroo gets to rail against democracy and preach blood-brotherhood as Lawrence did, but Somers gets to retaliate with

Lawrence's view that love isn't going to be enough, because it doesn't allow people to remain separate and single. Somers becomes so fed up that he wonders if he has more time for the socialists, but he decides that they also make too much of human love and are wrong to leave out the divine. A big meeting of all the political parties ends in violence. There's a large mob, fighting frenziedly around a red flag, some clutching fragments of the Union Jack. Several people die, and Jack announces that 'there's *nothing* bucks you up sometimes like killing a man – *nothing*'. Somers is repulsed by the whole thing, retreating home exhausted and then leaving Australia as soon as he can. The version of Lawrence who wins out here is one for whom lives matter. This is still the Lawrence who sees the creaturely in us, who seeks the nakedness of our vulnerability and exposure to the world.

In a way, there's a moment of honest *mea culpa* here. Lawrence seems to acknowledge that his ideas about democracy are likely to get him invited to join a blood-letting fascist cult. But he continued to preach against democracy nonetheless, and this is one of the aspects of Lawrence's thinking I find most difficult, especially as it connects (as it does in *Kangaroo*) to his ideas about natural aristocrats and our need for strong leaders. He hated fascism – his ideas of leadership couldn't have been more different from Hitler's or Mussolini's: for Lawrence the ideal leader was morally sensitive and spiritual; this wasn't about imposing power. But his ideas about democracy feel, in the end, irresponsible to me, and they left him stranded. It's not as though many people can claim really to *like* democracy, as it actually plays out. Most of the people I know in Britain have hated all the fruits of our democracy over the past decade: we have hated the particular politicians we have collectively voted in and the agendas they have inflicted on us. But in Lawrence's day it seemed more hopeful and, even more than now, it was horribly obvious that the alternative was not merely unsatisfactory but dangerous. On the one hand, there was democratic reform in Britain, which in 1918 had extended the vote to all men over twenty-one and all women over thirty, tripling the electorate. On the other hand, there was fascism in Italy. It was the wrong point in history to distance himself from constitutional settlements, whatever pain and limitations they entailed. At least in *Kangaroo* there's a moment of reckoning with this. The novel knows that if Lawrence is left to his own devices, left merely to proliferate Lawrences in a wilderness, a bloodbath will result.

In the end, Lawrence would decide that the problems of democracy couldn't be solved on their own terms. He never managed to have a complete political vision of the world as he wanted it to be – he took refuge instead in a religious vision, which we can see the beginnings of in *Kangaroo*. It's a novel that finishes with its narrator as well as his characters at a loss to understand the world. We end up face to face with the abyss of modern political power, knowing that we don't know how to form communities that respond to the powerful needs of modern life. He throws us into this maelstrom with terrifying force, and reading it, I feel as much at a loss as he was.

For Lawrence himself, Australia ended up as a stepping stone to New Mexico, where Frieda at least finally found a home. Not long before he went to Australia, Mabel Dodge had written her invitation to New Mexico, and with it offered a new purpose: to help her in reconciling the Indigenous American culture and the white one. Her letter was accompanied by a Indigenous American necklace for Frieda, a few leaves of *desachey*, a herb said to lighten the heart, and some local medicine for him to try. 'I believe what you say,' Lawrence wrote in return, 'one must somehow bring together the two ends of humanity, our own thin ends and the last dark strand from the previous, pre-white era. I verily believe that. Is Taos the place?' It took him a year to get there – it seemed necessary to go east first, to Ceylon and then Australia – but by 1922 he and Frieda arrived, this time seeking a new world rather than Rananim. He was thirty-seven at this point. He'd had so many new lives, but he started again; there was more painting, more clearing, more building – more than ever before, because he had never made a home somewhere this remote. They moved between houses, disgruntled at first about being too close to Mabel Dodge and feeling themselves to be in her power. Eventually, she gave Frieda a lodge of her own and the Lawrences set about renovating it, accompanied, as they tended to be, by a friend, this time the painter Dorothy Brett. It was a wise decision of Mabel Dodge to give them the lodge. It made them more likely to stay, which she wanted them to do, though she was jealous of Frieda and hurt by Lawrence's taunts about her wilfulness. It was wise to offer it to Frieda, given Lawrence's hatred of the idea of property ownership. There were a few years, now, when Lawrence committed to New Mexico, seeking new visions of communal life there. But always in the background was Eastwood.[22]

The further he went, the more he was driven back to Eastwood imaginatively. It is unsurprising that he ended up there for his final novel. It was there that he had discovered people to be vulnerable, seeing the vulnerability of bodies as they emerged from the mines, or as his family washed his father's blackened back, or as children in nearby households suffered from often deadly illnesses. And it was there he had believed most easily in community. 'Here, in this ugly hell, the men are *most* happy,' Lawrence told Edward Garnett after returning to Eastwood in March 1912. 'They sing, they drink, they rejoice in the land.' When he did feel at home elsewhere, it was often in places that reminded him of Eastwood. 'It reminds me so of home when I was a boy. They are all so warm with life,' he wrote from Lake Garda that October.[23]

In our trip to Eastwood in May, I felt rather outraged on Lawrence's behalf about how much the town had co-opted its famous novelist, even though he was such a reluctant member of the community when he lived there. He left as soon as he could, he rarely went back, he never saw himself as having fitted in. Yet now the Lawrence jeweller offers to buy all your gold and silver for cash, and the Wetherspoons' Lady Chatterley pub offers two meals for the price of one. It felt all the more peculiar to us because it was all shut; the decimation of lockdown gave it an end-of-the-world feeling, as though Lawrence was the only surviving inhabitant in a ghost town, rather than the absent, shadowy figure in a living town that I'd expected to encounter.

Perhaps, though, Lawrence would have liked it after all. Perhaps he'd have been glad that he'd succeeded in his early ambition of making his mother and her community proud of him. He didn't turn New Mexico into Eastwood – this was to become the period of the most efflorescent and lurid of his communal visions. But, though he was glad for Frieda to have a home, he began to accept that Eastwood remained the only home he would ever have, and to understand that his childhood had left him more drenched in home than most people ever were. Home was both his natural element and an alien imposition he could not cope with. The challenge was to home himself in his writing again, even as he moved on ever more restlessly, fleeing all the homes on offer.

# 6

# Religion

September comes and we get stuck in a field that P tells me is being harrowed. According to the map, we should walk through it, but we can't find a way out. The tractor drives up and down systematically, breaking up the soil, churning it, chewing it up with its huge teeth and spitting it out. We talk about the harrowing of hell, Christ's descent to 'the lowest parts of the earth'. Christ was killed, the earth shook and darkened, he plunged down to hell and rescued the righteous. As we talk, I picture the dead in the underworld chewed up by the teeth of this ruthlessly industrial harrow and thrown back out again, destroyed and renewed.

I think of Lawrence, watching the fields being harrowed in Eastwood. Perhaps he helped Jessie Chambers's brothers with the harrowing as well as the harvesting. And I think of how much he hated Christ, and how this antipathy began even then, when he spent much of his time in chapel, or at chapel-related reading and social groups. The language of the Bible ran through his thoughts then, like the language of the hymns that he later described as having 'penetrated through and through my childhood', glistening in the depths of his consciousness in 'undimmed wonder'. His was a world, a class, whose daily hopes and fears were inflected by the examples offered by God in his different manifestations. But Lawrence couldn't go along with the New Testament. 'At the present moment I do not, cannot believe in the divinity of Christ,' he wrote to the minister of his Congregationalist chapel in Eastwood in 1907, aged twenty-two. He wasn't giving up on God altogether. He was announcing himself as an outsider and turning his back on the puritanism he would never quite renounce. He told the vicar that he could still believe in a 'Cosmic God' but not in the Christian Father and Son. I think, though, he'd have liked Jesus's harrowing of hell. He liked things to be shaken up.[1]

We have been walking through the water meadows. Our feet are sodden and I feel continually on the verge of tears. Yesterday a judge sent my son back to London to return to school there until she makes a final decision about whether I can move the children to the countryside. I hadn't expected this. These are my children, I say to myself, as Frieda said about hers. This weekend I feel only half myself without them; my body feels amputated in their absence. Our house has been harrowed, but not by a loving and forgiving Christ. This is the impersonal law of the Old Testament, as ruthless as the tractor making its way methodically up and down alongside us, the law of the Father that Lawrence thought was preferable to the love of the Son. I have submitted to Solomon, only to find that though these children are both mine, and though I love them both with a mother's love, he is prepared to divide them after all. Our family, as I have remade it in these months, has been cut in half.

'Which of you convicts me of sin? And if I say the truth, why do ye not believe me?' The law. I was mistaken to think that this was a loving system. I have put myself in the hands of power. Lawrence wanted his Cosmic God to be powerful rather than loving. He thought that Christ was wrong to offer light to redeem the darkness of a broken world. 'He that followeth me shall not walk in darkness,' Jesus promised, 'but all have the light of life.' Lawrence railed against it. 'We are not only creatures of light and virtue,' he wrote in 'The Reality of Peace'. 'We are also alive in corruption and death. It is necessary to balance the dark against the light if we are ever going to be free.' Hence wanting to take Christ out of Christianity, hence insisting that there were better conduits than Christ to God. I wonder if my mistake was to try to live in the light. Light will drench my memories of this summer, burning, hot, on the water in the river, falling on the children's faces as we walk through fields. And now, abruptly, after a court hearing that I entered in sunlight and departed in a downpour that left me soaked as I returned, disbelieving, to my car, I am shown the darkness that was waiting to claim me all along.[2]

Lawrence felt himself to be less religious than other people in Eastwood but to be more religious than other people almost everywhere else. This resulted in characteristic ambivalence, but also made him the great religious novelist of his generation – a writer who claimed the significance of religious experience even as he renounced the specificities of Christian doctrine. At a time when Joyce was furiously scorning the Catholicism he'd been brought up with, when Woolf and the rest of Bloomsbury were freeing themselves from religion, when Forster was merely curious about religious experience, when Hemingway turned religious experience into a pagan ethics of manhood, Lawrence continued to worry away at religious questions and to see religious experience as fundamental – as much so as sex. 'I am primarily a passionately religious man,' Lawrence wrote to his publisher in 1914, 'and my novels must be written from the depths of my religious experience.' If the modern age was a secular one, then Lawrence was a huge, dissenting voice within that. His ambivalence made him an ideal instrument for processing the complex religious possibilities of modern life: for diving into the relationship between Christianity and secularism, for exploring whether doubt could be a vehicle for religious meaning (as in Dostoevsky, who Lawrence much admired), and whether modernity's focus on individual freedom and will could connect to Christianity's emphasis on the individual soul, for asking whether pagan energy could be reignited within modern religious practice, and whether society could once more be structured through religious experience. Lawrence lived in a society that, on the whole, didn't know what being religious meant any more, and this turned out to be the ideal setting in which to launch his restless, urgent exploration of what being religious is.[3]

His ambivalence was centred on his ambivalence to Jesus, who in many moods he simply hated. Why was this? Perhaps he was mainly envious, as he was with Freud. He was a prophet himself, whose books were going to guide England into a new era of religious feeling. After 1914 he had a decidedly biblical beard, and he always loved playing biblical charades: if he wasn't 'Gawd-a-mighty', he was St Peter on Judgement Day. When he wasn't reviling Christ, he was identifying with him. In 1915 he described the first year of the war as destroying him, leaving his soul 'in the tomb – not dead but with the flat stone over it'. In coming through, he had 'risen' full of hope after his period of illness and despair. His friends were often happy to join in the role play. 'Do not betray me,' Lawrence told Murry at a London dinner in 1923 that he and his friends later cast as his 'Last Supper', between trips to New Mexico. 'It wasn't a woman who betrayed Jesus with a kiss,' Catherine Carswell reported herself as saying in an aside to Murry.[4]

Perhaps Lawrence saw Jesus as a kind of alter ego – as the puritan he might have been. Lawrence recognised in Jesus his own sexual fastidiousness. He hated the idea of promiscuity, and was very circumspect about his brief season of adultery with Rosalind Baynes in 1920. The lure of sexual renunciation for Lawrence is clear in *Aaron's Rod*, written mainly in Italy in 1920, before and after the affair with Rosalind. It's because of a brief sexual encounter with a loose woman that Aaron sinks into weeks of decapacitating illness. 'I did myself in when I went with another woman,' he tells Lilly. 'I felt myself go – as if the bile broke inside me, and I was sick.' Aaron seems incapable of tenderly erotic sexual feeling either for the wife he's abandoned or for the women he meets on his travels, and I think that Lawrence saw something of himself in this sickly squeamishness. That's why he was so derisive of Christ when it came to his sexual renunciation – he was castigating himself alongside him. In *Fantasia of the Unconscious* he mocks Jesus's claim not to need the feminine 'world of love, of emotion, of sympathy'. Even he should have learnt to be 'man enough ... To come home at tea-time and put his slippers on,' he wrote, and he gives Jesus the chance to do something like this in 'The Escaped Cock', his free-wheeling retelling of the Resurrection, written during an agonised Easter in Florence in 1927.

Lawrence's Christ, waking from the tomb here, quickly comes to regret his years of high-minded fastidiousness. 'Life bubbles variously,' he reflects, wondering why he told everyone to live in the same, abstemious way. His soul has been as dead as his body, and he fears the living touch of others until he meets a young woman he finds tending the temple of Isis. Watched over by 'all-tolerant Pan', the woman heals him with sex. 'I am risen,' he proclaims, basking in 'the deep, interfolded warmth, warmth living and penetrable, the woman'. Now he wonders if Judas betrayed him because Jesus loved him bodilessly, when he should have kissed him with 'live love'.

This is a Jesus who is redeemed by sex, as Constance Chatterley is. Lawrence's problem with Jesus was that he was too disembodied in his spirituality: rather like Miriam in *Sons and Lovers*, Jesus was born, as Lawrence wrote in his Hardy essay, not to flesh but to spirit. Lawrence liked God the Father better because he was a God who talked about the body: 'In God the Father we are all one body, one flesh. But in Christ we abjure the flesh.' Lawrence thought that since the Renaissance there had been too much emphasis on Christ. He called the Renaissance the Epoch of Love, meaning fleshless, spiritual love. It succeeded, he said, the era of the Old Testament God, the Epoch of Law, meaning the biblical laws, which he saw as grounded in earthiness. The Old Testament God could blend, more easily than Jesus, into Lawrence's 'Cosmic God'. In *Kangaroo* Somers tells Kangaroo (who sees himself as a kind of Christ figure) that men should again 'refer the sensual passion of love sacredly to the great dark God'. This is a god of the solar plexus: a god of the unconscious who we pray to from our stomachs.[5]

There are two eternities, Lawrence wrote in 'The Lemon Garden', during that first trip to Italy with Frieda: the eternity of the flesh and the eternity of the spirit. Neither is enough without the other. If you have a religion too much of the flesh, as he thought the Italians did, you will go mad out of sensual excess. If you have a religion too much of the spirit, like the northern puritans, you will destroy yourself through too much rational will.

In *The Rainbow*, shortly afterwards, he set all these Gods and eternities against each other. The first generations dwell, in their different ways, in the Old Testament. Will, drawn to a dark and sensuous Old Testament God, ignores the sermon in church to glory 'in his dark emotional experience of the Infinite'. He doesn't have the blank sensuality of his ancestors, though. He irritates Anna by being too emotional in his religiousness, too selfless in his soulfulness. She wants instead to assert her selfhood, to 'dance and play' before the unknown, Cosmic God. So, pregnant, she begins her naked dancing, dancing in secret 'in the pride of her bigness' before her creator. And one day she does this when Will is in the house:

> On a Saturday afternoon, when she had a fire in the bed-room, again she took off her things and danced, lifting her knees and her hands in a slow, rhythmic exulting. He was in the house, so her pride was fiercer. She would dance his nullification, she would dance to her unseen Lord. She was exalted over him, before the Lord.
>
> She heard him coming up the stairs, and she flinched. She stood with the firelight on her ankles and feet, naked in the shadowy, late afternoon, fastening up her hair. He was startled. He stood in the doorway, his brows black and lowering.
>
> 'What are you doing?' he said, gratingly. 'You'll catch a cold.'
>
> And she lifted her hands and danced again, to annul him, the light glanced on her knees as she made her slow, fine movements down the far side of the room, across the firelight. He stood away near the door in blackness of shadow, watching, transfixed. And with slow, heavy movements she swayed backwards and forwards, like a full ear of corn, pale in the dusky afternoon, threading before the firelight, dancing his non-existence, dancing herself to the Lord, to exultation.
>
> He watched, and his soul burned in him. He turned aside, he could not look, it hurt his eyes. Her fine limbs lifted and lifted, her hair was sticking out all fierce, and her belly, big, strange, terrifying, uplifted to the Lord. Her face was rapt and beautiful, she danced exulting before her Lord, and knew no man.

It hurt him as he watched as if he were at the stake. He felt he was being burned alive. The strangeness, the power of her in her dancing consumed him, he was burned, he could not grasp, he could not understand. He waited obliterated.

This is a scene where religious faith has all the power of sex. There are echoes, too, of the earlier scene where Will and Anna gathered the sheaves of corn in the field. Rhythm comes into it again, in Anna's 'slow, rhythmic exulting'. Spurred on by the example of Lawrence's own namesake, David, who danced naked before the Lord, Anna uses her dancing to nullify her husband, oppressing him with the vision of a connection to her creator far more potent than Will's own connection either to Anna or to God. It's an astonishing image: Anna, pregnant and naked with the firelight on her ankles and feet, bathed less in Jesus's heavenly light than the light with which God burns bushes in the wilderness. She is herself on fire, and the flames that protect her threaten to consume her husband. He stands in the shadows, powerless in the darkness, and she reminds him of those full ears of corn they once harvested together, as she dances him into non-existence. Now it is Will who is on fire. Watching, his soul burns, he is consumed by flames from within. She lifts herself heavenwards, exulting to the Lord and knowing no man; he feels as if he is being burned at the stake, becoming himself a kind of lurid Christ figure, weakened by God the Father and by the dancing, flaming woman.

The words, as always, are so ordinary – 'big, strange, terrifying'. Once again it's the rhythms, sonorously biblical here, that burnish the words and give the scene its visionary power: 'He watched, and his soul burned in him. He turned aside, he could not look, it hurt his eyes.' Anna is confident, now, in her knowledge of God. That's why, when they visit the cathedral in the next chapter, and Will loses himself in 'the perfect, swooning consummation, the timeless ecstasy' he feels in the hushed darkness of the vast godly building, she is able to resist him, remembering that the sky they can see beyond is 'a space where stars were wheeling in freedom, with freedom above them always higher'. She dismisses the building as dead matter, determined to seek her ecstasies in the natural world beyond.

Will's is a dark, unknown God, Anna's a cosmic creator. Neither seems very interested in Christ and it's their daughter Ursula who falls for the modern God of Love. She has a passion for Christ, who she yearns for as a daughter and a lover. Seeing the lambs in the fields, 'stooping, nuzzling, groping to the udder', she pictures herself as a lamb tended by Christ the shepherd who is himself the lamb of God. Then she finds a new form of ecstasy in her sexual encounters, first with her teacher Winifred and then with Anton Skrebensky. Winifred frees her from the dogmas of her religion, teaching her about how each of the world religions has its own version of Christ. She gives up on Jesus, as Lawrence did at the same age. Now her God is no longer mild and gentle, neither lamb nor dove. He is the lion and the eagle: 'she loved the dignity and self-possession of lions'. Ursula isn't going to end up straightforwardly inhabiting the Old Testament world of her parents and grandparents, though, any more than Lawrence could. Her task is to find a form of religion fitting for modernity; to find forms of religious experience that can enable the new kinds of living and loving she will pursue in *Women in Love*.

A few days after the court hearing I get ill. It's a cold, caught from my son, that my daughter and I now come down with in his absence. 'Poor Mummy,' we say as we cough and sneeze together, 'poor G'. There is something luxuriant about this even as I resent it for disrupting my plans. We lie in my bed watching children's TV together, intermittently napping. We drink a lot of juice and G takes her vitamins and medicine willingly, startled into a new docility by her brother's absence. 'H is at school,' she says, as we walk past his worktable on our way to the kitchen. I think of Lawrence's sister Ada, waiting in Nottinghamshire for his periodic returns, always willing to rent a cottage for him and Frieda to stay in when they needed it. She had her crisis of faith not long after his. He urged her to believe in an abstract God even if she couldn't believe in the Christian Father and Son: 'not a personal God: a vast, shimmering impulse which wavers onwards towards some end'.[6]

Lawrence had a lot of colds and flus. He told everyone about them, partly because he believed illness to be instructive, partly because it was a relief to be able to talk about illnesses that were curable, unlike the spectre of the TB he may or may not have had lingering in his body since childhood. He thought that illness was psychosomatic, the product of mental distress. 'One is ill because one doesn't live properly – can't,' Birkin says in *Women in Love*. But this didn't mean that Lawrence wished to avoid being ill. He thought that it was useful that we could channel our distress into physical symptoms; that the physical symptoms, by being curable, could provide a way out of the unhappiness that gave rise to them. Writing from Cornwall in January 1916, he told Ottoline Morrell that he had been ill for weeks but was emerging from the 'dissolution' into a new dawn, knowing that he would be strong again. He advised her to simulate illness herself: 'you must lie very still and give up your body and your mind … as if they were not yours at all, as if you had no more will'. Lie 'loosed and gone' for a few days, he advised, and then she would be well.[7]

My daughter recovers before I do. She goes bouncily back to nursery and I spend more days in bed. It is absurd to be so ill with so sodden a cold, when the virus that is making the world around me uninhabitable is characterised by a dry cough, but these are the symptoms I have been assigned. Although it's a warm September, I shiver all the time. I stay determinedly inside for days. Waking up from a nap, I look in the bathroom mirror and find that I can't connect the image of myself with the physical sensations of my body: dry throat, aching limbs, head overspilling.

Lawrence put his illnesses partly down to despair at the state of the world and partly down to personal 'chagrin'. 'My illnesses I know come from chagrin,' he wrote to Frieda's sister towards the end of his life; 'chagrin that goes deep in and comes afterwards in haemorrhage or what not'. It's a word I don't quite understand but that meant a lot to him. The OED defines it as 'a species of skin or leather with a rough surface', which is used metaphorically to refer to 'acute vexation, annoyance, or mortification, arising from disappointment, thwarting, or failure'. It's a Lawrentian feeling: a form of regret that contains anger. Mortification plays a part in it and the deadliness of that word doesn't seem too strong for a feeling that, in Lawrence's view, would literally kill him, bringing on the haemorrhages that led to his death. Once you start looking for chagrin, you see it in all his novels. Miriam looks with chagrin at the sunset in *Sons and Lovers*, angry and disappointed with Paul. Will is hurt 'with a chagrin' when Anna pulls away from him in *The Rainbow*. Ursula experiences 'anger and chagrin' when Birkin withdraws from her, and Birkin is silenced into chagrin when she accuses him of being 'cocksure' (a word that Lawrence elsewhere applied to overconfident women). Gerald's father dies of chagrin in *Women in Love* because he has failed to be a good Christian, exploiting the colliers instead of acting lovingly towards them.[8]

I wonder if it's chagrin that I'm experiencing. Is there a Lawrentian element of regret and recrimination in my feelings, and is my fever burning it away? Illness for Lawrence's characters is almost always followed by revelation. The chagrin dissipates and the world is seen anew. In my moments of greater alertness, I wonder what I can learn. It seems to me that in all my wilfulness I have been too attached to the world, to cause and consequence. I wrote statements, listing the reasons why my son should be with me, but then I lost him. There is a relief now in giving up on effort, and in giving up on people altogether, as Lawrence did when ill as well. I am out of touch, though touch for five months has been reserved for only three people. Touch with them feels more necessary still than ever. I relish even the 4 a.m. wakings from my daughter, who is touchingly grateful for the medicine that I syringe into her mouth, asking for her blanket to be arrayed neatly. I sink into P. But other people feel too much. I feel unable to talk to people when I am so far from being what I would consider to be myself, or perhaps it's that this emptied self requires no communion other than the touch that I wouldn't anyway have from anyone else.

Even as I complain about my symptoms, I know that I am grateful to them for making this retreat from the world possible.

The crying has stopped. Now my face feels full of fluid instead. I have been worried by somatisation in the past, especially when it comes to P's frequent migraines, but it turns out to be very pleasing to feel the body expressing and expelling disgust and pain as the soggy tissues gather on my bed. It feels like a time of waiting: waiting for my throat to stop hurting and my nose to stop running, and waiting to mind less, to move through the chagrin. While I wait, I eat chocolate biscuits and tangerines, I respond apathetically to queries from lawyers, I read the *Bhagavad Gita* and the Old Testament, hoping to acquire wisdom from the sources where Lawrence located it.

I am curious about the *Bhagavad Gita*, partly because P quotes it so often. 'Action without regard for the consequences of action,' he tells me when I am despairing about things going wrong. It is all right to fail if you have acted rightly. I find it calming when he says it; it is calming to think that we can strive to act rightly, without striving to bring about the consequences we desire. It seems like a way to have the good form of Lawrentian will without the bad form, so it's not surprising that Lawrence was drawn to Hinduism, which also appealed to him for its phallus worship (Lord Siva is worshipped in India as a lingam, or symbol of the phallus) and sun worship.

'Not by refraining from action does man attain freedom from action,' Krishna tells Arjuna, persuading him to fight. The *Bhagavad Gita* is an account of Krishna's success in persuading Arjuna to go back to the battlefield, insisting that he is wrong to worry about killing in battle because there is an eternal self that remains unaffected by death, and because it is possible to fight without being corrupted by desire. This is a book about going back into the world, while relinquishing desire. 'Even as all waters flow into the ocean, but the ocean never overflows, even so the sage feels desires, but he is ever one in his infinite peace.' Ill in bed, I wonder what it would be like to return to the world while still feeling something of the stillness I've acquired.[9]

The rhythms of illness and renewal were religious rhythms for Lawrence. This is the journey into the wilderness we see again and again in the Bible: the retreat from the world followed by the return. I have often wondered what exactly Lawrence meant by saying that his novels were written from the depths of his religious experience, but I think that a crucial element of it was his sense of life's rhythm being one of retreat and return, unmaking and making. If his Cosmic God was a God of power rather than love, then it was a God who engaged in acts of destruction because only then could the world be remade. 'We've exhausted our love-urge,' Lawrence has his prophet-figure, Lilly, tell Aaron in *Aaron's Rod*. 'It's no good. We've got to accept the power motive. It is a great life motive.' Not the will to power, he says, not in Nietzsche's sense, though this is one of the places where a Lawrence character misreads Nietzsche. Lilly wants unconscious, impersonal power, urging 'from within, darkly, for the displacing of the old leaves, the inception of the new'. This sounds dangerously close to a naked celebration of power. If all we need is for the world to be destroyed and cleansed, then why not start a war, why not found a cult of death? We know how much destruction has been wrought in the name of power as a force of life. This has always been the danger lurking within religious ideals – and it's a danger close to the surface in most religions.

It's because Lawrence's God was a God who destroyed and remade that he was dismissive of Buddhism, and why he was more receptive to Hinduism. In 1922, explaining to his Buddhist friend Achsah Brewster that he didn't want to come and see her in Ceylon, he said that 'more and more I feel that meditation and the inner life are not my aim, but some sort of action and strenuousness and pain and frustration and struggling through'. His goal, he went on, was not that men should become serene as Buddha, but, as in the *Bhagavad Gita*, that 'the unfleshed gods should become men in battle'. Men had to fight for the new incarnation, for gods becoming men. 'And the fight and the sorrow and the loss of blood, and even the influenzas and the headache are a part of the fight and the fulfilment.'[10]

What Lawrence meant, in part, by describing himself as a passionately religious man was that his vision of the world was a religious vision. In *Fantasia of the Unconscious* he says that Freud makes too much of sex as a drive because there's another drive, equally strong, which is the religious impulse. This is the impulse that takes us out into the world: it's the impulse to work, to create, to build a world beyond the home.

After sex, he says here, new impulses and a new vision come into being. The brain tingles to new thought, the heart craves for new activity. This is work, and it's the work that Anna urges Will to do after their honeymoon in *The Rainbow*. Don't you have something to do? she asks him, though really it's she who is feeling the push towards worldly action, but Lawrence couldn't quite allow her generation of women to feel it. Will does eventually start working again. He does his woodwork, he begins to teach. The next generation is split in their attitudes towards work. There are women, now, whose brains tingle with new thoughts. Gudrun longs to make art, Ursula longs to teach, until she discovers the grubby, mechanised reality of the education system. But Birkin decides to give up work in order to live more fully. 'It has become dead to me,' he says. And Gerald's work is the mines is seen not merely as dead, but as deadening to all the workers he employs. Work here is something to be avoided, and Lawrence says this in the Hardy essay as well, where he writes that we work in the first place to earn enough to eat, and then to provide for the future, and then to provide for the poor, but complains that we are told to keep on working even when we have done all that. 'For the mass, for the 99.9 per cent of mankind, work is a form of non-living, of non-existence, of submergence.'[11]

Lawrence's argument here is reminiscent of Frieda's sister's sometime lover, the sociologist Max Weber, who was part of Frieda and Lawrence's circle in Germany. Max and his brother, the economist and sociologist Alfred Weber, had been brought up in an influential, cosmopolitan but authoritarian household before going on to become prestigious academics. It was Max Weber who first fell in love with Frieda's sister Else von Richthofen, who was herself an economist (she was employed by the state as an inspector of factories) and whose husband, Edgar Jaffé, was a former student of Max Weber's. Max and Else began an affair in 1909 which proved life-changing for Max (whose marriage was unconsummated), but then the more bohemian Else moved on to Max's brother Alfred, whose flat in Icking Lawrence and Frieda would borrow. Max Weber remained the more famous of the two brothers, a bold sociologist with Nietzschean yearnings, who forced social scientists in Germany to confront the largest questions and thinkers of their age.

Meeting the Webers, Lawrence might have been aware of their puritanical religious upbringing, not dissimilar to his, despite their otherwise very different backgrounds. Though Max Weber later described himself as 'unmusical religiously', his own religious experiences were in the background when he wrote his influential 1905 book *The Protestant Ethic and the Spirit of Capitalism*, where he linked the excessive work ethic of contemporary capitalism to forms of religion like the Congregationalism that Lawrence was brought up in. Weber complained that puritan religion had been used to justify the rapaciousness of capitalism, because it was naturally disposed to support both 'the strict avoidance of all spontaneous enjoyment of life' and 'the expression of virtue and proficiency in a calling', which could easily be reduced to mere work. Protestants, he wrote, had the idea of a calling as the highest form which the moral activity of an individual could assume. It had somehow come to pass that even a job in the mines had taken on the aspect of 'a task set by God', so that puritanism had bequeathed to its utilitarian successors 'an amazingly good … conscience in the acquisition of money, so long as it took place legally', and a doctrine of religious asceticism that provided factory owners with sober and industrious workmen.[12]

We might call to mind Mr and Mrs Morel here, with Mrs Morel complaining on religious grounds about Mr Morel's inclination towards pleasure, and Mr Morel worked to exhaustion and illness by the mine owners. Lawrence couldn't quite let go of his puritanism in *Sons and Lovers*. He disapproved of his father's laziness, even if he disapproved of the mine owners' rapaciousness as well. But by *Women in Love*, he had turned against work and the Protestant work ethic that underpinned it. I had a phase, rereading it to teach, when I was perplexed by the lack of vocation among all its central characters except Gudrun.

These are people whose brilliance and high-mindedness we are meant to accept, yet no one wants to do anything. They give up their jobs and go off to do what? – just to forge new forms of relationship and community. But I have since realised that the point is that forging new forms of relationship is a religious task for Lawrence. What Lawrence termed the religious impulse is the problem: it pushes us into the non-existence of deadening work. It's also the solution: it can allow us to retreat from the world altogether (those quasi-religious influenzas!) and can give us a purpose beyond work.

This is what Lawrence decided in many of the books that followed, from *Kangaroo* to *The Plumed Serpent*. If Lawrence couldn't quite come up with a new theory for society in *Kangaroo*, then he did so in New Mexico, where he committed fully to giving religion the responsibility for replacing a broken political system and restoring collective vitality to the world. His vision of the collective was religious rather than political now, and the religious experiences he found most compelling were the ancient religious traditions he had encountered in New Mexico and Mexico.

'A vast, old religion which once swayed the earth lingers in unbroken practice there in New Mexico,' Lawrence wrote soon after going there for the first time in 1922. He had been to Ceylon, and seen naked villagers dancing under torches, witnessing religion as 'an uncontrollable, sensual experience'. But he thought that religion did not establish a settled way of life there. In New Mexico, in Apache country, he had come across 'the most deeply religious race living'. The tribes here had traditions going back beyond the birth of Christ, beyond the pyramids, beyond Moses. There was no single God in this religion. Instead 'God is everywhere, God is in everything.' Attending the ceremonial known as the 'snake dance' and watching a priest hopping around a small square no bigger than a back yard with the neck of a pale, bird-like snake nipped between his teeth, Lawrence saw what he most wanted from religion. He was seduced by the feeling that 'Creation is a great flood, forever flowing, in lovely and terrible waves. In everything the shimmer of creation and never the finality of the created.' These waves of cyclical life in constant motion were, after all, what he'd been trying to write about for the past decade.[13]

It was in New Mexico that Lawrence revised his essay on Whitman for *Studies in Classic American Literature*, an essay where he found a new, secular formulation for his deepest religious urges. This is a book that begins as an anxious tirade about the false ideal of American freedom and then settles into an aphoristic, elliptical discussion of American writers from Benjamin Franklin to Whitman. Throughout, he is as edgily dismissive of American freedom and democracy as he was of Australian freedom and democracy in *Kangaroo*, but with more at stake, more of a sense that American freedom, as manifested in the landscapes he has come to rely on, is precisely what the world needs. The essay on Whitman follows directly on from an essay on Melville, where Lawrence reads *Moby Dick* as lamenting 'the doom of our white day'. The whale here becomes 'the deepest blood-being of our white race', who is hunted by our white mental consciousness, aided by dark races co-opted for the fight. After this there can only be ghosts, and he sees Whitman as bringing 'a certain ghoulish insistency ... a certain stridency and portentousness' to his talk of democratic loving and merging. 'Your mainspring is broken, Walt Whitman. The mainspring of your own individuality. And so you run down with a great whirr, merging with everything.'

Then the tone shifts, and Lawrence finds in Whitman's notion of sympathy a kind of redemption, locating it on what Lawrence calls the open road:

> Whitman's essential message was the Open Road. The leaving of the soul free unto herself, the leaving of his fate to her and to the loom of the open road. Which is the bravest doctrine man ever proposed to himself.

The open road here is both a physical place and an existential state. Lawrence goes on to say that it's a better, more strenuous alternative to fasting or meditating. To be on the open road is to be exposed to full contact with anyone else we meet along the way, watching the vibration of their soul and flesh as we pass. This, he says, is the best of America, the best of American democracy. Whitman didn't quite get there: he got sidetracked by loving and merging. But there's still time. We can seek a kind of communion of the spirit with strangers on the open road. This would be Lawrence's own quest for the next decade.

It was also in New Mexico that in 1923 Lawrence wrote his essay 'On Being Religious', an attempt to make sense of his own faith at a time when his travels had thrown him into exhilarating contact with ancient religions so different from the one he'd been brought up in. Years after his agony with his own religious doubt, this begins as a curiously carefree declaration of his belief in God, on the grounds that 'whatever the queer little word means, it means something we can none of us ever quite get away from' and that (as emerges in an imaginary dialogue he stages between two believers) believing in God 'looks like fun'. Lawrence then goes on to extol the Holy Spirit in terms that sound strikingly similar to his celebration of Whitman's open road. In 1912, in his 'Lemon Garden' essay, Lawrence had talked about the need for the Holy Spirit to mediate between two eternal ecstasies: the daylight, loving spiritual ecstasy of Christ the lamb, and the dark, destructive bodily eternity of God the lion. These two forms of infinity, positive and negative, needed to be kept separate, but also needed to relate to one another, and it was the Holy Spirit that could relate 'the dual Infinities into One Whole, which relates and keeps distinct the dual natures of God'. Now he went further in his claims for the Holy Spirit, saying that it was all that remained to us of the Christian Trinity. God the Father has left heaven, he writes; he's climbed down and is sitting alone, somewhere in the cosmos. Jesus once offered one way to reach him, but his way is no longer open. From time to time, God sends a new saviour (perhaps Lawrence had himself in mind) but otherwise we are left with the Holy Ghost:

> We go in search of God, following the Holy Ghost, and depending on the Holy Ghost. There is no Way. There is no Word. There is no Light. The Holy Ghost is ghostly and invisible. The Holy Ghost is nothing, if you like. Yet we

hear His strange calling, the strange calling like a hound on the scene, away in the unmapped wilderness. And it seems great fun to follow.[14]

The Holy Ghost here, with his mixture of fun and ghostliness, his invitation to the 'unmapped wilderness,' sounds like the kind of spirit we might encounter on Whitman's open road. And for Lawrence, it was a spirit met more naturally in the ancient Mexican religions than in Christianity, although even now, he didn't give up on the Church, and he sought ways in *The Plumed Serpent* to join up the ancient Aztec religions with Christianity.

This is the major work that Lawrence made in New Mexico, though it's telling that almost all of it was written across the border in Mexico. If Mabel Dodge had invited him to stay because she wanted him to help with her political efforts, putting his writing in the service of the Indigenous Americans in New Mexico, then he didn't end up fulfilling his duties to his host. He didn't write much about the Indigenous Americans in New Mexico and his potentially more directly flattering project of writing a novel about Mabel herself was put on hold once it became clear that Frieda wasn't going to tolerate the semi-clad 'research' sessions that Mabel instigated in her bedroom. Instead he ended up with *The Plumed Serpent*, his messy, megalomaniacal and often very misguided novel in which he went the furthest he ever went in imagining society reorganised according to religious principles.

He began the novel a few months after first crossing the border into Mexico in 1923. It tells the story of an Irish tourist called Kate Leslie, who visits Mexico from England and is swept into the cult of Quetzalcoatl, a religion founded by an intellectual-cum-priest-cum-god called Don Ramón Carrasco with his friend Don Cipriano, a Mexican general who Kate ends up marrying. This is a religion that flows through everything, and that captivates Kate in its all-encompassingness even as it repels her in its authoritarianism – Ramón has set himself up as a kind of god and expects to be worshipped and obeyed. As Lawrence revised the novel during subsequent stays in Mexico, he focused increasingly on the ritual of the new religion he was devising, totally captivated by constructing elaborately detailed hymns and rituals on behalf of his imaginary cult. In the violent idyll of the lakeside village of Sayula, very like the once grandly elegant resort of Chapala where Lawrence had begun the book, a whole community has devoted its days to sewing religious vestments, making religious symbols and singing Ramón's hymns. Indian drums (to use the nomenclature of the novel for a moment) sound from the church at midday, reminding the community that 'every man should glance at the sun, and stand silent with a little prayer'.

The question of the relationship between the Quetzalcoatl cult and Christianity preoccupies Lawrence throughout. This is a living religion necessary, the book suggests, because Christianity no longer leads the Indian race to God. 'Tomorrow Jesus and Mary / will be bone' goes one of the Ramón's songs. Ramón explains that 'it is time now for Jesus to go back to the place of the death of the gods, and take the long bath of being made young again'. But Ramón doesn't see this as a repudiation of Christianity, any more than Lawrence did. His religion contains elements of Christianity. The god Quetzalcoatl, embodied by Ramón himself, is said to have 'risen and pushed the stone from the mouth of the tomb', and Ramón describes himself as a 'Catholic of Catholics', insisting that he wants 'One Church' but that 'different peoples must have different Saviours, as they have different speech and different colour'. He is the saviour needed here, and he's offering a religion of the morning star, somewhere between spirit and blood.

*The Plumed Serpent* is such a frustrating book to read. Lawrence wanted so much for it – revising it in 1925, he said that it lay 'nearer my heart than any other work of mine'. We can feel this in the writing, can feel it in Kate crying aloud in her soul 'to the greater mystery, the higher power that hovered in the interstices of the hot air, rich and potent'. Often, reading it, I have felt like Lawrence is on the brink of something amazing, yet usually it becomes very dull, because most of the characters are curiously wooden and the religious songs go on for far too long. It's easy to guess, reading it, that Lawrence found it hard to finish – he rewrote the ending many times. It's rather poignant watching him portray Kate arriving by boat at the lake over and over again, captivated by the image, yet knowing he still hasn't got the most out of it, that there is a better version of the book that it's still worth attempting to write.[15]

The most convincing scenes are the ones where Kate voices her frustration with Ramón, fed up with his attempt to turn her into an Aztec goddess:

> For heaven's sake let me get out of this, and back to simple human people. I loathe the very sound of Quetzalcoatl and Huitzilopochtli. I would die rather than be mixed up in it any more. Horrible, really, both Ramón and Cipriano. And they want to put it over me, with their high-flown bunk, and their Malintzi. Malintzi! I am Kate Forrester, really. I am neither Kate Leslie nor Kate Tylor. I am sick of these men putting names over me. I was born Kate Forrester, and I shall die Kate Forrester. I want to go home. Loathsome, really, to be called Malintzi. – I've had it put over me.

The voice here is fully Kate's. Lawrence's own rhythms are lost in her speech. 'I am sick of these men putting names over me.' As with *Kangaroo*, as with *Women in Love*, Lawrence allows a female character to triumph in challenging the speechifying hero. Perhaps we can see in this the genesis of his final novel, where he gave up on grand visions of society or religion and returned once more to the possibilities of a couple remaking each other in a Nottinghamshire wood. He had wanted to think that collective life could be made possible by a new version of an ancient religion but when he actually tried to write it, he couldn't make it work.

The churches are open again here and P goes every Sunday. There is a sense, on Sunday mornings, of people on the move once more. Church round here feels more about community than about religion. But that may be particularly the case for my generation. So few of my friends are religious, even the more observant Jews would be hard-pushed to profess a belief in God, though a believing Muslim friend says that she finds the idea of practising without belief peculiar. I don't think I'm alone among unbelievers in hedging my bets, going so far as to pray or to make bargains with God, shuffling off occasionally to church or synagogue.

It is October now and the leaves are becoming crisp, the days shortening. On Fridays I drive my son home from the station in evening light. The drive back west brings a feeling of escape and of sadness, the sky pinkening behind clouds that H says look like atomic bombs. In the car on my own, I have been listening with peculiar urgency to podcasts on prayer. American evangelicals, Anglican former archbishops, English Low-Church seekers: they are all asking for the same thing, for a conversation with God that can feel as open, as undemanding, as possible. They are making a space to hear God in. The former archbishop says that he works with his breath when he prays; he thinks there's a Christian tradition of deep breathing and meditative prayer that can be forgotten by the modern Church, and he uses the 'Jesus Prayer' as a kind of mantra, 'Lord Jesus Christ, Son of God, have mercy on me, a sinner.'

I'm reminded of Lawrence in his *Etruscan Places*, published posthumously but written in 1927, where he found in the Etruscan religion a vitality akin to what he'd found in Mexico. Talking about the Etruscan science of augury, he says that this was a practice of divination analogous to any other act of attention, whether in politics or 'prayer, or thought, or studying the stars, or watching the light of birds, – or studying the entrails of the sacrifice'. All of these are about attention and all depend on 'the amount of true, sincere, religious concentration you can bring to bear on your subject'.

I used to pray a lot as a child. The God of my childhood was a loving God of the kind Lawrence rejected. My father's Jewishness was too complicated for our religiously split family to take on, so I had very little contact with his Old Testament God and I got my religion from the monthly church services I attended as a Brownie. 'Our Father who Art in Heaven,' 'Jesus, Lamb of God, have mercy on us.' I was the kind of child who thought in words, chatting away inwardly to a large selection of imaginary friends at the imaginary boarding school I'd invented for myself. Conversations with God were a natural extension of this. He was the ideal father, the understanding parent always prepared to forgive me and see the best in me, without the rivalry that I (always realistic) attributed to my imaginary best friends. He could see my weaknesses through the prism of my strengths. Since then, I've got this sometimes from psychoanalysts, lovers and friends. Perhaps now if I didn't have P, I would have more need to pray.

We go, masked, to a hymnless church service. The congregation seems at ease with going to church in the age of Covid, opening their hands for the wafer that is dropped into them without touch, sitting two pews apart. The lambs in the fields round here have all grown up, indistinguishable now from their parents, but the lamb in the stained-glass window remains a lamb, making me think of Ursula in *The Rainbow*. The image is of the Good Shepherd, the one who values his flock's life above his own. I admire the lambs but am irritated by the sermon, which makes a case for Jesus as a socialist, praising the farmer who pays each of the men who work for him according to their need rather than their abilities. What about inequality? I ask P afterwards. What about poverty and starvation? What are we to make of the fact that Jesus has manifestly failed? We are back to Lawrence's letter to the Eastwood vicar, written after walking through the Nottingham slums. P talks me through the Church's answer: by giving us the gift of freedom, God allows us to be fallen as well as free, so of course we will get it all wrong. He says that Kant says that the existence of these ideals of fairness and equality shows that there is a more perfect world beyond us that we glimpse from time to time.

In a way it's a relief, after hearing about an impossibly beneficent version of Jesus, to think about Lawrence's destructive, punishing God. Here he is in one of his 'Pansies', telling us to seek thunder rather than love.

> never will you know any joy in your lives
> till you ask for lightning instead of love
> till you pray to the right gods, for the thunder-bolt instead
>   of pity ...

It has always been strange to me that Lawrence found in his thunder-bolting God any form of comfort. But if I have given up on my childhood God as I've got older, then it's partly because I have discovered that goodness and effort are not rewarded, that justice as I once envisaged it will not prevail. Lawrence's God allows for all that. This is an angry, adult God, an unknown God who cannot be understood in human terms. Perhaps there can be solace believing in a God who confirms the worst in us, showing that we are wrong to seek justice on earth when we can't expect it from heaven. There was solace for Lawrence, too, simply in opening oneself up to the unknown. The more irrational and incomprehensible the God, the more unknown he was, maybe. And at best, Lawrence's God was a deity who could make life, with its cycles, its dialectics of destruction and renewal, make sense.[16]

October is properly under way now and the leaves are changing colour, the roadside trees washed with red and yellow, their shapes revealed in diagrammatic form as they thin. My main encounter with the trees is on the roads, because the children want to go to playgrounds at weekends and I am working all the time during the nursery days. There are times when the lure of reading and writing exceeds the lure of the outside world for me, as it could for Lawrence. So it feels like the changing of the seasons is slipping away unnoticed until P and I escape one afternoon for an hour's walk. The sun is already low in the sky at 4 p.m., the clouds backlit by the heavens my son likes to see behind them, able to believe in the afterlife despite not believing in God. We find a walk by the Windrush where the grass, tufty and sheep-nibbled, undulates more erratically than by the Thames. There are trees of every kind of red and yellow, some still green beneath the yellow flecks, some burning fully in their new shades.

My desk here is in my son's room, a yellow desk chosen because it's his favourite colour. I inhabit his life in his absence, his Lego arranged around my ankles when I teach, his fluffy toys surrounding me when I lie in his bed to read between tasks. The day after our walk, lying exhausted under his duvet, I try out a prayer. 'Dear God.' I feel something of the same relief, the same feeling of relinquishing responsibility that I do in the yoga class I have started attending in the hall of a nearby village on Friday mornings. At the beginning and the end of the class, as the draught from the germ-mindedly open windows blows onto our shadowy figures, we are urged to breathe well and deeply. This is the breathing that the former archbishop thinks should be part of prayer. 'All is well and you are well and you are safe and you are enough,' we say in our minds. We stretch our thighs, ridding ourselves of anger, we open our lungs, breathing out fear. We are even told to soften our solar plexus to empty ourselves of anxiety, which makes me wonder if anyone else is thinking of Lawrence. 'I surrender to the flow and have faith in the ultimate good,' the teacher chants. It is faith in goodness that the act of prayer restores to me now on my son's bed, taking me back to my childhood self. I have learnt from the prayer podcasts. I am careful not to ask for too much, not to ask for the court case to go my way. I pray instead for courage to bear what is to come. Afterwards, I ask a handful of friends if they pray. In general, they don't, but my new Oxford friend tells me that she believes in grace. She says that she means calm, reflection, openness to the unknown. I say that Lawrence would have called this God.

I haven't realised how tired I have been getting until I go back to yoga and find that I don't have the energy to lift myself onto my toes between the upward and the downward dogs. I sink my knees onto the mat. The teacher asks if my back is sore. 'I am tired,' I say. 'That's all right,' she says, 'you are who you are today.' I cry for a few seconds, unseen, the tears falling down into my hair from my upside-down head. I had not realised how rare it was for me, the acceptance of limitation. For the rest of the class, I am gratefully docile. I believe everything I am told, repeating the mantras needily. 'All is well and you are well and you are safe and you are enough.'

They know so little about me here; they know that my scoliosis makes me curve to the left, that my shoulders are stiff and clenched, that I have a daughter whose nursery drop-offs make the timings tight. It's a form of community that I like, this intimacy without explanation – the intimacy of church. I wonder if this is what Lawrence imagined in his religious communities. We have little personality here; our desire, peculiarly intense, is for elongation, for balanced stillness. 'What we have already is good enough,' the teacher says. I think of the Jesus Prayer. 'Lord Jesus Christ, Son of God, have mercy on me, a sinner.' Even in my Christian childhood, it was the Father I was interested in rather than the Son. I haven't minded Lawrence's writing away of Jesus. I want a father, not a lover, and it feels right to me that Lawrence's Jesus is a pulsing, sexual man – otherwise he is too good to be true. But the mercy that Jesus is meant to bring feels necessary. Never more than now have I been aware of myself as a sinner, aware of how much I am asking from the world, aware that I may turn out to have been wrong to ask it and that mercy may be required. We lie on our backs, blanketed against the cold. The former archbishop said on the podcast that we feel the Holy Spirit within us when we feel yearnings to be better, godlier versions of ourselves. Is it the Holy Spirit that I have found in the draughty old school hall? Does it waft in through the open window, carried on the vibrations as we hum?

I drive back under the autumn trees, whole trees red, yellow, the pavements covered with yellow leaves like scattered offerings. As with spring, it is too much, too abundant; I do not know what to do with it. It brings to mind a conversation at the weekend with my son where I failed to explain why I find the changing colours so beautiful, leaving him perplexed as to why right now I find red and yellow more beautiful than green. For his part, Lawrence was saddened by the falling autumn leaves: he saw them as deathly. 'The acrid scents of autumn, / Reminiscent of slinking beasts, make me fear / Everything,' he wrote in 'Dolor of Autumn'. But he saw too in the changing colours the hope of renewal that he sought in religion. 'If as Autumn deepens and darkens / I feel the pain of falling leaves,' he wrote in 'Shadows',

Then I shall know that my life is moving still
With the dark earth, and drenched
With the deep oblivion of earth's lapse and renewal.

Was this what I should have said to my son at the weekend? That here, on the open road of the Oxfordshire countryside, I feel my life moving as the leaves fall?

# 7

# Nature

It is hard to say when autumn becomes winter. Even some of the trees with delicate-looking leaves turn out to be evergreen, so patches of green remain. The cold comes in waves, the rain falls for days at a time, making the river swell and the fields flood – it can feel as though we are by the sea. I stop going to church on Sundays and lie inside, reading, looking out at the trees that Lawrence in some moods thought might be gods. A tree is Pan, he wrote in 1924 in 'Pan in America', looking up from his cabin under the Rocky Mountains at the big pine tree that rose 'like a guardian spirit' in front of their ranch, alive, though its crest had been cut off by lightning. 'It vibrates its presence into my soul, and I am with Pan. I think no man could live near a pine-tree and remain quite suave and supple and compliant. Something fierce and bristling is communicated ... Give me your power, then, oh tree! And I will give you of mine.'[1]

There are two large old fir trees outside the window where I lie in bed reading at P's house, their trunks twined with ivy. It's a foggy day but the trees are close enough to be seen clearly. The branches overlap each other so it looks like one two-trunked tree, a two-legged creature when faced head-on. From my window all I see are the branches, stark in outline, though the leaves hang down in fluffy clumps. There are almost as many leaves as there were in the summer, but I know that it's a winter view, the branches darkly silhouetted in the heavy white light, the wind more determined than in summer, making the leaves wobble with what can seem like fear.

I have moved to the country partly because I want us to be more located in the natural world, but I have not been going out into it very much. G spends her days bird-watching at nursery, but I have stayed at home, reading in bed, getting up only to teach online. I have lost the court case. The children are to remain apart. For days after the final hearing, my mind refused to be still. I was stuck in the courtroom with false accusations playing out repeatedly. I longed for the silence that I can hear around me at last this Sunday morning in mid-December, looking out at this pair of fir trees. Behind them is the church where P has gone with many of his neighbours, all valiantly determined to continue to congregate, though several of the oldest inhabitants of the village have now died of Covid. I wonder if the churchgoers are also looking out at the trees, and if they would agree with the German naturalist-philosopher Ernst Haeckel, beloved by Lawrence in his youth, who said that man needs no special church because 'his church is commensurate with the whole of glorious nature'.[2]

I have quietened the voices in my head by learning to banish words from my thoughts altogether. At other times in my life, I've talked my way out of distress, but now, after two days of being assailed by speech in court, I distrust words too much. I cannot bear to tell this story, but can speak of nothing else, so silence seems the only possibility. I find it reassuring that Lawrence, who wrote more words in a year than almost anyone else can have done, frequently hated language, wanting us to be silenced. His yearning for the world of Pan was a yearning for the world before (as he put it in a draft of his essay on Pan) the 'First Word, or Logos was uttered', when man 'lived in the world of the unconceived, unspoken Pan'. His most appealing characters lash out at his most talkative ones. Constance Chatterley becomes fed up with her husband, Clifford, for talking too much about the wood they both love, because she wants just to experience it without being told that violets are Juno's eyelids. 'How she hated words, always coming between her and life.' Perhaps Lawrence loved silence so much partly because he had spoken and not been heard. His books were banned, many of his essays went unpublished; what point was there in human speech? He liked to listen instead to what Rousseau called 'the cry of nature', which preceded words. The scream of a tortoise during coition, the 'blorting' of a heifer on heat. And he longed for silence. Happy with Ursula, Birkin looks at her face, turned upwards like a flower, and smiles faintly, 'as if there were no speech in the world, save the silent delight of flowers in each other'.[3]

Lawrence loved flowers almost as much as he loved trees. They too had that particular, living kind of stillness, and offered the listener an audible silence. All those flights from society were escapes into the natural world, into a life lived alongside plants and animals, where humans become just one animal among many, human language only one more set of noises. There was always a side of him that wanted a world with only plants and animals and no humans. 'Don't you find it a beautiful clean thought,' Birkin asks Ursula, 'a world empty of people, just uninterrupted grass, and a hare sitting up?' You'd be dead yourself, she retorts, so what good would that do you? But Birkin doesn't care. He would die like a shot, he says, to know the earth really would be cleaned of all the people. 'I much prefer to think of the lark rising up in the morning upon a humanless world. Man is a mistake, he must go. There is the grass, and hares and adders.'

After lunch, the fog thickens, but we drive out, half unwillingly, for a walk, P's car quickly invisible as we move away from it. We walk slowly, setting off across a field we cannot see to the other side of, making out sheep as their black noses come into view. They race across the field away from us, the speed surprising in a world that feels dulled and slowed. We walk on, each patch that we cover somehow new, separate from the world a few metres ago. From the house, the fog looked uniform, but it turns out to have a peculiarly physical presence, weaving around us, shaking itself out. Looking in some directions, I feel like it's something I could touch. I am becoming curious again, even excited. We enter a wood and find that each tree that we pass is, if anything, more visible than usual. It is unexpected that something so obfuscatory can feel so clarifying – it turns out there is nothing clearer than the outline of a tree emerging from fog.

What was nature for Lawrence? I ask P, breaking into speech. I have been immersed in eco-criticism, reading the scholars of today who hope the world can be redeemed by literature. Some of them make cases for Lawrence, applauding him as an eco-warrior, a lover of nature. But Lawrence didn't use the word 'nature' as much as you might expect, and when he did, he was usually referring to essence – to what it was in our nature to do. When he did refer to nature as a whole, with a capital N, he was often being caustic. 'We must always beware of romance: of people who love Nature, or flowers, or dogs,' he wrote in an essay on Wordsworth, who he criticised for worshipping 'Nature in her sweet-and-pure aspect'.[4]

Nonetheless, he did have a sense of the natural world as a collective, living entity. And if there's anything that's likely to make him popular now, then it's probably his nature writing. Pantheism is in vogue again, whatever name it goes by. 'This is a rebellion ... for the forests and the forest medicines, for the trees of wisdom, the trees of life and the living waters of the Nile and the Yangtze, the Tigris and the Ganges,' I read this morning in an Extinction Rebellion vision statement. Couldn't this have been Lawrence, celebrating Pan, or mourning the loss of the Etruscan religion, in which 'all was alive; the whole universe lived; and the business of man was himself to live amid it all', drawing life into himself 'out of the wandering huge vitalities' of the living cosmos?

We talk now about Extinction Rebellion (known as XR), and what Lawrence would have made of it. We imagine his disgust – the disgust and distrust he brought to almost any movement, unless it was initiated by him. His inclination was to hate things; he found a peculiar energy in rage and negation. This meant that when he did assent to anything, he was ecstatic, as when he occasionally liked other people's books, or found a house or a patch of land he was prepared to live in. We agree that neither the eco-critics nor XR are likely to have been sources of ecstasy for him. 'You think we can make the world less anthropocentric through literature?'

I can hear him asking the eco-critics. 'Through words!' As for XR, 'You want to save the world through love?'

I say that I can hear Lawrence in parts of the XR vision statement, though, even if he might not have recognised it. I can hear Birkin there as well, which makes me wonder if XR members too really long for a world without humans, with just the grass and the hare sitting up. P tends to make speeches rather like Birkin does, relying on me, more than I used to see, for the other half of the dialectic, as Lawrence makes Birkin rely on Ursula. He says now that XR idealises humanity and idealises nature, and that Lawrence did neither of these. He says that the whole notion of the Anthropocene, the word beloved by climate-change activists to define the era in which humans have had a significant impact on the earth's geology and ecosystems, overemphasises the role of humans in nature. Though the activists claim to want to make humans less central, they make us more so, by seeing the whole cosmos as determined by us. And they idealise who we can be. They hope for an ideal nature, which we can love into being, and hope for an ideal, cooperative humanity. But in fact there is no period in history when humanity has cooperated in the way they want us to. Destruction and degeneration have always been part of who we are, and nature has never been pristine and undestroyed.

It's true. 'We catch glimpses of a new world of love, respect and regeneration,' I read in the vision statement this morning. It is partly just that the moral views are much simpler than Lawrence's, which makes the XR statements enticing as a call to action but means that we miss the turbulence, the vortex of intellectual action that comes from reading Lawrence, whose imaginings of regeneration contained more destruction than love. Still, he did look back to a better past, as they do. Growing up in Nottinghamshire, in an agricultural world that had recently been industrialised, he looked back to the world before the industrial revolution as a world where men had lived in harmony with nature, not asking for too much.

They felt the rush of the sap in spring, they knew the wave which cannot halt, but every year throws forward the seed to begetting, and, falling back, leaves the young-born on the earth. They knew the intercourse between heaven and earth, sunshine drawn into the breast and bowels, the rain sucked up in the daytime, nakedness that comes under the wind in autumn, showing the birds' nests no longer worth hiding. Their life and interrelations were such; feeling the pulse and body of the soil, that opened to their furrow for the grain, and became smooth and supple after their ploughing, and clung to their feet with a weight that pulled like desire, lying hard and unresponsive when the crops were to be shorn away.

There is nostalgia here, in the opening of *The Rainbow*, a longing for a lost home. It isn't love, it isn't respect that's described, but it's a world whose fecundity – as unstoppable as the rhythms of that first sentence – is perfectly balanced with its destructiveness. Here and elsewhere, Lawrence is explicit in seeing man-made machines as ruining the countryside, making England ugly and the English people mechanical. If he was surrounded by people bemoaning the decline of Western civilisation, then he sometimes resisted this, as with his calls for a bodily unconscious, and sometimes outdid everyone else, locating his particular version of decline in physical ugliness. 'In the cities / There is even no more any weather,' he complained in a poem, recoiling from the weather in town that was 'always benzine, or else petrol fumes'. 'The real tragedy of England, as I see it, is the tragedy of ugliness,' he wrote not long before he died. 'The country is so lovely: the man-made England is so vile.'[5]

Raymond Williams, in his 1973 book *The Country and the City*, demonstrated that there have been people in each century who look back to the world of their grandparents as a world that has not yet been spoilt by man. He compares the feeling of panicky nostalgia for the lost countryside to the feeling of being on an escalator moving us further and further backwards towards one lost golden age after another. It's true that there is something 'sentimental and intellectualised', as Williams puts it, about nostalgia for an idealised past. And Lawrence knew, as Williams did, that nature and culture were intertwined, that progress is a part of human life, and that the fields where he saw the hare and the grass had been made and enclosed by man. So are the foggy fields we walk in today, fields made to provide food for the city dwellers whose lives have always been full of connections to the lives of those in the country, even when they were not going between them every week, as I do, taking my children between their two lives on the trains, that Lawrence thought in some moods had ruined the landscape and in others found a source of 'fearsome pleasure, announcing the far-off come near and imminent'.[6]

In *the Rainbow*, the women break the spell, interrupting the idyll of heavy satedness by wanting more.

> But the women looked out from the heated, blind intercourse of farm-life, to the spoken world beyond. They were aware of the lips and the mind of the world speaking and giving utterance, they heard the sound in the distance, and they strained to listen.

They want knowledge and newness, and Lawrence doesn't blame them. He sees this as the natural movement of generations, and he honours human progress by creating modern characters as magnetic, as fully themselves, as Ursula and Gudrun. Yet he remained ambivalent, of course; his novels allow for the ambivalence that P thinks XR are unable to permit themselves. He made Ursula contend with Birkin, and he gave her his own horror of ugliness and of machines and mechanised humanity. She is so furious with Gerald when she sees him subjugating his horse next to the railway line, frightening the animal with an industrial world it should not have to face so close up. Gerald forces the horse to stand right by the line when the train goes past, spinning and swerving but unable to escape the strength of his will, as he presses his spurred feet down on her with an 'almost mechanical relentlessness', making her bleed. The animal spins 'round and round, on two legs, as if she were in the centre of some whirlwind'. Gudrun is half seduced and half repelled; Ursula is horrified. 'Let her go! Let her go, you fool, you *fool*—!' she cries out. She hates the ugliness of the setting and she hates

Gerald and the machine-power he brings from his mine-owning to his horse-riding.

'A pathological obsession with money and profit is engineering this breakdown,' XR say in their vision statement. They could be talking about Gerald. 'We rise in the name of truth and withdraw our consent for ecocide, oppression and patriarchy.' Would Ursula go along with this? She's definitely against ecocide, and there are moments when she's at the very least exasperated by the patriarchy. The best of the eco-critics worry, though, that Lawrence's nostalgia for a lost age is a sign that his greenness is part of the proto-fascism that remains his most unpalatable element for us. Perhaps, indeed, though it doesn't seem to trouble XR, with their 'new world of love', there's a fascist element in the basic desire to escape the machine and dwell in nature. Is Gerald the fascist, subjugating people and animals to his will, or is it Birkin, wanting to return to an earlier era, when man and nature were more harmonious? This is a danger lurking within all nature writing, and we need to remember that anything we say about wanting to live more closely with plants or animals was said by the people who burned my grandparents' siblings in their ovens. 'This striving toward connectedness with the whole of life, with nature itself, a nature into which we are born, this is the deepest meaning and the true essence of National Socialist thought,' wrote the Nazi botanist Ernst Lehmann in 1930. Heinrich Himmler, who set up and controlled the concentration camps, began as an agronomist and chicken farmer, whose model of purity and virtue was drawn from traditional rural Bavarian life.[7]

Literary critics like comparing Lawrence to Heidegger, who was still a Nazi when he wrote 'Why I Stay in the Provinces?', rejoicing in his cabin in a mountain valley in the Black Forest, his 'centuries-long and irreplaceable rootedness in the Alemannian-Swabian soil' and his 'simple and essential' existence away from the city, away from machines, moving and flowing alongside 'the slow and deliberate growth of the fir-trees, the brilliant, simple splendour of the meadows in bloom, the rush of the mountain brook in the long autumn night'. Heidegger was yearning backwards, as Lawrence did in some moods, to an unspoilt, unmechanised age, though for Heidegger there was plenty of Nietzschean will in the mix as well, competing with his desire to come at truth by letting be. The critics who compare them are sometimes enthusiastic about both of them, sometimes anxious about what the comparison with Heidegger means for Lawrence. The terrifying truth may be simply that the fascists got some things right, that it's precisely this that made them so dangerous. Or it may be that we need a more dimensional sense of nature than Heidegger had in his cabin, one more capable of incorporating modernity. Can we hope that XR has this? I think that Lawrence, in his most expansive writing, did.[8]

If Lawrence resisted the modern, but also brought the modern, urgently and ambivalently, into being, then he was doing this with nature, as well as with modern womanhood and the modern unconscious. He may have mourned the loss of the easy confluence of man and nature seen at the beginning of *The Rainbow*, but he also showed how humans could find a new life alongside nature, one with loss built in. This isn't Birkin's dream of nature redeemed by the extinction of humans. It's the vision that unfolds around Birkin, seen at its most idyllic when Ursula and Gudrun have their peculiar encounter with the Highland cattle.

'They are quite safe,' came Gudrun's high call. 'Sing something, you've only to sing something.'

It was evident she had a strange passion to dance before the sturdy, handsome cattle.

Ursula began to sing, in a false quavering voice:

'Way down in Tennessee—'

She sounded purely anxious. Nevertheless, Gudrun, with her arms outspread and her face uplifted, went in a strange palpitating dance towards the cattle, lifting her body towards them as if in a spell, her feet pulsing as if in some little frenzy of unconscious sensation, her arms, her wrists, her hands stretching and heaving and falling and reaching and reaching and falling, her breasts lifted and shaken towards the cattle, her throat exposed as in some voluptuous ecstasy towards them, whilst she drifted imperceptibly nearer, an uncanny white figure, towards them, carried away in its own rapt trance, ebbing in strange fluctuations upon the cattle, that waited, and ducked their heads a little in sudden contraction from her, watching all the time as if hypnotised, their bare horns branching in the clear light, as the white figure of the woman ebbed upon them, in the slow, hypnotising convulsion of the dance. She could feel them just in front of her, it was as if she had the electric pulse from their breasts running into her hands. Soon she would touch them, actually touch them. A terrible shiver of fear and pleasure went through her. And all the while, Ursula, spell-bound, kept up her high-pitched thin, irrelevant song, which pierced the fading evening like an incantation.

These are the rhythms we are accustomed to from Lawrence's sex scenes: 'stretching and heaving and falling and reaching and reaching and falling'. Here, again, the rhythms usher in a world beyond consciousness; this is a moment of unconscious union between human and animals. Nonetheless, this isn't the organic unconsciousness of *The Rainbow*. There is an electric pulse between Gudrun and the cattle; they are mutually energised by the modernity the women bring to the scene. There is a feeling that it will soon become too much, as sex does for Gudrun and Gerald, that the inherent silliness of it all (that thin, irrelevant song!) will overwhelm them, or that Gudrun's fear will be realised in another of the moments of violence that pulse through the book. As it is, Birkin and Gerald interrupt them and the genuine possibilities of the scene are lost. But the sisters are left with the knowledge that a moment of shape-shifting has taken place – a moment when two women, conscious of their place in the modern world, have attempted to remake themselves alongside animals.

Lawrence's vision of man and nature wasn't always this flexible. As a fiction writer, and as a poet, he could see how you could be a modern person and live with modernity's contradictions, but as his essay writing became more embattled, he got more caught up in the brilliant but claustrophobic whirl of his polemic and lost the freedom that fiction writing could bring. Nonetheless, it's freedom that we can hold him to, I think, and that he can hold us to, a century later. Lawrence was an admirer of the biologist and sociologist Herbert Spencer, who wrote in 1862 that: 'Absolute rest and permanence do not exist. Every object, no less than the aggregate of all objects, undergoes from instant to instant some alteration of state.' This is what we see again and again in Lawrence's characters and settings, instant-to-instant alterations that show us that stasis is impossible, that people, animals and trees progress despite themselves. It's this, surely, that made nature so compatible with his version of modernity and its constantly shifting forms. 'Yet its column is always there,' Lawrence says about his tree in the Rocky Mountains, 'alive and changeless, alive and changing.'[9]

We lose the path on our way back down. It was foolish not to keep map reading in the fog, even though it's familiar territory. We're not far from the path – it's not dangerous – but we are conscious of haste because it gets dark early and because I am collecting my daughter from the station later. There is a moment of scrabbling through bracken and a rather tortuous clamber over a fence topped with two rows of barbed wire that reminds us again that these fields are organised and controlled by human methods. And then we are walking past three large horses, pale in the fog. They start coming towards us, frightening me, because it's impossible for me to walk past horses without thinking of that scene at the end of *The Rainbow* when the horses block Ursula's way. Ursula feels that the horses are 'aware'. It is that quality of awareness that I feel now. P interprets the awareness as curious pleasure and walks towards them, saying hello, while I edge towards the boundary of the field. He strokes the noses of two of them, and the third one comes to join in.

I look back, half wishing I could join them, could be a less diffident country dweller. The third one has a bramble stuck in its mane and P begins to pull it off, hurting it as he does so, making me scared that it will turn on him. It's not until children are about three that they can understand you are hurting them in order to help them; I don't know if horses are able to understand this or not. But the bramble is out now, and we're walking towards our car. I think of another horse, of St Mawr, in Lawrence's 1925 novella about a noble, fiercely untamable horse, who lashes out, shaking off his riders unpredictably because they are no longer noble enough to ride him. Lou, the American who St Mawr helps escape from her overcivilised London life to New Mexico, sees the stallion upturned, his hooves working wildly, after he has almost killed her husband, and thinks that this is a vision of evil that makes a lie of acts of loyalty, piety or self-sacrifice. What would XR make of St Mawr's evil nobility, I wonder, as we drive home. Can they make room for it? What would they make of the horses chasing Ursula? For Lawrence this is all part of nature's vitality; it's because it's so unpredictable that the natural world serves as so strong a call to exploration, and that it was so fertile for him as a writer. There's a way in which the natural world can seem more predictable than the human world: one season follows another, animals act on primeval instincts. But the shapes in nature are more disorderly than machine-made shapes and, moment by moment, collisions are more unexpected, more liable to have consequences resulting in sudden death or violent injury. This combination made it well suited for the unevenness of tone, the mixture of coarseness and poise that characterises his writing.

I am wary of Christmas. I feel that, by failing to defend myself as a woman, I have failed my son. I do not know how we are going to be together. The holiday begins with frost, which my daughter is encountering knowingly for the first time, in this year that has turned out to be her year of awakening in the world. 'The grass is white,' she says in the morning, and she does experiments with the frost at nursery, painting it with hot water dripped from a paintbrush.

I book my son in for some mornings of forest school. If he is going to be only occasionally rural, we need to get a lot of mud into our week together. He is reluctant about putting on his wellies, apprehensive about the new children, but he emerges from his first session muddy and excited, a Lawrentian child. They have spent the morning lighting fires and he promises me that he will light one for me in our garden. Next holiday, I'm told, he can learn to carve wood and build dens. I think of Mellors, prescribing woodwork for the alienated workers: 'they ought to learn to be naked and handsome, and to sing in a mass and dance the old group dances, and carve the stools they sit on, and embroider their own emblems ... They should be alive and frisky, and acknowledge the great god Pan.' Lawrence was thinking, here, of his friends who were involved in the Kindred of the Kibbo Kift, a youth group set up by pacifist former scoutmaster John Hargrave in 1920 to help the post-industrial youth get back in touch with the natural world. 'To get out of touch with Nature is to get out of touch with life itself,' Hargrave wrote. Kin members (male and female) gave themselves Indigenous American animal names, sewed their own costumes, carved their own totems, and went camping and hiking, lighting fires and doing woodcraft. Lawrence's friend Rolf Gardiner was very involved in the Kindred, and in some moods Lawrence liked the idea of it all. 'On the whole he's right,' he told Gardiner. 'If it wasn't for his ambition and his lack of warmth I'd go and Kibbo Kift along with him.'[10]

While we wait for H to Kibbo Kift, I take my daughter to a nearby café, where they have llamas outside. We watch them eating, identifying likely parents and children among them, and I take pleasure in how natural she finds it to be seeing llamas roaming the Gloucestershire countryside. It is not yet clear to me whether she knows that the lions and zebras in the nearby wildlife park are more bewildering as local presences than the sheep and horses we see more regularly. Part of this is simply that children spend their whole lives alongside animals, real or imagined. The pigs she watches on TV and plays with in her Peppa Pig dolls' house, the goat she read about going to nursery at the time she started, the lion and elephant and one-eyed sheep she takes to bed with her each night, the ducks and frogs (parents and children carefully allocated by species) who have swimming lessons every evening in her bath – these are her friends and playmates, her contemporaries, as much as the other children she meets at nursery. Animals and humans commingle easily in her dolls' house. There's something uncanny about all this. It's not simply that she's learning about the human world through reductive animal models. There's something more shamanistic, a feeling that G is in touch with a wilder world (albeit one brought to us through consumerist domesticity) than I am able to see.

It's not surprising that G treats our cat as a kind of unruly sibling. After the cat eschews the dry food that G has just put in her bowl because she's already full of meat, G follows her crossly, telling her to come back and have her pudding. Together, the children present the cat with her Christmas gift, and wait, apparently expecting her to unwrap it. Is this anthropomorphism? I suppose it is. Lawrence hated anthropomorphism. 'Anthropomorphism, that allows nothing to call its soul its own, save anthropos,' he wrote in that same, mocking essay on Wordsworth. But what's the alternative? Will G learn to see our cat as another being, a killer who doesn't eat pudding or open presents? Perhaps what G is doing, as she attempts to get the cat to eat her pudding alongside her, is not committing the sin of anthropomorphism, but zoomorphism: she's making herself more like an animal. Lawrence mocks Hermione in *Women in Love* for wanting people to be more like animals. But he's more favourably disposed to Lou in *St Mawr*, who despairs of modern humanity, watching the horse, and says impatiently to her mother that she wishes 'we could get our lives straight from the source, as the animals do, and still be ourselves'. Lawrence was writing in an age when Darwin had recently told humans that they were animals. 'There is no fundamental difference between man and the higher mammals,' Darwin wrote in *The Descent of Man*. Freud had also recently observed that a child 'can see no difference between his own nature and that of animals' and derived whole theories from his sense of how challenging it had been for the human species to learn to walk upright. As a result, being an animal was a peculiarly modern experience that nonetheless linked us to the timeless, because animals had changed less than humans over the last century, and could connect us with the wildness of earlier ages.[11]

Lawrence's humans resemble animals in every novel. He saw the animal in us, whether it was the kittenish children in *The Rainbow* (Ursula, compared to a 'kitten playing by herself in the darkness with eyes dilated'), or their father, Will, who has 'bright inhuman eyes, like a hawk's'. For Lawrence we can become more human when more animal-like, because more unconscious and bodily, but we can become less human too, taking on the otherness of other species. The human relationships he depicted were characterised by constant oscillations between closeness and alienation, so our animality becomes one feature of those.

Unlike Ursula, G doesn't particularly resemble a cat – she's heavier and rounder. She's a little beaver, burrowing her way into things, building dams on the floor and sofa. H is more of a cat, and his love for our cat, who he chose as a tiny, funny-looking kitten with a half-ginger, half-tabby face, is complicated by a feeling of extreme identification that finds him, sometimes, crawling around the house and miaowing. If he's catlike, then it's partly because he has a catlike tendency to spring away from contact he half desires. And in another version of rural life, I can picture him as a hunter. Perhaps that will be the next stage in his Kibbo Kifting.

Lawrence wrote wonderfully about cats, as he did about all animals. There's an account of Timsy, his New Mexican cat, in 'Reflections on the Death of a Porcupine'. He describes her as 'the most pretty, the most fine' of the animals they live alongside. 'It is not her mere corpus that is beautiful; it is her bloom of aliveness.' Her 'infinite variety'; 'the soft, snowflakey lightness of her, and at the same time her lean, heavy ferocity'. He hones in on the 'vacant, feline glare of her hunting eyes' as she strikes a blow at his foot through the bedclothes, the 'soft, high-leaping sideways bound' she makes as her 'snow-flake of a paw' comes down on a chipmunk. There's familiarity here, but there's otherness too: I know that vacant stare, and it's not the stare of a creature that opens Christmas presents.[12]

'Reflections on the Death of a Porcupine' is a strange, brilliant essay, written in New Mexico in 1925. The description of Timsy is one of many marvellous animal descriptions, in an essay that begins as an account of a botched attempt to kill a porcupine and goes on to be a gruffly compassionate description of Lawrence's attempts to rid an ungrateful visiting dog of the porcupine quills that have stuck painfully into it, rather like the horse that P managed to de-bramble:

The dog wanted the quills out: but his nerve was gone. Every time he saw my hand coming to his nose, he jerked his head away. I quieted him, and steadily managed to jerk out another quill, with the blood all over my fingers. But with every one that came out, he grew more tiresome. I tried and tried and tried to get hold of another quill, and he jerked and jerked, and writhed and whimpered, and ran under the porch floor.

The dog both knows and doesn't know that Lawrence is helping him, and Lawrence evokes precisely the feeling of weary tenderness that builds up when helping an animal (or human infant) in pain.[13]

The essay also contains some of the most repellent sentences that Lawrence ever wrote. His uneasy account of why we are justified in killing porcupines becomes a discussion of the food chain, in which he decides that 'the truth behind the survival of the fittest' is that some creatures are 'higher' than others, and that this means that life is more vivid in them. 'Life is more vivid in a snake than in a butterfly,' he states authoritatively, 'life is more vivid in a cat than in an ostrich.' This leads, apparently easily, into 'life is more vivid in the Mexican who drives the wagon, than in the two horses in the wagon' and from that into 'life is more vivid in me, than in the Mexican who drives the wagon for me'. The man can destroy the horse, or any other animal, and 'one race of man can subjugate and rule another race'. 'Can' is ambiguous here – it seems to mean that these men both are capable of and are entitled to this subjugation. This is a law, he says, and if the essay ended here it would be wholly unredeemed. But instead he goes on to suggest that there is another way of seeing these creatures: the 'fourth dimension, of being'. In this dimension, any individual being is incomparable to any other, because each is fully themselves, if they can achieve their own 'fulness of being'. I think – although the essay at this point becomes a little hard to make sense of – that he's suggesting an alternative hierarchy in which there can be a profound equality among any creatures who attain the fullness of being that all of Lawrence's best characters aspire to. Simultaneously, we live in time and space, subject to the hierarchy of the food chain, and in the fourth dimension, where modern animals are greater in stature than modern humans because they are so much better at being fully themselves.[14]

I find it hard to know what to make of all this. I know that Lawrence finds it as unpleasant as Ursula does when Gerald insists that the horse he abuses 'is there for my use. Not because I bought her, but because that is the natural order.' But that is the kind of sentiment he's expressing himself in this essay. I get P to read it, and he thinks that I am too determined to redeem Lawrence with my emphasis on the fourth dimension. He reminds me that we should introject Lawrence's repugnance into our vision of him, pointing out that part of what I admire in Lawrence is the way he introjected the repugnant into his vision of nature (he was often repulsed by animals, while somehow still honouring them). We have to absorb Lawrence's more repellent ideas not by turning them into what we believe, but by turning what we believe into something capable of acknowledging them. P says that this is what being open to otherness really means – being open to the otherness that repels us. I can see that I'm too tempted to explain away the repugnance, to say that those statements about subjugation are somehow invalidated by the statements about the fourth dimension. If Lawrence is worth reading now, then perhaps we do need to make a case for him that includes his wrongness, and acknowledges it. After all, he himself did, much of the time, especially when writing his powerfully ambivalent explorations of encounters between humans and animals.

The spirit of encounter is so strong for Lawrence. The meeting of two species becomes a way of structuring narrative and a way of seeing the world afresh. We can see this in the porcupine essay, which sets up the two central questions running through Lawrence's accounts of the animal world in his fiction and poetry: Are we right to kill them? Are we right to love them? These are questions he asks again and again through his portrayals of encounters with animals; questions that we still ask now. Lawrence is grappling, as we do, with the fact that animals don't live in an ethical world, yet come under our ethical jurisdiction.

There are so many near misses with killing animals in his writing, and some disturbing successes, where the pathos that Lawrence evokes when he removes the porcupine quills from the dog is never absent.

'A snake came to my water-trough', begins his famous poem, 'Snake', probably written in Sicily in 1920.

> On a hot, hot day, and I in pyjamas for the heat,
> To drink there.

The snake is at the trough before him; soft-bellied, he rests his throat on the stone bottom and sips water through his straight gums, 'silently'. Lawrence feels like a 'second-comer' (there is a lot of religious imagery in his nature poetry) as he watches him drinking. He hears the 'voice of my education' telling him to kill the venomous snake, but knows too that he is glad he has 'come like a guest in quiet' to drink at his water-trough.

> Was it cowardice, that I dared not kill him?
> Was it perversity, that I longed to talk to him?
> Was it humility, to feel so honoured?
> I felt so honoured.

The eloquence of the poem comes from its mixture of certainty and uncertainty. The lines oscillate in length as the feelings oscillate, enabling Lawrence to establish a voice that's both commanding and self-questioning. Fearful and flattered, he watches as this 'god' draws his slow length round and climbs away from him. Overcome by sudden horror at his withdrawal, Lawrence picks up a log and throws it at the back of the snake. It doesn't hit him, but the back of the snake convulses and then disappears 'in an undignified haste'.

> And immediately I regretted it.
> I thought how paltry, how vulgar, what a mean act!
> I despised myself and the voices of my accursed human
>     education.

Lawrence is left here with a 'something to expiate: / A pettiness'. This is bathetic. The notion of expiation sets up the expectation of a realm of sin and guilt that doesn't usually include pettiness. What he shows through the bathos is that in fact pettiness can be a sin greater than any other. It's the narrow-mindedness of pettiness that he has set himself up to fight over the past decade and that now he has detected in himself. The argument for assassination was strong, but he was wrong to attempt it. This is a snake who is magnificently himself, not merely godlike but a god in his vitality. Lawrence, full of ideas, stuffed with education, is inferior to him, though it's perhaps only when he came to write the 'Reflections on the Death of a Porcupine' essay that he formulated his concept of the fourth dimension and worked out why. 'If men were as much men as lizards are lizards / they'd be worth looking at,' Lawrence wrote in his late poem 'Lizard'. Snake or lizard, the creaturely world is far better at being themselves than modern humanity in the age of the machine.

In the porcupine essay, Lawrence comes down on the side of killing porcupines. They destroy his food and it is 'part of the business of ranching' to kill them: 'you plant, and you protect your growing crop with a gun'. But it was never this straightforward in his poetry or fiction. If we are compelled to kill by natural law, as with the porcupines, but also lured to kill by the misplaced voice of our education, as with the snake, then it can be hard to disentangle the two motives, and best left alone, as in 'Man and Bat', where Lawrence resists the urge to kill the bat, saying instead, 'Let the God that created him be responsible for his death.' Here there's a kind of ease of equality between man and bat, even though Lawrence is repulsed by him ('A disgusting bat / At mid-morning!'), which results in Lawrence chasing the bat round and round his room to shoo him away, refusing to let him rest, exhausted by him but not prepared to exert his status as a creature better fitted for survival.

This equality is felt more strongly and more eerily in Lawrence's 1922 novella *The Fox*, where two women, March and Banford, living a probably platonic quasi-marriage on a farm, fail to kill the fox that attacks their chickens for several years. One day, March sees the fox looking at her and is 'spellbound' as he meets her eyes and then makes off with slow impudent jumps. It's only with the arrival of a strange man, Henry, that the fox's life becomes really endangered. Henry succeeds in seducing March, largely because he reminds her of the fox. When he first comes to visit, she dreams that the fox is singing outside. She goes out and tries to touch him, but he bites her wrist and then withdraws, whisking his brush against her face and burning her mouth because his brush is on fire. March agrees, foolishly, to marry Henry, partly because she is attracted by his fox-like odour, 'something like a wild creature'. Henry then kills the fox by predicting his movements and trapping him. The next day, March communes with the dead fox, hung up in the shed. 'White and soft as snow his belly: white and soft as snow.' She strokes his belly, and his 'wonderful black-glinted brush', taking the full fur of his thick tail between her fingers and passing her hand down it repeatedly. 'Wonderful, sharp, thick, splendour of a tail.'

The marriage is not a success. The encounter with the dead fox has been the real erotic consummation of March's life. As a fox-substitute, Henry and his human tail are a disappointment. There has been no nobility in killing the fox. The food chain is seen as irrelevant compared to the spiritual, erotic connection between the women and the animal. In the encounter between human and fox, the fox was the powerful one, and should not have been subjugated. Yet this isn't a fairy story in which the fox is a prince in disguise. He is fully fox, fully other. He is 'a strange beast to her, incomprehensible, out of her range'. It's a story about estrangement: about how animals and humans remain unknowable to each other, and how humans remain unknowable to each other too. Human interactions become much more raw when there are animals involved. *The Fox*, *St Mawr*, *Women in Love*: in all of these Lawrence uses the encounters with animals to bring out the strangeness that exists between people, showing that we are alienated from each other by our cruelty and by our love.

It's more surprising, perhaps, that Lawrence should question the ethics of loving animals than of killing them. But, after all, he ordered parents to refrain from loving their children and husbands their wives. When it comes to animals, this is really the question of anthropomorphism again. Is it possible to love another creature while still accepting its otherness? It's the question Lawrence asked of sexual relationships too, and answered with Birkin and Ursula's new model of separate togetherness. Lawrence addressed it explicitly through his stories about domestic pets, 'Adolf' and 'Rex', both autobiographical accounts, written in the first person and based on his own childhood.

Reading these stories makes me realise that it's telling how few of the animals Lawrence wrote about were pets. Lawrence was very curious about animals, compelled by them and used to living in a world inhabited by as many animals as people. But on the whole, he didn't see them as part of the family. It is almost impossible to have a pet without anthropomorphising it, so one way to avoid anthropomorphism is to avoid pets, and find other forms of relationship with animals.

Adolf is a baby rabbit, brought home by Lawrence's father, and quickly tame enough to sit on the table drinking his milk alongside the Lawrence children while they eat. They don't love him – 'he was wild and loveless to the end'. Instead, he's a delightful visitor from another world, and it seems to come naturally to them to return him to the woods when he grows up. Rex, however, is loved. He comes as a puppy, dropped off for a few months by their uncle, and sleeps on the children's beds. The puppy is torn between 'two great impulses', the impulse to hunt and the impulse to love and obey, loving the children 'with a fierce, joyous love'. The children stand watching in 'mute despair' when the uncle takes them back. Later, Lawrence visits the dog in the uncle's pub and finds that he has become vicious, refusing to obey the uncle because he is too used to love. 'It was our fault. We had loved him too much, and he had loved us too much.'

It's a curious story for the contemporary pet owner to read. It hasn't occurred to me that we might love our cat too much. The suggestion is that animals lose their 'wild freedom' when we love them. They become too much like us, and not enough themselves. The rabbit, unloved, remains fully rabbit, but the dog becomes half human. It's an interesting thought that I think explains why Lawrence's animal writing is so good. W. H. Auden loved Lawrence's writing about animals because 'he never confuses the feelings they arouse in him with what he sees and hears and knows about them'. It's true: it's the lack of anthropomorphism. His animals are given agency and seen on their own terms. This is clearest when he's writing about animals that are totally different from humans. His poem 'Fish' is about these questions. 'No fingers, no hands and feet, no lips,' Lawrence observes, rather enviously; 'Food, fear and joie de vivre / Without love.' At the same time he never pretends that he himself isn't intensely involved in the encounters. He owns up to the intensity and wilfulness of his own project, his fidelity to his own voice, his will to power. His commitment to nature's agency is all the more of an achievement because it's caught up in his own wilfulness.[15]

He wrote his stories about Adolf and Rex in 1919 in Derbyshire, where he and Frieda were briefly living near his sister. He was drawn to think about himself as a pet owner for the first time in years, and then in New Mexico, he had the first pets – his dog Bibbles and his cat Timsy – that he'd had since childhood. In 1923 he wrote 'Bibbles', his poem about his 'Little black snub-nosed bitch with a shoved-out jaw / And a wrinkled reproachful look'. He is angry here that Bibbles loves everybody. He loses her, only to find her bestowing affection on other people. 'You love lying warm between warm human thighs, / indiscriminate,' he complains, before going on to list scenes from Bibbles's daily life with great joy: 'So funny / Lobbing wildly through deep snow like a rabbit.' But the dog has been kicked for her exploits: she's come home vomiting after eating the wrong food elsewhere; she's looking to Lawrence for protection. To which Lawrence retorts:

All right, my little bitch.
You learn loyalty rather than loving,
And I'll protect you.

To which Auden retorts: 'His poem about "Bibbles", "the Walt Whitmanesque love-bitch who loved just everybody," is the best poem about a dog ever written, but it makes it clear that Lawrence was no person to be entrusted with the care of a dog.'[16]

I go along with Auden, despite his priggish glibness. I allow us our love of our cat. I allow the cat her softness, her love of us, her pleasure when I get into bed to read or work and she lies on my chest, purring, her white feet placed delicately on my throat, pleased to be the only dependent creature in my room for a while. Meanwhile, we all dream of animals. H dreams that the cat is dying of a slow illness and wakes up fearful, wanting to find her and check that she's all right. G wakes me one night, crying, and tells me with real terror that 'there's a horse in my bedtime, Mummy, a horse escaped'. She sees horses all the time here, walking down the street past our house, galloping alone in fields; it's not inconceivable that one would come in here, seeking a rest in her bunk bed. P dreams, a few days later, of beautiful horses with noble faces, arriving at his house. He thinks they are the souls of the people in his village – all old, mostly horsey – who have died of Covid. I think of St Mawr, who draws breath from another world, 'where the horse was swift and fierce and supreme, undominated and unsurpassed'. I think of March's dream in *The Fox*, where the fox summons her only to elude her, searing her with flames as he goes. Later, March has another dream, where she buries Banford in a coffin with the brush of the dead fox folded under her head, the skin of the fox making 'a whole ruddy, fiery coverlet' over her body. Fur and fire, love and fear, seduction and repulsion: animals glide richly through our imaginative lives.

The children go to their father. It is the first whole week that I have spent away from G. I miss her less continually than I feared I would, and it turns out to be a period of recovery that I had not known I needed. Walks, books, mornings in bed, evenings by the fire at P's house with the two cats whose friendship is one of our achievements: the stately ginger farm cat who's become soppily home-loving in his old age, spread out next to the fire, tolerant of the pounces and nuzzles of my little city cat. She wriggles, deliriously, offering him her white belly, drawing out the moment before she will pounce and then leap away. Each night she brings him the mice that he can no longer catch, the tiny, barely edible creatures that are the only available pickings at this time of year.

We half wonder about spending a day in London before we collect the children, but P doesn't want to go to the city in its present state of semi-lockdown. And he thinks that arduousness is better experienced in the countryside: the rhythms here are better suited to struggle. Instead, we drive to our nearest sea: an estuary with a beach of mud. I have missed the sea less this year than I usually do, learning to get some of that same expansiveness from hills and fields and rivers. But there's still a very particular pleasure in looking out over water that I can't see to the end of, in feeling that edge-of-world feeling. Nature is culture here: as we follow the shoreline, we pass row after row of empty, run-down hotels. Almost everything is shut, but, huddled under what passes for a cliff, we find a hut with two women selling tea and homemade cake, valiantly undaunted by the pandemic, and we join the queue gratefully.

I want to walk from one bay to another, so we set off across the mud, innocent of what this will mean. This is the most open space I have been in for a long time. 'I do like having the big, unbroken spaces round me,' Lawrence wrote from his ranch in New Mexico, celebrating the savage spirit of peace. It is not savage here, but it's peaceful, although halfway across, the mud gets deeper and boggier. We are up to our thighs, lurching between footsteps, only half enjoying the half-fear it induces. P decides that the answer is to go quickly and lightly, and I attempt to follow, but my boots are too heavy and I fall flat on my front, emerging as a muddy monster. A few minutes later we are back at the shore, climbing a woody hill. The world seems larger, full again of possibility.[17]

A week later we are in lockdown again. This time the silence is against my will, and it scares me. It's a cold January that starts to feel horribly gruelling. I am suddenly desperate for company, missing the few people we still saw. I know that I should be grateful to have P, grateful that G still sees her friends at nursery, grateful to have fields to walk in. But I feel anxiously lonely. I wonder what Lawrence would have made of this new phase in our year.

Would he have seen in this world where we see no one the world that he wanted to create for himself? More than ever in my life, we are protected from the signs of modernity that he loved to hate, however much it grinds away in the background, however many people suggest drinks or meetings on Zoom. He might by now have stopped shouting at the state for taking control of our lives and made the most of the leap back in time. He was a better solitary walker than I am. He loved reading about Thoreau in Walden and made a world rather like ours is now, in Cornwall, in Italy, in New Mexico; the couple, a few friends, a desk, a water trough shared half unwillingly with a snake, a bed shared half unwillingly with a cat.

But the English winter was too much for Lawrence, so why not for me? The mud. The rain. 'I'm still sleeping,' G says, pulling the duvet over her head when I go into her room in the morning, 'It's not morning time.' I seek refuge in passivity, in stopping trying, in clothes layered on top of each other – if two or three, then why not five or six? – in staying in bed, doing nothing, for an hour after I wake up, in long baths with G, the sharp contrast of hot water and cold skin. We develop a collective addiction to jigsaws, the hobby that binds us ever closer with my daughter. I am not unhappy now, I am waiting, hibernating rather than lethargic. Even the cat doesn't want to leave the house. She has given up on the non-existent mice, leaving P to emulate them in their absence, his hand racing under the rug or duvet.

Lawrence loathed the English winter more and more year by year. Those animal poems were written out of such a different landscape. In a letter from London, written for publication in January 1924, he complained about the 'mouldering damp' and the 'dull, heavy, mortified half-light that seems to take the place of day in London in winter'. He had just come back from America and was longing to return to the open spaces and the horses he recalled as 'turquoise centaurs'. But he was longing, also, for warmth. He'd caught a bad cold soon after returning to London in December, which, exacerbated by the effects of port, had resulted in his vomiting over the table at the same dinner at the Café Royal where he designated Murry as Judas, hosted by

Lawrence in order to try, unsuccessfully, to persuade his friends to move to America with him.[18]

Perhaps the TB sufferer always loathes the cold, knowing, even when he is in denial as Lawrence was, that he is dying, knowing, as we know now, watching the hospitals crowd, watching the numbers of deaths rise, that viruses thrive in winter. P says that the world has gone mad, that we fear death too much, because we cannot accept that we or our parents are going to die. Lawrence thought the same thing, thought that we needed to accept death as part of life. This was partly what he got from nature: a sense of the cyclical nature of death and rebirth, a sense of death as part of the life cycle. This remains the challenge he offers to us now. He reminds us that nature is too complex and devious to have a clear idea of, and that we need to remember its complexity and deathliness even as we take up arms in the name of environmentalism. We can all gain from learning about nature from a thinker as agonised and disorientating as Lawrence can be.

Nonetheless, Lawrence didn't stick around to risk the death-liness of the British winter when he could help it. He and Frieda left for Paris and then Baden-Baden later in January. And by the autumn, back in America, he was longing for warmth again. 'I want to go south, where there is no autumn, where the cold doesn't crouch over one like a snow leopard waiting to pounce,' he wrote to Murry in 1924 from New Mexico, planning his next trip to Mexico.[19]

We are not going anywhere, so we have to accept the snow leopard, and find what brightness we can in the mortified half-light. We live such Lawrentian rhythms now, cycles of despair and regeneration. We have been plunged downwards again, but there has been a peace in hibernation. We have been biding our time, waiting, and now, in the rain, G and I go out for a long walk around a lake with my aunt. The mud is thick, the puddles huge, more like ponds as far as G is concerned. We can barely see, with our hoods on, but then the rain stops and we take them off and start to look around. There is a heron; there are swans, accompanied by overgrown cygnets. 'That's a brown baby swan and that's her brother,' G says, pronouncing it 'bruder', as she does with the brother she talks about often, telling me that he's in London with her Daddy. There are male ducks, fighting when we give them bread, showing us that it's mating time, that spring is coming. G cycles on her balance bike slowly at first, tentative about the mud, but then fast, powering through puddles in her wellies, jubilant at the immersion in a new element. She pauses in the middle of a puddle and reaches her hand into it, wonderingly. This is a child discovering her body through nature and it's moving to watch, even as I hurry her towards the car as the rain becomes heavier, even as I throw our wet clothes in the washing machine and lock the door against the rain.

# 8

# Apocalypse

It is February now; winter drags on relentlessly and I read a new
book by the activist philosopher Srećko Horvat about apocalypse.
'If the apocalypse already happened and there is no new beginning,
no new epoch after this already dystopian epoch, then what we
are living now is already the post-apocalyptic present in which
our only horizon is the "naked apocalypse" – or *extinction*.'[1]

Horvat has been struck – as most of us have – by the
apocalyptic elements of the pandemic. For months at a time, the
streets in the centres of major cities around the world have been
empty; supermarket shelves have been bare because people are
stockpiling supplies for the end of the world; bodies pile high in
mass graves or are burned in large-scale funeral pyres. A study
suggests that fans of zombie apocalypse movies are coping better
with the pandemic than everyone else – they knew what to expect
and are less bewildered by it. We scour the signs of revelation,
wondering if a new world is being ushered in and hoping that
it will be the fairer, less aggressively industrialised, more state-
supported world that the more privileged among us glimpsed
in the first lockdown. We worry that in fact the apocalypse has
already happened, revealing only the destitution of everything,
and that the world we are living in is one without hope.

For Horvat, there is a kind of hope in accepting that we have
already passed the point of no return towards ecological collapse.
We have brought upon ourselves a deadly disease that portends
other diseases, likely to wipe us out, and can see in this disease
a 'revelation' of the things to come. We are living in an age of

post-apocalyptic disaster and must do what we can to survive it, which means working collectively to mitigate damage.

Many of the best minds of our times are caught up in thinking about apocalypse – writing it away, writing it into being, imagining it in fiction, averting it but also sometimes welcoming it because it would prove right the doomsayers and provide the gateway to a new kind of life. I have been wondering how Lawrence would have fared among the apocalyptic thinkers of my generation. He loved reading the runes, as Horvat does. He had his own moment of global crisis – the First World War – and he responded to it apocalyptically. He liked quoting the Bible to tell people that death would be followed by collective rebirth ('Except a seed die, it bringeth not forth,' he wrote to Bertrand Russell in May 1915; 'Our death must be accomplished first, then we will rise up') and he liked looking for apocalyptic images and signs. Watching with excited fear as the Zeppelin planes dropped bombs above them, splashing the world with fire, he saw it as a Miltonic war in heaven.

> But it was not angels. It was the small golden Zeppelin, like a long oval world, high up. It seemed as if the cosmic order were gone, as if there had come a new order, a new heavens above us: and as if the world in anger were trying to revoke it … Everything is burst away now, there remains only to take on a new being.

At a moment when all hope could seem to be lost, he found release in the possibility that we had now gone so far towards destruction that a new order was on its way, and he sought clues as to the truths of the universe in the golden Zeppelins.[2]

It's not surprising that Lawrence was so keen on the idea of apocalypse. Most of the crankiest men of his times were, then as now. For some this was the Christian apocalypse – the revelation granted to John the Evangelist foretelling the end of the world and the signs and wonders accompanying it, written up in the Book of Revelation, also known as the Apocalypse of John. For others it was a more generic cataclysmic world ending, accompanied by some form of revelation and followed by the inception of a new world. Lawrence was writing in the wake of a cluster of thinkers who had seen in the French Revolution an apocalyptic event on earth, and in an intellectual climate caught up with Marx's proclamation that an old world was being replaced by a new because, as a result of capitalism, 'all fixed, fast-frozen relations, with their train of ancient and venerable prejudices and opinions, are swept away' – all that is solid melts into air. Alongside Lawrence, there were other modernists whose desire for collapse and desire for regeneration collided in apocalyptic thinking. 'Surely some revelation is at hand,' Yeats wrote in his 1919 poem 'The Second Coming', describing the 'blood-dimmed tide' loosed everywhere. Eliot in his 1922 *The Waste Land* also saw the catastrophe of the First World War as leaving the world in the midst of an apocalypse whose revelations had been deferred but might still occur, though he was less hopeful than Yeats about this, and less jubilant in his account of the destruction, which contained more boredom than horror in his portrayal.[3]

Many of Lawrence's generation saw the First World War as an apocalyptic event that required a second apocalypse to provide the revelation it had failed to bestow. This elision between historical disaster and apocalypse is also there in Horvat's account, though for him there is no definite crash of world ending – it has happened already without our quite registering it. Lawrence reminds me a little of Horvat, who I know a bit, and who is another bearded, wirily energetic, brilliant, opinionated man at home everywhere and nowhere, and with a love of coming up with theories that incorporate the whole of collective life. Perhaps they'd have been enthusiastic correspondents if they'd had the chance to coincide in time. Lawrence liked writing long letters to other apocalypse-hungry men. His final, unfinished book, *Apocalypse*, emerged out of a correspondence with Frederick Carter, a mystical painter-cum-astrologer who had sent Lawrence his own cranky take on the Book of Revelation, *Dragon of Revelation*, proposing a collaboration.

But if it's not surprising that Lawrence was an enthusiast of apocalypse, then it's all the more remarkable that he did so well at coming through the idea of apocalypse into something richer, something more open to ordinary human experience in the present. He may have written about apocalypse in his letters and essays; he may have written a whole book called *Apocalypse*. But he didn't give in to the temptation to write apocalyptic fiction. He was too committed to a sense of life as a flow of impermanent, unsettled states, and to seeing flux as a characteristic of modern experience. This competed with his yearning for rupture and cessation and it's telling that his most apocalyptic story, 'A Dream of Life', remained unfinished. Crucially, *Lady Chatterley's Lover*, written in the years when he knew himself to be dying and knew himself to be unpublishable, when his poems were banned and his pictures seized by the police, who threatened to send them up into the apocalyptic flames that had already consumed over a thousand copies of *The Rainbow*, is not an apocalyptic novel. 'The cataclysm has happened, we are among the ruins,' we read in the second sentence of the book, suggesting that this might be a novel in which a version of Horvat's thesis is played out. But the opening as a whole belies this:

> Ours is essentially a tragic age, so we refuse to take it tragically. The cataclysm has happened, we are among the ruins, we start to build up new little habitats, to have new little hopes. It is rather hard work: there is now no smooth road into the future: but we go round, or scramble over the obstacles. We've got to live, no matter how many skies have fallen.
>
> This was more or less Constance Chatterley's position.

It matters hugely that this is a cataclysm and not an apocalypse – meaning that there has been violent destruction but no final ending – and that Lawrence is diagnosing our times as tragic and not apocalyptic. It matters also that this is Constance Chatterley's position. The opening lines have the flavour of a grand diagnosis but then it becomes clear that it is a single person's perspective. The transformation of apocalypse from grand cultural vision to a 'more or less' individual question opens it up and gives it novelistic life. It matters also that he is ventriloquising on behalf of a woman and not of a hypostasising man. We've got to live. Connie's version of post-cataclysmic life is one of making do with the here and now; it involves circuitous scrambling rather than large-scale remaking. This is so hard-won. For a man who feared and longed for the apocalypse so passionately to have put it aside in favour of a woman's experience of keeping going, and for this to be the way he navigated his own sense of his impending ending – this is one of the most moving, the most momentous achievements of Lawrence's life.

It all began in Mablethorpe, on the Lincolnshire coast, in August 1926. This would be Lawrence's last trip to England, and it was his first trip back to the Lincolnshire coast in years, though this was where he'd first seen the sea that he'd sought out again and again elsewhere. He had arrived in rather bleak, beleaguered spirits. Since he had left New Mexico for the last time in September 1925, the world had rushed in on him, mostly in the form of crisis and scourge. He turned forty just a couple of days after they left the ranch. He had now succeeded in reaching the age his mother had once predicted her sickly son would never make, yet he worried that he was only half alive. He had been formally diagnosed with TB and knew that he couldn't return to America because he wouldn't pass the health checks required to get back in. He was thin and pale and easily enraged and depleted. He'd had enough of writing ('I am so bored by the thought of all things literary – why not sell cigarettes!'). He'd had enough of sex ('desire has died in me, silence has grown, / and nothing now reaches out to draw / other flesh to my own') and more than half knew that Frieda was having an affair with their landlord in Italy, Angelo Ravagli. He moved around restlessly, with and without Frieda, between Italy, England, Spain and France. He didn't like places he'd been ill in, and he'd been ill in so many by this point. His cough kept getting worse and it was hard to deny his TB, but he did his best, blaming his symptoms on his 'bronchials', on malaria, on the male menopause – anything but his decaying lungs – and putting it all down, as always, to chagrin.[4]

And then they went to Lincolnshire and looked out at the waves lapping the shore along the same flat, wide, sandy beaches he had run up and down in his childhood. They were expecting just to spend a few days there, but they ended up renting a bungalow in Sutton-on-Sea and staying for three weeks. He even talked about returning for several months the following year. 'It is rather fine here at the seaside,' he wrote to Frieda's sister, 'big smooth sands that gleam when they are wet, and little people that seem gone in the gleam – and a hoarse sea.' He knew that only a few miles away communities were being destroyed by the coal strike that he predicted would be 'the beginning of a slow revolution here in England'. But he found that he rather liked being 'back in my own country, the Midlands', and felt there was 'a queer, odd sort of potentiality in the people' he saw at the seaside. 'One feels in them some odd, unaccustomed sort of plasm twinkling and nascent.'[5]

It was here that he first thought about writing a novel again. 'The Midlands are still much more alive than London,' he wrote to his English publisher, Martin Secker, 'I feel if ever I were going to do an English novel, I'd have to come to England to do it. Perhaps this neighbourhood.' He had travelled around the world, he had lived within every kind of culture, he had attempted to turn the novel into something between ethnographic survey and religious tract in The Plumed Serpent, which had been published that spring to rather baffled and on the whole negative reviews, leaving him stranded at the end of the trajectory he had followed since leaving England at the end of the First World War. Now, returning to the Midlands, he was rejecting the cosmopolitan world. It had turned out that one revelation was no truer than another, that people could be as alive in England as anywhere else, that if he was going to change the world, it would be in ways both more intimate and more literary than he had envisaged over the past few years. He'd given up now on ideas of leadership. 'I'm afraid the whole business of leaders and followers is somehow wrong, now,' he would write to Rolf Gardiner in March 1928. Already, in 1926, he had seen fascism at first hand in Italy and understood that 'the sense of false power forced against life is very depressing'. He was left with quieter scenes, with a man and a woman in a hut in a wood in the Midlands, who were coming slowly into being.[6]

It may be because he already had Constance Chatterley in mind that he decided to go back to Eastwood for the first time in eight years. He sought out his old friend and mentor Willie Hopkin, and they walked around Eastwood, past his childhood houses, past his father's favourite pubs, past his school, and through the woods to Robin Hood's Well (which appears in every version of *Lady Chatterley's Lover*) and along to the Haggs Farm, where he once came day after day to visit Jessie. At the end of the walk Hopkin asked Lawrence if he would return to Eastwood again. 'Never,' he replied, 'I hate the damned place!' But if he would never need to return physically, this was partly because he was now inhabiting the place again imaginatively. And hating it was a way to do this, partly because it allowed him to love it but also to defend himself from being flooded by the extremity of his passion.[7]

And at the same time, he was reviving his faith in the novel. Since writing *The Plumed Serpent*, he'd written a series of essays in defence of the novel as a form, at a point when he perhaps knew that his latest novel, the one that he in some moods believed in most of all his works, was a failure. 'The novel is the highest complex of subtle interrelatedness that man has discovered,' he wrote in 'Morality and the Novel' in 1925; 'the novel is a great discovery: far greater than Galileo's telescope or somebody else's wireless,' he wrote in 'The Novel' in 1925; 'the novel is the one bright book of life' ('Why the Novel Matters'). What he said in these essays, again and again, was that the novelist had to avoid being didactic in order to attain a 'quick relatedness'. 'If you try to nail anything down, in the novel, either it kills the novel or the novel gets up and walks away with the nail.' Yet he had just finished writing the most didactic novel he'd written. It's as though he was semiconsciously planning his next move, the advance that would be a return to his oldest setting and that would restore the full, living quality his recent novels had lacked.[8]

'Now Verga turns to the peasants of his boyhood, and it is they who fill his soul,' he wrote in 1925 in an introduction to Giovanni

Verga's *Mastro-don Gesualdo*. In another version of this essay, he criticised *Madame Bovary* because Emma Bovary was 'too insignificant to carry the full weight of Gustave Flaubert's sense of tragedy'. But he extolled it as a masterpiece nonetheless: 'a great book and a very wonderful picture of life'. So, what if you had an Emma Bovary who was less insignificant, less pitiful. What if you returned to the landscape of your boyhood and found in it a quick relatedness that enabled you not to nail anything down. What if you did this partly through going in hard on style, as Flaubert had, and finding a style that was compatible with a female point of view. 'Ours is essentially a tragic age, so we refuse to take it tragically.' What if this could be Connie's thought – 'more or less Constance Chatterley's position'.[9]

It was appropriate, having committed again to the novel, that in the novel he began to write that October, back in Italy, sitting beneath a tree in a wood quite like the wood he was writing about in the Midlands, he should hone in on female experience. *Madame Bovary* was a reminder that this was what the novel had always done best – as he had known, when he set out to write about the Brangwen sisters, over a decade ago. In an age when novels were dismissed as silly stories for silly women, Flaubert had taken the story of a silly woman who read too many novels and turned it into something that reinterprets tragedy in ways both piquant and mordant for a nineteenth-century bourgeois world, creating that wonderful picture of life. Lawrence, who had been taught and enabled to live first by his mother and then by Frieda, now began to write his book partly as a gift to his wife, though appropriately enough, the character he created also had elements of his other recent lover, Rosalind Baynes. This was a celebration of a woman with a bodily life, and every day he came back from the woods and read the chapters he'd just written aloud to the woman who had first enabled him to feel at ease with his bodily wants.

Frieda hadn't got all she'd hoped for out of their marriage. There hadn't been much sex for several years, she'd been dismissed and sidelined by many of his friends, she'd lost out on the childhoods of her children, she'd rarely had a house she could call a home for more than a few months at a time. But the conversation begun between them in 1912 had been sustained for almost twenty years, through one book after another, one country after another. And now he turned once again to her point of view, honouring it at the same time as he honoured his mother and the women of Eastwood, asking how a woman, living in the Midlands, could manage to have a meaningful life. In the process, he gave Frieda two versions of himself. One was bookish, withered and world-destroyed, living a kind of posthumous existence, in which he knows his wife must have other lovers. The other was strong and lusty despite in later versions being weakened by pneumonia; a man so much a man that he allows himself a tenderness that makes some people think he has 'too much of the woman in me'. And he set these men loose in his beloved Eastwood woods at a time of crisis, a time after the cataclysm.

Spring comes suddenly here. There are snowdrops, unexpectedly, at the end of January, as the snow melts. There are sunny days in February, alternating with more days of snow. This is our new, post-apocalyptic unseasonal weather, or perhaps it has always been like this. Snowdrops are, after all, called snowdrops. They are everywhere now, by the side of the road, in the woods, in gardens. G picks them – she is allowed to pick two each time – and holds them wonderingly. It has been so long a year for her that she seems to have forgotten flowers.

P and I go on a windy, late-February walk. I am irritable and rushed after too many hours spent at train stations, and we pick our route badly: it seems only to involve flat fields that leave our boots full of mud, as they were at the seaside. It feels like we are carrying half the countryside with us as we plod.

We talk about apocalypse. We talk about the Horvat book I have been reading. P – another man who might have corresponded with Lawrence – says that apocalyptic thinking is irresponsible. We are better off with tragedy than apocalypse, he says, because our desires for endings and for truth are both dangerous, and it's preferable to have less-absolute versions of both. I have also been reading *The Sense of an Ending*, the classic 1967 musings on humanity's 'brooding on apocalypse' by Frank Kermode, the academic grandee who always saw himself as an outsider and was in a way a less embattled and more decisively idea-driven successor to Leavis. Kermode says here that tragedy is characterised by delay rather than endings, that the end becomes immanent rather than imminent. 'In tragedy the cry of woe does not end succession; the great crises and ends of human life do not stop time,' because, 'the world goes forward in the hands of the exhausted survivors'. P says that the difference between them is a difference in truth rather than endings. Apocalyptic truths are sudden and divine, tragic truths are revealed more obliquely. He likes his gods hidden and his truths gradual. I start to think about whether this was true for Lawrence.[10]

Then we see, unexpectedly, our first lambs. It is too soon. I wasn't ready. The day is overcast – it is even starting to rain – and I didn't have any of the spring feelings to hand. This wasn't a day of renewal, and I feel that the energy of newness has come upon me too abruptly. There are three of them, tiny, grubbily white creatures. It's the noise that strikes me most. The leaping, the jubilant wriggling as they feed, the sheer lambiness of them is all familiar, but these noises, which P seems to know well, I've never heard. It is a kind of ecstatic, half rageful announcement of presence. Here I am. In the world. But what a world it has turned out to be. This is the newborn's cry of insistent selfhood that Lawrence is so good on. We watch from the edge of the field, not wanting to go too close. The noisy one makes its noise, and then finds its mother to feed; it turns out that each has a separate mother; they are three only children whose siblings may have died at birth, too small or too cold to survive.

It is all beginning again. Another spring in lockdown, last year repeated, all the same, all new. February turns to March and the countryside finishes its tossing and turning and settles into its familiar spring shape. We are woken by birds again now, reminding us that we live alongside a world more determinedly sociable than our own. The grass is exploding into thick tufts of green that P refuses to mow because it will bring him one step too close to being a suburban dad. H learns to ride a bike and we set off, without coats, to the river, where the water no longer swells and it's just about possible to imagine swimming again. The cat brings in a series of tiny mice. It feels like it should be a decision to be swept into the energy of spring. Yet we have no choice. I think of Lawrence's wonderful essay 'Whistling of Birds', written in Cornwall as he emerged from winter in 1917. Spring rushes in after a period of frost (the frosts in Cornwall that winter had been the worst in twenty years) that has left birds dead in hedgerows, half-eaten by scavengers. When the warmth arrives, the birds adapt to the new season more quickly than the humans. Immediately, they begin to whistle. 'Vive', Lawrence hears it as. Live! The song bubbles through the twittering creatures so swiftly that it seems not to be their own doing. 'In their throats the new life distils itself into sound. It is the rising of the silvery sap of a new summer, gurgling forth.' We cannot hold back the spring, Lawrence says, though we may still see the corpses and feel winter's pain. We can't prevent the bubbling of the wood pigeons, the perfume of the daphne tree, the arrival of the lambs. It turns out that winter, with its 'mortification and tearing', was entangled upon us, like bats in our hair, but was never really our innermost self. Within, we were always this, 'this limpid fountain of silver, then quiescent, rising and breaking now into the flowering'.[11]

We have to accept the new life, have to accept the flowering, as Constance and Mellors do in the novel Lawrence brought into being in an Italian autumn but filled with remembered English springs. It is spring, with its insistence on natality, on new life after the cataclysm, that makes *Lady Chatterley's Lover* so moving. I am glad to be reading it again in spring. It makes it easier to picture that greyish-brown first little chick that Connie comes upon in the woods, 'the most alive little spark of a creature in seven kingdoms'.

At this point Connie, desperate for an outlet apart from her stultifying marriage to her soul-stunted and war-wounded husband, has taken to going to the woods each day, and using Mellors's hut as a place to rest in. Mellors is responsible for the chickens, as he is for the whole life of the wood, and he has been overseeing the hatching of the eggs in the coop outside the hut. They have both been waiting for the chicks to arrive, though for

Mellors there is dread in this because he is weary and deadened and too caught in the mortification of winter to be ready for new life.

When Connie first sees it, the chick has just escaped the coop and is prancing around while the mother hen clucks in terror. Connie crouches down to watch, delighted by this 'fearless new life', and it scrambles back into the coop, disappearing under the hen's feathers. The chick is not really frightened, though – it doesn't know fear yet – and it pokes its little head back out, 'eyeing the Cosmos'. Delighted by this new life, Connie becomes more conscious of 'the agony of her own female forlornness': she is childless and untouched.

It's the chicks that bring Connie and Mellors together a few days later. There are thirty-six of them now, and Connie rushes over to the woods one evening to see them. Mellors reaches in, evading the pecks of the mother hen, and gives her one to hold:

'There!' he said, holding out his hand to her. She took the little drab thing between her hands, and there it stood, on its impossible little stalks of legs, its atom of balancing life trembling through its almost weightless feet into Connie's hands. But it lifted its handsome, clean-shaped little head boldly, and looked sharply round, and gave a little 'peep'. 'So adorable! So cheeky!' she said softly.

The keeper, squatting beside her, was also watching with an amused face the bold little bird in her hands. Suddenly he saw a tear fall on to her wrist.

And he stood up, and stood away, moving to the other coop. For suddenly he was aware of the old flame shooting and leaping up in his loins, that he had hoped was quiescent for ever. He fought against it, turning his back to her. But it leapt, and leapt downwards, circling in his knees.

This is spring, with its trembling, balancing life, sweeping down on them, making her cry, making him feel the old quiescent flame shooting through him. Life itself becomes a force, a kind of laser, leaping from his loins down to his knees. He touches her shoulder and strokes down her back to 'the curve of her crouching loins', his hand 'softly, softly' stroking the curve of her flank 'in the blind instinctive caress'. He has been taught animalistic, bodily instinct again by the sight of the chicks. 'Shall you come to the hut?' he asks, quietly, and leads her inside, where he spreads a brown, soldier's blanket on the floor. She lies down. They do not kiss. He kisses her cheek, he draws down her silk underclothes, with 'a quiver of exquisite pleasure', he touches her warm body and kisses her navel. 'I thought I'd done with it all,' he says, half regretfully, as he walks her back afterwards towards the house. 'Now I've begun again.' Begun what? she asks. Life, he says. 'There's no keeping clear. And if you do keep clear you might almost as well die. So if I've got to be broken open again, I have.'

It is a great, painful achievement, to make us feel how onerous this efflorescence is, for Lawrence's characters and for himself as a writer. There is something a little clumsy about the description of the chick. It's as though Lawrence can only stand back and describe it, step by step, as it lifts its little head, looks around and gives a little peep. We can feel how huge an effort it was, as well as how natural and right it felt, to describe the woods and the flowers of his boyhood one more time. It all feels much more perilous, much more weighted, than it did in *The White Peacock*. This was, after all, a novel that he couldn't even hope would be published. He knew, as he wrote the sex scenes, as he pushed further into the next draft and gave himself the full freedom of the fucks and cunts, that this was not a novel that would be given to the general public freely to read. Yet he wasn't writing it in secret. 'Read me,' he cried, even as he made himself unreadable. He knew that it would be read; he knew his own powers and knew that his books would live on after his death, live on into the freer modern world that he was creating through them, however slowly. He was writing into the future, and it was a future he cared deeply about. He believed that he had the power to change how people felt about bodily life. This book, which drained what remaining energy he had, was also the book that gave him the willpower to fight his illness and live, and he believed it would help future generations to live in their turn. 'I always labour at the same thing,' he wrote to his literary

agent Nancy Pearn in April 1927, 'to make the sex relation valid
and precious, instead of shameful. And the novel is the furthest
I've gone. To me it is beautiful and tender and frail as the naked
self is – and I shrink very much even from having it typed.'[12]

He did have it typed, though – and printed – he did it all himself
and turned out to be a good salesman, punctilious in his book-
keeping and posting. In his 1924 essay 'The Bad Side of Books',
he wrote that writers submit to publication 'as souls are said to
submit to the necessary evil of being born into the flesh'. He
might hate it, but it was necessary – he did not write simply for
his own benefit and with this book he had a mission in the world
at large. 'The book must be read,' he wrote to his Kibbo Kifting
friend Rolf Gardiner from Florence in March 1928, enclosing
some order forms for Gardiner to tout for business on his behalf,
'it's a bomb, but to the living, a flood of urge – and I must sell it.'
He acknowledged to Gardiner that it would 'set me apart even
more definitely that I am already set apart', but proclaimed also
that he saw this as his 'destiny'.[13]

It has been a question waiting for me throughout – what will
I make now of his most infamously famous book? Can I read it
in a way that isn't Millett's, isn't Frieda's, isn't Leavis's (he saw it
as a 'bad novel' brought on by the final stages of TB, a novel that
the 'normal' Lawrence would have found as distasteful as Leavis
himself did). I have been prepared for it to be a struggle because
last time I read it, in preparation for teaching a couple of years
ago, I found it an uncomfortably preachy read.[14]

Now, though, I am struck most of all by how absurd it is
that Kate Millett should have paid no attention to the chicks. It
is clearer to me than last time how much she leaves out. Most
importantly, she fails to see how fully Lawrence inhabits Connie
as well as Mellors. This is one of the great portrayals by a man
of a female character. We believe in the particularity of her
combination of vivacity and imaginative intensity and intelligence
and scepticism and fear. She's up there with Ursula Brangwen,
with Emma Bovary, with Anna Karenina. Yet for Millett this is
simply Lawrence as ventriloquist, finding a way to make a woman

preach his message. '*Lady Chatterley's Lover* is a quasi-religious tract recounting the salvation of one modern woman (the rest are irredeemably "plastic" and "celluloid" through the offices of the author's personal cult, "the mystery of the phallus").'[15]

I feel confused now that there have been years when I couldn't take *Lady Chatterley's Lover* seriously because I was too won over by Millett's arguments. I could only see Connie's passivity in that scene with the chicks. But now Mellors's activeness seems to me more gentle, more reluctant, and Connie's place in the scene more creative – there are times when he is more diffident than she is. It's true that Connie is redeemed by contact with the phallus they lovingly (I will never not find this excruciating!) refer to as John Thomas. 'Tell lady Jane tha' wants cunt,' Mellors tells his penis, 'John Thomas, an' th' cunt o' lady Jane!' I'm glad that Lawrence didn't go ahead with his plan to call the book *John Thomas and Lady Jane.* It's true too that Mellors's body is described in more lengthily lyrical detail than Connie's. There is nothing like that first, very moving sighting of him washing, those 'clumsy breeches slipping down over the pure, delicate, white loins, the bones showing a little', though Mellors does make it clear through speech and touch that he feels, if anything, even more delight in her than she in him: 'What it is to touch thee!' he says, rubbing his cheek against her belly and thighs. What would Millett have said if it was the other way round – if it was the usual story of a female body objectified by the male gaze? It took the more playfully insightful Angela Carter to celebrate Lawrence for reversing the gaze.

For the last few years, when I have taught Lawrence, I have looked on as my female students fall in love with *Lady Chatterley's Lover.* 'It's as though he is a woman,' one said, wonderingly, last year. It helps, I think, that Connie isn't special – like Emma Bovary, she is an ordinary woman in whom lots of possibilities have come to a crisis, but unlike Emma Bovary she is intelligent and often incisive in her judgements. And then the following week I have given them Kate Millett to read and have looked on as they change their minds. It happened again this autumn and now, as I mark essays grappling with Millett, I wonder what I can do next year to allow them to retain trust in their first experience of reading it. During that first read, they don't mind that Connie's body isn't described lyrically, because they are caught up in her point of view, they feel Mellors rubbing his cheek against their thighs. This may have been more strongly felt when they read the novel during the November lockdown, when we were all forlorn, in need of spring and missing human touch and tenderness.

Millett makes no mention of Mrs Bolton, Sir Clifford's brilliantly imagined nurse, a woman who manages to combine being a kind of novelist-substitute as the gossip of Tevershall with being a maternal lover to Clifford and an ally to Connie, who she urges to take seriously her experience of mutual sexual love. She says little about Clifford, who is another novelist within the novel, and who isn't simply dismissed by Lawrence as impotent and upper class. He and his friends aren't quite idiots – some of them have very similar ideas to Mellors about the primacy of bodily life. There is such dextrous novelistic world-building and scene-making here that Millett seems to miss, and she says nothing about the class struggle that is as much a subject in the book as sex is. If Lawrence had seen a revolution in the making that summer in the Midlands, then he showed its antecedents in this novel, where we see a 'gulf impassable' between Clifford and the colliers who work for him – a 'strange denial of the common pulse of humanity' that can only breed hatred.

Yet surely Connie and Mellors have to be viewed within this larger picture, in which Mellors's is just one, flawed point of view. There are times, I think, when Lawrence found him as overreaching, as foolish, as pig-headed as the modern female reader does. Perhaps it's in this context that we can read his repulsive speech about his estranged wife's clitoris – which he describes as a hard beak tearing at him with 'a raving sort of self-will'. After all, these are views we've heard expressed previously in the novel by Connie's first lover, Michaelis. Just after Connie's orgasm, achieved by rubbing herself against his flaccid penis, he says, in a painfully hurtful comment: 'you'd have to bring yourself off! You'd have to run the show!' This 'unexpected piece of brutality', just when she's glowing with post-coital calm, is, we're told, 'one of the shocks of her life'. There is no suggestion at this point that the book is on the side of the male character. And we have this in the background when we read Mellors's speech about his wife. Don't we wonder, then, how it might look from Bertha's point of view? Millett sees this as Lawrence talking through Mellors, but I think that Lawrence gives us room to think that this might just be a failed marriage, in which there was no pleasure for either of them and they were left taking what ineffectual solace they could in the satisfaction of physical needs. Connie doesn't seem to agree with Mellors at this point, and it's presumably partly because of the pain she remembers from the scene with Michaelis that she remains distant from Mellors after their conversation. 'Do you think you've always been right with women?' she asks him, inviting him to reflect on his own part in the difficulties.

It turns into a scene that resembles the best marital scenes in *The Rainbow* in its portrayal of the minute-by-minute gyrations of love and hate. Connie walks outside alone, disturbed by the conversation, and feels like going away, 'right away from him and everybody'. She goes back in and speaks up for Bertha and his other lovers. 'Perhaps the women *really* wanted to be there and to love you properly ... Perhaps it wasn't all their fault.' They bicker, he tells her that women are self-important, and she tells him that he is. She's arranged to stay the night – it will be their first whole night together – but he tells her to go home. They make up and go quietly to bed; it's not till the morning that they undress and, in a glow of spring sunlight, she examines his body openly for the first time and they have sex.

It's a shame that Lawrence wrote 'A Propos of *Lady Chatterley's Lover*', his 1929 defence of the book after it was banned. He subscribes to a lot of Mellors's views there, and it can mislead us into thinking that the novel has a single point of view. But it doesn't. Mellors learns as much as Connie does. He learns more about the female experience of sex and he learns another way of being, a more reciprocal and humble one. He learns to be a character in a novel – a character who, curiously, becomes less delineated, has less of that 'old stable ego of character' as the book progresses, rather than more so – and not the writer of an essay. And Lawrence himself was learning, once again, about the possibilities of novels, learning to put in practice his injunction not to nail anything down.

Lawrence's polemical brilliance and his novelistic imagination were always battling against each other. It's crucial not to let the essays overwhelm us, or to overwhelm the novels. Millett was right to dislike the writer of that essay, but she did the novel a huge disservice. I wish she had given herself the chance to read it again in later life; I wish I could have persuaded her to do so when we met. She's not the only critic I'm grappling with now, though. There's also Frank Kermode, who read it in strikingly apocalyptic terms, seeing the seven sex scenes in the novel, culminating in the scene where Connie is cleansed of shame through anal sex, as a conscious rewriting of the opening of the seven seals in the Book of Revelation. Clearly, there is something about *Lady Chatterley's Lover* that drives people mad, though it's a book pleading, with an intensity that is itself a form of madness, for us to be sane. At any rate, this is Kermode on less sane form than he was in *The Sense of an Ending*. He's right to see apocalyptic elements in *Lady Chatterley's Lover*. Mellors has his flashes, like Birkin, of wishing humanity away, and before they dance in the rain, he and Connie feel like they are in an ark in the flood. But, even more strongly than Birkin with Ursula, Mellors's impulses are given a kind of oppositional balance by Connie. He accepts fatherhood, which will draw him into the future; he has a Rolf Gardiner-like vision of a new life, though admittedly a slightly ridiculous one, in which everyone will wear red trousers and make their own furniture. The point does seem to be that this is a book that begins with a tragic age, not an apocalyptic one, and ends as a comedy as traditionally defined, with its characters released out into the world alive and ready for it, full of the new life of Connie's pregnancy, though also suspended in semi-separation.[16]

Lawrence had thought more apocalyptically in *The Rainbow*, where the rainbow itself brings the promise that the 'old, brittle corruption of houses and factories' will be swept away and a 'new, clean, naked' world will come into being, built on a 'living fabric of Truth'. It seems to have helped him, writing *Lady Chatterley's Lover*, that he had the beginnings of his work on the *Apocalypse* book as an alternative receptacle for his apocalyptic energy, a kind of wastepaper basket for his crankiest ideas. He also had his story, 'A Dream of Life', written in late 1927 out of that same trip back to Eastwood, and opening with the same ugliness that characterises Tevershall in *Lady Chatterley's Lover* but that here seems to call out for apocalyptic transformation. 'Nothing depresses me more than to come home to the place where I was born,' this begins, 'this coal-mining village on the Nottingham-Derby border.' He describes the new generation of miners, 'got under' by their wives, too forbearing, 'poor with a hopeless outlook and a new and expensive world around them'. There are several pages like this and then he describes walking on that footpath, up past the quarry and through to the Haggs Farm, which he had written about so many times. He walks into the tree-filled quarry and finds a little cavity in the rock where he can curl up and fall asleep. Waking, dizzy, he is lifted out and washed by two men, in a biblical scene where he is figured as the resurrected Christ. They lead him down a path to a plough-land, with oxen-drawn carts, and he sees at the top of the hill a golden city, 'yellow in the late afternoon light, with yellow, curved walls rising massive from the yellow-leaved orchards'.[17]

He knows immediately that this is the ugly colliery town of his childhood transfigured into the golden city he sang hymns about in the Congregational chapel. What follows is a description of a utopian city, something between a biblical vision and Rolf Gardiner's idea of a new kind of local, collective life. There are men in tunics on horses, silent but with the 'magic of close-interwoven life'. There are naked girls with bundles on their heads, all exhibiting an inner ease, like plants. Later, he witnesses a collective dance at dusk, apparently unfurling by instinct, very like the traditional dances that Gardiner and Lawrence fantasised about reviving together. What's crucial here is that although this is a vision of all he has ever wanted for humanity, the narrator is frightened: 'afraid for myself'. These people do not seem to be 'human beings in my sense of the word'. He feels like a ghost among them. When he is told that he has woken into the distant future, he sits down and cries, weeping his soul away.

It's telling that Lawrence couldn't finish the story. He had come to see that his fantasy of post-apocalyptic life was unsatisfactory. Breaking down in tears, his narrator is longing to be returned to the here and now, the ruins that Connie and Mellors are struggling through. Lawrence's distrust of apocalypse was to acquire great, though typically ambivalent, force in his *Apocalypse* book, a 110-page study he'd been thinking about since early on during his time in New Mexico, but wrote largely in 1929 as he saw *Lady Chatterley's Lover* into the world. It had begun as an introduction to Frederick Carter's study, and remained in dialogue with it, but took off into larger musings on the Book of Revelation and our relationship to revelation and to endings more widely. At its heart is Lawrence's disparagement of man's 'simple lust, lust is the only word, for the end of the world'. He sees the Book of Revelation as a trap set for modern man. His central argument here is that the biblical book is a mishmash of writings by two separate generations of Christians. There are the earlier pagans, celebrating the cosmos as 'the great Power that is', and writing into being some symbols that Lawrence finds wonderfully inventive. In particular, he likes the 'great Mother of the cosmos', the woman 'clothed with the sun, and the moon under her feet', who is driven to the desert, leaving us only with the virgins and harlots, the 'half-women of the Christian era'. And then there are the later, narrow Hebrews, providing 'grand biblical authority' for the cry of the 'weak and pseudo-humble' with their 'weird and mystic hate of the world'. These are the apocalypse-mongers. Lawrence no longer believed in the vision of the Book of Revelation as much as he had when he wrote *The Rainbow.* He resisted definitive endings now that he was closer to his own ending, and he resisted definitive truths.[18]

After that summer in Sutton-on-Sea, Lawrence's periods of recovery became briefer and more limited. Amid all their travels, there was nowhere that he wasn't ill. People meeting him after absences were shocked at how skinny he was; his tumultuous coughs seemed always on the verge of breaking his tiny frame.

His plans for the new life he would have after he recovered started to sound less and less realistic, and the lines in his letters that I find speak most directly, reading them through now, are the ones where he acknowledges his illness. 'Between malaria and continual bronchial trouble, I'm a misery to myself,' he wrote to his sister in May 1927. 'I wish I could sort of get over it, and feel a bit solid again.'[19]

In denial about his own TB, he put a lot of energy into helping alleviate the TB of his old Eastwood friend, Gertie Cooper, who was sent to a sanatorium in September 1926. His enthusiasm for helping Gertie may have been connected to his refusal to name his own illness as TB, which can feel as intense and as peculiar as his inability to name himself. There was obviously stigma attached to the disease at the time, but his fear of naming it went way beyond general squeamishness or fear and shows a kind of terror of the power of words themselves, as though the word was more frightening than the symptoms. In Gertie's case, though, he could name it, and he seems to have gained strength from advising her on her illness.

In January 1927 Gertie was told she would have to have one lung removed. 'My God, what a fight for life!' Lawrence wrote, telling her not to try to understand why this was happening and urging her not to weaken or fret. 'While we live, we must be game. And when we come to die, we'll die game too.' After she survived the ordeal, he wrote to Koteliansky, detailing her operation with an extravagant interest that suggests he was imagining it as a possibility for himself. But if he was, then he found it was not something he would be able to bear. 'Too horrible – better die ... Why aren't we better at dying, straight dying! What is left, after all those operations? Why not chloroform and the long sleep! How monstrous our humanity is! Why save life in this ghastly way?'[20]

During six intense weeks at the end of 1927, Lawrence wrote his final version of *Lady Chatterley's Lover* at their unheated house outside Florence. He was worried about money (he'd now had the idea of printing the book privately, but there was no guarantee it would work), he was freezing in the unheated house ('the vapour froze in my beard: never been so cold here,' he reported to Gertie Cooper, knowing she would feel as he did about the cold), and he was coughing hard in the damp, foggy weather – much of the time he was too ill to work. But he put astonishing energy, confidence and conviction into redrafting the novel, focusing in part on turning Mellors into a more complex and more autobiographically inspired character. He made Mellors weaker, introducing his delicate lungs, and he made him more of an intellectual. But he also made him potent, making him able for acts of lovemaking Lawrence himself had long given up on, but which perhaps reflected his own feeling of potency as he wrote. It probably doesn't matter when Lawrence had become impotent, though it's been the subject for much biographical speculation. An abortive encounter with Dorothy Brett, their former companion in New Mexico, in March 1926 seems to have been his final attempt at sex. 'One has just to forget, and to accept what is good,' Lawrence wrote to Brett afterwards, obliquely. 'We can't help being more or less damaged.'[21]

After they left the villa outside Florence in June 1928, Lawrence moved from one hotel or rented house to another, seeking the high altitude his doctors had told him he needed but then finding that he hated being high up, given that he was no longer able to walk uphill. He went from Saint-Nizier (where he was told to leave because of a by-law prohibiting the hotel from taking guests with 'affected lungs') to Chexbres to Gstaad to Port-Cros (where the storms made it impossible to keep warm). He went to Bandol for a couple of weeks that turned into four months, and composed most of his 'Pansies' there, revisiting all his old themes – the gods, class, Englishmen, old furniture, work, the need for men to be real men ('women want fighters for their lovers'), money ('Get money, or eat dirt!'), the sun, sex, will and women ('favourite vessels of wrath').[22]

Lawrence's poetry followed on where *Lady Chatterley's Lover* had left off in attempting to make cunts and balls acceptable to the wider world. He had taken to painting a year earlier – describing himself as 'bursting into paint' – in parallel with his search for novelistic regeneration through his final novel. These are the

paintings of a major imagination working in a medium it has only
a partial understanding of, which makes them touching, fascinating
and gawky. He was drawn again and again to the nude, whether
he was illustrating biblical scenes or painting the people around
him, and his representation of carnal life is suspended between the
outrageously material and the sacral. Now both his writing and his
painting came under threat. His most controversial poems were
written just as he heard that copies of *Lady Chatterley's Lover* had
been seized in January 1929. And then, that summer, his paintings
were taken by the police at the first exhibition of his work in
London. He knew that his paintings were risky, just as he knew
that his novel was, but he still minded the fact of censorship fiercely,
and was furious when the gallerist suggested allowing his paintings
to be burned, in order to make a public statement about censorship.
He refused to cooperate. Over a thousand copies of *The Rainbow*
had been incinerated already; he knew that eventually his clothes
would probably go up in flames as he died, as was the custom for
TB sufferers; he wasn't going to let his paintings be scorched as
well. 'There is something sacred to me about my pictures, and I will
not have them burnt, for all the liberty in England.' He became
preoccupied with the possibility of burning his paintings over
the months that followed, horrified by the idea, as though it was
himself they wanted to send up in apocalyptic flames. Yet there is a
lightness in his late poems, even when he writes about this:

The upshot was, my pictures must burn
that English artists might finally learn

when they painted a nude, to put a *cache sexe* on,
a cache sexe, a cache sexe, or else begone!

There was crisis here, and revelation, but they were given a new
buoyancy, as though the chagrin could at last be released. If he
had accepted that his destiny was to be reviled in his lifetime,
perhaps being close to death made it easier to accept that his work
would have its real reception in a future he could only, though
vividly, imagine.[23]

Out of this all came his great death poems, an extraordinary attempt at a new kind of ending, and a peculiar lifeline as his life ended. He had been struggling to breathe for over a year now. For a long time, he hadn't been able to walk uphill without gasping and now he couldn't walk at all. This is the terrible reality of TB, and it seems more viscerally terrible to me after this year, in which people have been dying in their hundreds of thousands around the world because they are rendered unable to breathe by Covid, and in which I have heard George Floyd dying from lack of breath. Yet in his final poems, emerging out of the rather breathless quips of the 'Pansies', Lawrence developed a new, calmly breathed rhythm. 'Bavarian Gentians', 'Shadows', 'The Ship of Death' – these are poems that he rewrote in bed, writing them out again and again by hand in his notebooks until he died, finding in their rhythms a kind of solace, giving himself voice in them of a kind he could no longer attempt in life. Here is the opening of 'The Ship of Death':

I
Now it is autumn and the falling fruit
and the long journey towards oblivion.

The apples falling like great drops of dew –
to bruise themselves an exit from themselves.

And it is time to go, to bid farewell
to one's own self, and find an exit
from the fallen self.

II
Have you built your ship of death, O have you?
O build your ship of death for you will need it.

The grim frost is at hand, when the apples will fall
thick, almost thunderous, on the hardened earth.

Lawrence had finished writing about spring; it was autumn now, and he was waiting for death as he waited for the winter he rightly feared would finish him off. He was wondering if he could 'his own quietus make', and find a way to the oblivion he half feared and half longed for. The repetitions here – 'Have you built ... O have you?' – add to the combination of density and ease; there's the feeling of him worrying away at thoughts but also a feeling of the thoughts unfolding easily, which is what makes these poems so readable, considering how high-toned they are.

He could never write only out of hopelessness. The fear that 'There is no port, there is nowhere to go' is followed in the next stanza by a vision of a flush of yellow and a flush of rose, a glimmer of a new dawn. This was a man who had schooled himself in struggle, in oppositional thinking, and he was able to see the peace in the oblivion he was coming to desire. 'Already the dark and endless ocean of the end / is washing in through the breaches of our wounds,' he writes, in the stately iambic rhythm that would characterise all of these late poems musing on death. Reading the poems aloud, I find that there is something very moving about the iambs, the feeling of homecoming in them, the return to the form of his early poems, overlaid with a new sensibility. There are the poetic rhythms he learnt from Shakespeare, from Milton, there's even the image of Christ that preoccupied him in his early years. But there's something uniquely Lawrence's in this hard-won breath, this eloquent reinvention of the modern poetic voice under pressure, on the other side of the casualness of the 'Pansies'. There it is, in the opening of 'Shadows':

And if to-night my soul may find her peace
in sleep, and sink in good oblivion,
and in the morning wake like a new-opened flower
then I have been dipped again in God, and new-created.

A few years after Lawrence's death, in 1936, the German writer Elias Canetti would praise the older Austrian novelist Hermann Broch for teaching his readers how to breathe. Canetti had found in Broch (himself an almost exact contemporary of Lawrence's) 'a rich store of breathing experience'. Reading Canetti's tribute fifty years later, Susan Sontag, who had not long ago styled herself as a female D. H. Lawrence, found that 'breathing may be the most radical of occupations, when construed as a liberation from other needs such as having a career, building a reputation, accumulating knowledge'. She thought that talented admirers take from other writers permission to breathe more deeply. Is this a permission that Lawrence, breathing deeply despite his own terrifying lack of breath, can teach us?[24]

It is still spring here, an insistent spring that means I can't quite sink into autumnal oblivion with Lawrence. There is no ship of death, only increasingly early dawns. We have been here for a year now. This is not the life I expected to have a year ago, and not the life I went to court to fight for. But we are all settling into the rhythms of our weeks as we become more accustomed to them. 'Let's go home,' H or G will say, out in the world, and I find it reassuring to hear them confirm that we have made a home. 'You have come your way, I have come my way … I have stepped across my people, and hurt them in spite of my care.' I didn't quite know how true this would be, when I quoted 'Frohnleichnam' to myself in our early months here. This has not been the ecstatic dance Lawrence goes on to describe, but I like to think that at our best we are 'Shining and touching'.

What you have is enough, my yoga teacher still says to me each week, online now, in our sitting room while P plays chess online on the sofa. In moments of panic I mentally list the things that I have, things that nothing but the accidents of fate I sometimes find myself imagining in bewildering detail can take from me. Lawrence doesn't encourage us to count our blessings, and nothing for him was ever enough – this is partly why he was so keen on renunciation. But in his final years he found new ways to accept struggle and difficulty as a necessary part of life. 'What irritated me in you in the past was a sort of way you had of looking on Buddhism as some sort of ether into which you could float away unresisted and unresisting,' he wrote to Earl Brewster from Sutton-on-Sea in August 1926, in the letter where he also talked about liking England again. 'Believe me, no truth is like that. All truth – and real living truth is the only truth – has in it the elements of battle and repudiation.'[25]

I think that one thing he has taught me is to battle to become more myself. Curiously, this was a lesson of the court case too, as Lawrence's travails with censorship were for him. *The Rainbow* was banned, but he didn't step back, he plunged forward, and wrote *Lady Chatterley's Lover*, championing 'tender-hearted fucking'. Having been told by the world that he was one kind of person, he doubled down on it, and this is what I am coming to see I must do too. I have been told by a judge that I am too honest, too ambivalent, too headstrong in my search for more life for myself and my children. Very well, I will become more honest, more ambivalent, more wilful, however much Lawrence has lectured me on letting go of my female will. Doesn't he let Connie plan her life with Mellors, doesn't she get pregnant, doesn't she fight for the life that flames into being between them?

H and I go out cycling into a day that looked springlike from inside but turns out to be beset by a wind that threatens to blow us down. Around us, the birds sing, the noise almost violent with that whistling cry of 'Vive' that Lawrence heard. There are primroses, like the ones that Connie sees in great tufts in the wood, and picks, to take the wood back inside with her. But it is tiring and cold, my hands become raw. At one point H throws down his new bike in rage. I think of the wind that plagued Lawrence's final winter. 'Such storms, such winds, such torrents of rain!' He hated the wind then, as he always had – 'here the winds are so black and terrible,' he wrote in Cornwall. It was the wind that made him move on from place to place most frequently. H shouts at me for suggesting this expedition, and I shout back, exhausted. This is struggle, this is repudiation, and I am not sure I can take much more of it. This isn't the 'fine, fine wind' that Lawrence pictured blowing him along, taking its course through the chaos of the world in his 'Song of a Man Who Has Come Through'. It's more like the night's flood-winds that lift his last desire from him, leaving his hollow flesh abandoned in 'Repulsed'. But we have no other way home; it's too far to walk, so we wrestle on in determined, exhausted silence on our bicycles. I remember that there is struggle, too, in 'Song of a Man Who Has Come Through'. He isn't only a 'winged gift', delicate and fine there. 'If only I am keen and hard like the sheer tip of a wedge,' he writes. And I feel us sharpening, hardening as we in turn make it through as best we can.[26]

Lawrence weighed only six stone by the time he went to the sanatorium in Vence in February 1930. His collected mass of printed words weighed almost more than he did by this point. It's as though he shrank as the pages piled up; he was a tiny wisp of a man, writing himself to death, though also writing himself out of it. 'I wish I could throw the thing off, it's really like a vampire,' he wrote to one of the distributors of *Lady Chatterley's Lover.* He now admitted that there was 'very slight tubercular trouble' but insisted that this would dissipate if they could only improve the bronchial-asthmatic side of things. After three weeks he hated institutional life too much to continue, and joined Frieda in a villa in Vence. He still didn't talk of dying, but, next to a game of noughts and crosses, he doodled a sketch of himself fully clothed, a corpse with feet and beard pointing vertically upwards. Aldous and Maria Huxley, close friends in these years, were with them at the end, as was Frieda's grown-up artist daughter Barby, who had become close to her mother again. He had a vision of his dead body, lying on the table, and asked Frieda and Barby to embrace him. 'Maria, Maria, don't let me die,' he said when Frieda went out of the room. When he died, Frieda was holding his left ankle.[27]

Did he believe, at the end, that a new heaven and new earth awaited him? 'I am walking still / with God, we are close together now the moon's in shadow,' he wrote in 'Shadows'. God was breaking him down to his own oblivion, sending him forth in the morning, 'a new man', into that red dawn of 'The Ship of Death'. Did he come through? I am not sure what it would mean to come through death, but he was right to commit himself to the future in his final works. Whatever afterlife he envisaged, he has had an afterlife here with us, in the troubled century that followed. We have been living out his hopes and fears, his contradictions, as many of his truths have become both more obvious and less palatable. He's had afterlives in the books written about him.

It's astonishing how many of the women he knew chose to write about him: there's Frieda's memoir and her rather forced attempt at writing a Lawrentian novel of their marriage; there's Jessie Chambers' impressively vivid account of their early life in Eastwood; there's Dorothy Brett's love letter of a book ('Forever I have the vision of you ... and I ... riding across the pale, ochre desert'); and Mabel Dodge Luhan's spiritedly self-centred account of his time in Taos. The men wrote about him as well – there's John Middleton Murry's troubled, vindictive account, Huxley's musings on his illness, Richard Aldington's adulatory, often insightful biography.[28]

*Lady Chatterley's Lover* really did live up to his massive expectations of it – surely more than even he can have expected. It's appropriate that Lawrence's most prominent afterlife should have come in the form of a trial. I think he'd have relished the preposterousness of the establishment still trying to undermine him three decades after he died. 'If I get an erection, we prosecute,' was the grounds for prosecution reputedly put forward by the pompous, priggish, clearly titillated QC Mervyn Griffith-Jones. As an exercise in literary criticism, the six-day trial was so gaudy, so excessive – more than anything we as literary critics have ever asked or hoped for. One expert after another was wheeled on stage to attempt to argue that the book had sufficient literary merit to count as literature and that it had no 'tendency to deprave or corrupt persons likely to read it'. There, suddenly, in the hallowed grounds of the Old Bailey, was a gowned QC using the four-letter words that Lawrence had tried to introduce back into ordinary language, telling the assembled jury and audience that the word 'fuck' or 'fucking' occurred no less than thirty times in Lawrence's last novel. There was Rebecca West, a wilful, modern woman, who was also a formidable establishment figure, explaining Lawrence's desire 'to have the whole of civilisation realising that it was not living fully enough, that it would be exploited in various ways if it did not try to get down to the springs of its being and live more fully and bring its spiritual gifts into play'. There was a bishop, saying that Lawrence was trying to portray the sex relationship as something essentially sacred and that it was a book all Christians should read. There was the esteemed literary scholar Richard Hoggart, another son of working-class parents who had joined the ranks of the literary elite, insisting that this book, far from being the 'vicious' pornography it was condemned as, was 'highly virtuous and, if anything, puritanical'. The word 'puritanical' came up a lot in the trial, and rightly so. Doris Lessing wrote in her statement of support that 'until recently he has been consistently represented as an indecent or immoral writer who advocated sexual licence; whereas the truth is that he was a very moral, not to say puritanical man, concerned to give sex dignity'. Lessing wasn't called by the defence; perhaps her own morals were seen as too lax for her to be a reassuring witness when it came to depravity and corruption.[29]

And there was E. M. Forster, once a candidate for Rananim, standing up on Lawrence's behalf. After he came to stay with Lawrence for that mutually disastrous night during the war, Forster wrote to his host saying that he liked the Lawrence who knew about birds and was physically restful and had written *The White Peacock*, but that he did not like 'the deaf impercipient fanatic who has nosed over his own little sexual round until he believes that there is no other path for others to take'. It is to his credit that Forster saw that Lawrence had gone beyond this deafness in his final novel, and that he could step forward at the Old Bailey and confirm that he believed Lawrence to be the greatest imaginative novelist of his generation.[30]

Not everyone rose in support of the book. Leavis's response to being called for the trial was, 'I do not think that Sir Allen Lane does a service to literature, civilisation or Lawrence in the business of *Lady Chatterley's Lover*.' Evelyn Waugh was 'quite certain that no public or private "good" would be served by its publication. Lawrence had very meagre gifts.' So much the better for Lawrence, who liked to be despised. He'd have hated the trial, though, as well as enjoying it. He took so personally the attacks on his books; he'd have hated the feeling during the six long days of the trial that the case was Penguin's to lose in the eyes of many of the legal minds involved. 'If you want justice / let it be demon justice,' he wrote in one of his 'Pansies', just after urging his readers to stand up not for Jesus but for 'jolly justice'. The justice at work in his life had often been demonic and rarely been jolly. Perhaps there's a cosmic justice in knowing that he won in the end, but it's resulted in a kind of over-reception for *Lady Chatterley's Lover*, which made it ready for Millett's takedown and has prevented many readers from getting to grips with what it really is: a deeply felt-through novel, supple and porous in the largest novelistic literary tradition.[31]

I feel that it's only now that I've understood this novel, at the end of a year in which Lawrence has been so vividly, often painfully alive to me. He might have been irritated by this particular afterlife, living alongside me in lockdown, as he's lived alongside the other women writing about him this past year – what right do we have to summon him at will? Perhaps it's been a grizzled, chuntering ghost that's been accompanying me, even when I've hoped that we might be becoming friends. But he may have found it only fitting – he expected admiration; he expected advocacy. I hope that I've found a way of admiring him that moves beyond advocacy because it incorporates and acknowledges so much that is wrong with him, and because when you live alongside a writer with this kind of intimacy, you don't feel required to make a case for them. The closeness of domestic intimacy makes it curiously difficult to sum up or to characterise the person you live with, as Lawrence well knew.

I have gained so much from his sense of life as a continual flux of moods and impulses of will that can erupt nonetheless into moments of visionary intensity – moments of utterance. I have gained from his preparedness to contradict himself, to rethink and refine his thoughts with such propulsive energy, and to allow opposing views to stand alongside each other. We have more need than ever for thoughts to be pushed to their uncomfortable limits, for the truths unquestioningly accepted on one side of the culture wars to be challenged by an insider, by someone who can think our thoughts but who can also think their opposites with energy and rigour.

I have found it so bracing to come up against someone who situates the unconscious in the stomach, who chastises us for our wilfulness even as he urges us to keep striving, who tells us not to over-identify with children or animals because there are other kinds of feelings that allow for freer relationships, who opens us to the constantly shape-shifting nature of desire and the mutability this sets up in our relationships, who builds whole philosophies out of his ambivalence about community and home and allows our relationship to our community to be filled at once with rage and wit and rapture, who reconceives religion for a secular age and has taught me in the process to pray again, who allows nature its strangeness and its destructiveness even as he celebrates it, who curbs his own apocalyptic yearnings and in doing so reveals how irresponsible apocalyptic thinking can be. I have grown from the experience of learning to accept that the man who believed fervently that state ownership of property should be abolished and was committed to writing into being freer lives for women was also a person who thought, in some moods, that a kind of aristocracy of the elite was preferable to democracy, that people are not equal, that children born of bad marriages are irredeemably lost souls, that women don't deserve to have orgasms when they don't manage to have them simultaneously with a man. Thinking freely for Lawrence – 'gazing on to the face of life, and reading what can be read', as he put it in that poem – meant sending his tendrils in every direction at once, inhaling experience and processing it into a hundred different thoughts, and then, over the years, honing in on the truths he could stand by, and could give imaginative life to in his fiction.

I want literature and culture to open up a space where it's possible to be passionately polemical, whether rightly or wrongly, or a Lawrentian mixture of the two, without feeling boxed in by each other's voices. This will be a space where ambivalence is possible within the polemic, where the polemical can easily give way to something more imaginative, and where we can be capable of that quick relatedness Lawrence prized, because we remain pliant and free. Over the past year, Lawrence has shown the way to such a space, making me hopeful that I can find a way to live with contradictions while still finding truths that I can believe in enough to live by.

And so we go on, limping along in the tragic age it still seems best not to take tragically. What more can we ask of our lives than the vision offered, with that typical mixture of casualness and portentousness, in the opening paragraph of Lawrence's final novel?

> Ours is essentially a tragic age, so we refuse to take it tragically. The cataclysm has happened, we are among the ruins, we start to build up new little habitats, to have new little hopes. It is rather hard work: there is now no smooth road into the future: but we go round, or scramble over the obstacles. We've got to live, no matter how many skies have fallen.

It's a paragraph that gains depth with every reading. Lawrence is so characteristically Lawrence when he writes 'It is rather hard work.' It's his gift for stating the ordinary and making it extraordinary. By starting the book with this paragraph, he turns an ending into a beginning; he shows that we can and must start again even as things seem to be ending around us, and shows that starting again involves neither a new heaven nor a new earth because both beginnings and endings are false and we will never come through in any final sense; there is just the rather hard work of keeping going.

# Note on Sources

I have not referenced Lawrence's novels, as readers will have their own favourite editions. There are free, searchable versions of all the novels (except *Mr Noon*, which is available as an affordable e-book), novellas and short stories available at www.gutenberg.com, where readers can easily locate the passages I refer to. Gutenberg also includes editions of *Twilight in Italy*, *Fantasia of the Unconscious*, *Etruscan Places*, *Mornings in Mexico* and *Studies in Classic American Literature*, so I have not given page numbers here. *Psychoanalysis and the Unconscious* is a short book, best read whole if at all, so I have refrained from giving page numbers there also.

Lawrence's poems (and some prefaces to poems) are all taken from *D. H. Lawrence: The Complete Poems*, collected and edited with an introduction and notes by Vivian de Sola Pinto and Warren Roberts (Penguin Books, 1993), abbreviated to *CP*. I have not given page numbers, but have identified the titles of poems where they are not given in the text. Lawrence's short stories are generally taken from D. H. Lawrence, *The Complete Stories* (Delphi Classics, 2015), abbreviated to *CS*. Lawrence's essays are generally taken from D. H. Lawrence, *Complete Essays* (Blackthorn Press, 2011), abbreviated to *CE*. Lawrence's letters are all taken from the Cambridge eight-volume collected edition (abbreviated to *CL*); in each case the exact date is given to make locating them straightforward.

# Notes

## INTRODUCTION

1. 'Skylark': DHL, 'The Poetry of the Present', *CP*, p. 181.
2. W. H. Auden, quoted by Janet Byrne, in *A Genius for Living: A Biography of Frieda Lawrence* (Bloomsbury, 1995), p. 385.
3. Simone de Beauvoir, *The Second Sex*, translated by Constance Borde and Sheila Malovany-Chevallier (Vintage, 2011), pp. 236, 237, 239; Kate Millett, *Sexual Politics* (Virago, 1977), p. 238.
4. Frieda Lawrence, letter to Harold Moore, 24 January 1951, in Frieda Lawrence, *The Memoirs and Correspondence* (Knopf, 1964), p. 327; DHL, 17 January 1913, *CL*.
5. Mabel Dodge Luhan, *Lorenzo in Taos* (Sunstone Press, 2007), p. 179; Anaïs Nin, *D. H. Lawrence, An Unprofessional Study* (Alan Swallow, 1964), pp. 49, 59; F. R. Leavis, *D. H. Lawrence, Novelist* (Pelican, 1981), p. 81; Claude McKay, *A Long Way From Home* (Rutgers University Press, 2007), p. 118.
6. T. S. Eliot, *After Strange Gods* (Faber, 1934), p. 58; T. S. Eliot, witness statement given to M. Rubinstein, Regina *v.* Penguin Books ('*Lady Chatterley* Trial Papers,' Rubinstein Archive, DM 1679, Special Collections, University of Bristol Library); closing speech for the prosecution in *The Trial of Lady Chatterley: Regina v. Penguin Books Limited*, edited by C. H. Rolph (Penguin, 1990), p. 219.
7. Susan Sontag in her journal: 'As Eva pointed out, if I hadn't made the grand switch from "Kant" to "Mrs D. H. Lawrence," I would never have been able to write fiction' (8 December 1967), *As Consciousness is Harnessed to Flesh: Journals and Notebooks, 1964–1980* (Penguin, 2013), p. 233; Sontag, 'On Paul Goodman', *New York Review of*

*Books*, 21 September 1972; Doris Lessing, Preface to *The Fox* (2002), in *Time Bites: Views and Reviews* (Harper Perennial, 2005), p. 20.

8. Angela Carter, undated letter, quoted in Edmund Gordon, *The Invention of Angela Carter* (Chatto & Windus, 2016), p. 77; Women Writers' Session, cited in *The Diaries of Barbara Hanrahan*, ed. Elaine Lindsay (University of Queensland Press, 1998), p. 181; Carter, 'Lorenzo as Closet-Queen', *Nothing Sacred* (Virago, 1982), p. 162.

9. Jessie Chambers, *D. H. Lawrence: A Personal Record* (CUP, 1980), p. 23.

10. DHL, 28 February 1919, *CL*.

11. DHL, 'The Good Man', *Phoenix: The Posthumous Papers of D. H. Lawrence*, edited by Edward D. McDonald (William Heinemann, 1936), p. 750.

12. DHL, 'Poetry of the Present', *CP*, p. 182; Al Alvarez, 'Lawrence, Leavis, and Eliot', *The Kenyon Review* (18: 3, 1956), p. 480.

13. DHL, 'Why the Novel Matters', *CE*, p. 130.

## I. UNCONSCIOUS

1. DHL, *Psychoanalysis and the Unconscious*.

2. DHL, 17 January 1913, *CL*; DHL, 1 February 1912, *CL*.

3. Friedrich Nietzsche, *Thus Spake Zarathustra*, translated by Thomas Common (The Modern Library, Random House, 1997), pp. 33, 39.

4. Jessie Chambers quoted in John Worthen, *D. H. Lawrence, The Early Years* (CUP, 1992), p. 152.

5. DHL, 28 January 1908, *CL*.

6. DHL quoted in John Worthen, *D. H. Lawrence, The Early Years* (CUP, 1992), pp. 157, 153.

7. 'I its creator': DHL, 20 January 1911, *CL*; 'That I'm a fool', 'wait restlessly': Jessie Chambers, *D. H. Lawrence: A Personal Record* (CUP, 1980), pp. 57, 103.

8. Jessie Chambers, *D. H. Lawrence: A Personal Record* (CUP, 1980), p. 156.

9. DHL, 'Study of Thomas Hardy', *CE*, p. 19.

10. DHL, 'Aristocracy', *CE*, p. 401.

11. Bertrand Russell, *The Autobiography of Bertrand Russell: 1914–1944* (Little, Brown, 1968), pp. 13–14; Ottoline Morrell, *The Early*

*Memoirs of Lady Ottoline Morrell*, edited by Robert Gathorne-
Hardy (Faber, 1964), p. 273; DHL, 8 December 1915, *CL*.

## 2. WILL

1. Quotations taken from *Psychoanalysis and the Unconscious*.
2. DHL, 23 April 1915, *CL*; DHL, 15 June 1924, *CL*.
3. H.D., *Bid Me to Live: A Madrigal* (Black Swan Books, 1983), p. 164;
   Rachel Cusk, *Second Place* (Faber, 2021), p. 154.
4. DHL, 5 June 1914, *CL*; DHL, 'Study of Thomas Hardy', *CE*, p. 39.
5. Friedrich Nietzsche, *Beyond Good and Evil*, translated by Helen
   Zimmern (The Modern Library, Random House, 1917), p. 14;
   DHL, 'Study of Thomas Hardy', *CE*, p. 19.
6. Ralph Waldo Emerson, 'Self-Reliance', in *Essays: First and Second
   Series* (The Riverside Library, Houghton Mifflin Company, 1883),
   p. 47; DHL, 3 March 1915, *CL*.
7. DHL, 'The Reality of Peace', *CE*, pp. 193, 194.
8. DHL, 'Study of Thomas Hardy', *CE*, p. 30.

## 3. SEX

1. Doris Lessing, letter to to Leonard Smith, 15 May 1948 (Lessing
   collection, Special Collections, University of Sussex).
2. DHL, 12 February 1915, *CL*.
3. DHL, 'A Propos of *Lady Chatterley's Lover*', 1929, in DHL,
   *Lady Chatterley's Lover*, introduction by Doris Lessing (Penguin,
   2006), p. 324; Simone de Beauvoir, *The Second Sex*, translated by
   Constance Borde and Sheila Malovany-Chevallier (Vintage, 2011),
   p. 240.
4. 'I have got a genius', quoted by Barbara Weekley Barr, 'Memoir of
   D. H. Lawrence', in Stephen Spender (editor), *D. H. Lawrence:
   Novelist, Poet, Prophet* (Weidenfeld & Nicolson, 1973), p. 8.
5. 'full-bosomed': DHL, *Mr Noon*.
6. DHL, 20 March 1912, *CL*.
7. Frieda Lawrence quoted in John Worthen, *D. H. Lawrence, The
   Early Years* (CUP, 1992), p. 375.
8. DHL, 7 May 1912, *CL*; DHL, 15 May 1912, *CL*.

9. DHL, 29 June 1912, *CL*.
10. DHL, 13 August 1912, *CL*.
11. DHL, 19 August 1912, *CL*; DHL, 11 September 1912, *CL*.
12. DHL, 23 December 1912, *CL*; Otto Gross quoted in John Worthen, *D. H. Lawrence, The Early Years* (CUP, 1992), p. 379.
13. DHL, 'Cocksure Women and Hensure Men', *CE*, pp. 455–6.
14. Frieda Weekley quoted in John Worthen, *D. H. Lawrence, The Early Years* (CUP, 1992), pp. 411–12.
15. Frieda's letter is part of DHL, 29 December 1912, *CL*.
16. Kate Millett, *Sexual Politics* (Virago, 1977), pp. 239–40.
17. DHL, 2 December 1913, *CL*.
18. DHL, 'Prologue to *Women in Love*', in The Rainbow *and* Women in Love: *A Casebook*, edited by Colin Clarke (Macmillan, 1978), p. 57.
19. Jacques Lacan, 'The Signification of the Phallus', *Écrits: A Selection*, translated by Bruce Fink (Norton, 2002), p. 276; DHL, 10 November 1923, *CL*.
20. DHL, 15 May 1912, *CL*.
21. Ibid.

## 4. PARENTHOOD

1. DHL, 14 December 1912, *CL*.
2. Frieda Weekley, 3 March 1902, and Ernest Weekley, 13 September 1902, both in Frieda Lawrence, *The Memoirs and Correspondence* (Knopf, 1964), pp. 154, 157.
3. Frieda Weekley and DHL quoted in John Worthen, *D. H. Lawrence, The Early Years* (CUP, 1992), p. 415.
4. DHL, 15 May 1912, *CL*.
5. Simone de Beauvoir, *The Second Sex*, translated by Constance Borde and Sheila Malovany-Chevallier (Vintage, 2011), pp. 236, 237, 239; Kate Millett, *Sexual Politics* (Virago, 1977), p. 241.
6. Samuel Smiles and Lydia Sigourney quoted in Christina Hardyment, *Dream Babies: Childcare Advice from John Locke to Gina Ford* (Frances Lincoln, 2007), p. 84.
7. Lily Kipping, letter to Frieda Weekley, in Frieda Lawrence, *The Memoirs and Correspondence* (Knopf, 1964), p. 167.
8. DHL, 'Education of the People', *CE*, p. 254.

9. Rosalind Thornycroft, *Time Which Spaces Us Apart*, quoted in Mark Kinkead-Weekes, *D. H. Lawrence: Triumph to Exile* (CUP, 2011), p. 602.
10. Ibid.
11. Frieda Lawrence, *The Memoirs and Correspondence* (Knopf, 1964), p. 108.

## 5. COMMUNITY

1. DHL, 'Education of the People', *CE*, p. 274.
2. DHL, 15 April 1915, *CL*.
3. 'I want to gather': DHL, 18 January 1915, *CL*; 'I want you to form', 'It is communism': DHL, 1 February 1915, *CL*; 'drop all your democracy': DHL, 14 July 1915, *CL*; 'There must be a revolution': DHL, 12 February 1915, *CL*.
4. DHL, 19 April 1915, *CL*.
5. George Ripley, letter to Ralph Waldo Emerson, 9 November 1840, quoted in Octavius Brooks Frothingham, *George Ripley* (Houghton Mifflin, 1882), p. 311.
6. DHL, 8 March 1916, *CL*.
7. Robert Lynd, *Daily News*, 5 October 1915, p. 6; DHL, 21 October 1915, *CL*.
8. DHL, 8 July 1916, *CL*.
9. DHL, 6 November 1915, *CL*.
10. 'a good peace': DHL, 30 December 1915, *CL*; 'I am willing': DHL, 6 January 1916, *CL*; 'not a teacher': DHL, 19 February 1916, *CL*; 'My dear Katherine': DHL, 7 January 1916, *CL*.
11. DHL, 8 March 1916, *CL*.
12. 'just under the': DHL, 5 March 1916, *CL*; 'a union in the': 20 December 1915, *CL*; for Murry and Mansfield on *The Rainbow*, see Mark Kinkead-Weekes, *D. H. Lawrence: Triumph to Exile* (CUP, 2011), p. 275.
13. John Middleton Murry, postscript to Katherine Mansfield, 26 February 1916, *The Collected Letters of Katherine Mansfield*, edited by Margaret Scott and Vincent O'Sullivan (OUP, 1984), volume 1, pp. 247–8; DHL, 9 April 1916, *CL*.
14. Katherine Mansfield, 11 May 1916, *Collected Letters of Katherine Mansfield*, volume 1, p. 263.

15. DHL, 'On Being a Man', *CE*, p. 306; DHL, 18 April 1916, *CL*.
16. 'They should have': DHL, 24 May 1916, *CL*; 'How I deceive': DHL, 19 June 1916, *CL*.
17. Lawrence's letter was reported by Mansfield, writing to Murry on 7 February 1920: 'he spat in my face & threw filth at me and said "I loathe you. You revolt me stewing in your consumption"', *The Collected Letters of Katherine Mansfield*, edited by Vincent O'Sullivan with Margaret Scott (OUP, 1993), volume 3, pp. 208–9; 'sworn, pledged': 5 December 1918, *CL*.
18. 'both I and': DHL, 16 April 1916, *CL*; 'One has a': 26 April 1916, *CL*.
19. DHL, 1 May 1916, *CL*.
20. DHL, 'Democracy', *CE*, pp. 223, 229.
21. DHL, 'The Reality of Peace', *CE*, p. 205.
22. DHL, 5 November 1921, *CL*.
23. 'Here, in this': 8 March 1912, *CL*; 'It reminds me': DHL, 4 October 1912, *CL*.

## 6. RELIGION

1. DHL, 'Hymns in a Man's Life', *CE*, p. 457; DHL, 3 December 1907, *CL*.
2. DHL, 'The Reality of Peace', *CE*, p. 199.
3. DHL, 22 April 1914, *CL*.
4. DHL, 31 Jan 1915, *CL*; Catherine Carswell, *The Savage Pilgrimage: A Narrative of D. H. Lawrence* (CUP, 1981), p. 212; see T. R. Wright, *D. H. Lawrence and the Bible* (CUP, 2001), p. 9 for a discussion of DHL's relationship with Christ.
5. DHL, 'Study of Thomas Hardy', *CE*, p. 63.
6. DHL, 9 April 1911, *CL*.
7. DHL, 24 January 1916, *CL*.
8. DHL, 18 July 1927, *CL*.
9. *The Bhagavad Gita*, translated by Juan Mascaró (Penguin, 2003), pp. 56, 54.
10. DHL, 2 January 1922, *CL*.
11. DHL, 'Study of Thomas Hardy', *CE*, p. 33.
12. 'unmusical': Max Weber, letter to Ferdinand Tönnies, 9 Feb 1909, quoted in Marianne Weber, *Max Weber: A Biography* (Transaction, 1988), p. 337; Max Weber, *The Protestant Ethic and the Spirit of*

*Capitalism*, translated by Talcott Parsons (George Allen & Unwin Ltd, 1950), pp. 53, 54, 176.

13. 'A vast': DHL, 'New Mexico', CE, pp. 179, 178, 180; 'Creation is': DHL, *Mornings in Mexico*.

14. DHL, 'On Being Religious', *CE*, pp. 294, 296, 298.

15. DHL, 10 June 1925, *CL*.

16. DHL 'No Joy in Life', *CP*.

## 7. NATURE

1. DHL, 'Pan in America', *CE*, pp. 167, 168.

2. Ernst Haeckel, *The Riddle of the Universe at the Close of the Nineteenth Century*, translated by Joseph McCabe (HardPress, 2016) p. 346.

3. DHL manuscript quoted in Jeffrey Mathes McCarthy, *Green Modernism: Nature and the English Novel, 1900–1930* (Palgrave, 2015), p. 201.

4. DHL, 'Love Was Once a Little Boy', *CE*, p. 379.

5. DHL, 'In the Cities', *CP*; DHL, 'Nottingham and the Mining Countryside', *CE*, p. 548.

6. Raymond Williams, *The Country and the City* (OUP, 1975), p. 10; DHL, *The Rainbow*.

7. Ernst Lehmann quoted in Jeffrey Mathes McCarthy, *Green Modernism: Nature and the English Novel, 1900–1930* (Palgrave, 2015), p. 192.

8. Martin Heidegger, 'Why Do I Stay in the Provinces?', in Thomas Sheehan, *Heidegger: The Man and the Thinker* (Transaction Publishers, 2010), p. 27; for an overview of the critics who compare Lawrence and Heidegger, see Caleb Fridell, 'D. H. Lawrence's Green Modernity', *The D. H. Lawrence Review* (43: 1.2, 2018).

9. Herbert Spencer, *First Principles* (Williams & Norgate, 1910), pp. 220–1. For a discussion of Lawrence and Spencer, see Roger Ebbatson, *Lawrence and the Nature Tradition: A Theme in English Fiction 1859–1914* (Harvester Press Ltd, 1980), p. 40; DHL, 'Pan in America', *CE*, p. 167.

10. John Hargrave, *The Great War Brings It Home: The Natural Reconstruction of an Unnatural Existence* (Constable, 1919), p. 2; DHL, 16 January 1928, *CL*.

11. DHL, 'Love Was Once a Little Boy', *CE*, p. 379; Charles Darwin, *The Descent of Man* (John Murray, 1871), volume 1, p. 35; Sigmund Freud, 'A Difficulty in the Path of Psycho-Analysis', *The Standard Edition of the Complete Psychological Works of Sigmund Freud*, volume 17, translated by James Strachey (Vintage, 2001), p. 140.
12. DHL, 'Reflections on the Death of a Porcupine', *CE*, p. 391.
13. Ibid., p. 388.
14. Ibid., pp. 393–4.
15. W. H. Auden, 'D. H. Lawrence', in *The Dyer's Hand and Other Essays* (Faber, 1962), p. 290.
16. Ibid.
17. 'They should have': DHL, 18 May 1924, *CL*.
18. DHL, 'Dear Old Horse, A London Letter', *CE*, p. 158.
19. DHL, 3 October 1924, *CL*.

## 8. APOCALYPSE

1. Srećko Horvat, *After the Apocalypse* (Polity Press, 2021), pp. 11–12.
2. 'Except a seed': DHL, 29 May 1915, *CL*; 'But it was not': DHL, 9 September 1915, *CL*.
3. See the Gutenberg edition of Marx and Engels' *Manifesto of the Communist Party*.
4. 'I am so bored': DHL, 28 August 1926, *CL*; 'desire has died': DHL, 'Man Reaches a Point', *CP*.
5. 'It is rather': DHL, 26 August 1926, *CL*; 'the beginning': DHL, 12 September 1926, *CL*; 'back in my': DHL, 29 August 1926, *CL*; 'queer, odd sort', 'One feels in them': DHL, 30 August 1926, *CL*.
6. 'The Midlands are': DHL, 2 September 1926, *CL*; 'I'm afraid the whole': DHL, 4 March 1928, *CL*.
7. For Lawrence's remark to Hopkin, see Derek Britton, *Lady Chatterley: The Making of the Novel* (Unwin Hyman, 1988), p. 124.
8. 'The novel is the highest': DHL, 'Morality and the Novel', *CE*, p. 117; 'the novel is a great': DHL, 'The Novel', *CE*, p. 120; 'the novel is the one': DHL, 'Why the Novel Matters', *CE*, p. 130; 'quick relatedness': DHL, 'The Novel', *CE*, p. 123; 'If you try': DHL, 'Morality and the Novel', *CE*, p. 117.
9. 'Now Verga turns': DHL, 'Introduction to *Mastro-Don Gesualdo* by Giovanni Verga', *Phoenix II: Uncollected, Unpublished and Other Prose Works by D. H. Lawrence*, edited by Warren Roberts

and Harry T. Moore (Heinemann, 1968), p. 279; DHL, '*Mastro-don Gesualdo*, by Giovanni Verga', *Phoenix: The Posthumous Papers of D. H. Lawrence*, edited by Edward D. McDonald (William Heinemann, 1936), p. 226.

10. Frank Kermode, *The Sense of an Ending* (OUP, 2000), p. 89.

11. DHL, 'Whistling of Birds', *CE*, pp. 191–2.

12. DHL, 12 April 1927, *CL*.

13. 'as souls are': DHL, 'The Bad Side of Books', Introduction to *A Bibliography of the Writings of D. H. Lawrence*', in DHL, *Life with a Capital L*, Essays Chosen and Introduced by Geoff Dyer (Penguin, 2019), pp. 210–11; 'The book must': DHL, 17 March 1928, *CL*.

14. F. R. Leavis, 'The Orthodoxy of Enlightenment', in *Anna Karenina and Other Essays* (Chatto & Windus, 1967), p. 236.

15. Kate Millett, *Sexual Politics* (Virago, 1977), p. 238.

16. Frank Kermode, 'Spenser and the Allegorists', in *Shakespeare, Spenser, Donne: Renaissance Essays* (Routledge & Kegan Paul, 1971), p. 289.

17. DHL, 'A Dream of Life', *CS*.

18. DHL, *Apocalypse and the Writings on Revelation*, edited with an Introduction and Notes by Mara Kalnins (Penguin, 1994), pp. 80, 119.

19. DHL, 19 May 1927, *CL*.

20. 'My God': DHL, 23 January 1927, *CL*; 'Too horrible': DHL, 27 April 1927, *CL*.

21. 'the vapour froze': DHL, 19 December 1927, *CL*; 'One has just': DHL, 18 March 1926, *CL*.

22. 'women want fighters': DHL, 'Women Want Fighters for Their Lovers', *CP*; 'Get money, or eat': DHL, 'Being Alive', *CP*; 'favourite vessels': DHL, 'It's No Good', *CP*.

23. 'bursting': DHL, 'Making Pictures', in *D. H. Lawrence's Paintings*, introduction by Keith Sagar (Chaucer Press, 2003), p. 137; 'There is something': DHL, 14 July 1929, *CL*; 'The upshot was': DHL, 'Innocent England', *CP*.

24. Susan Sontag, 'Elias Canetti', *Granta*, 1 March 1982.

25. DHL, 30 August 1926, *CL*.

26. 'Such storms': DHL, 27 October 1928 (in a postscript not included in *CL*: see instead Frieda Lawrence, *Not I, But the Wind* (Macmillan, 1934), p. 267; 'here the winds': DHL, 15 February 1916, *CL*.

27. 'I wish I could', 'very slight': DHL, 14 Feb 1930, *CL*.

28. Frieda Lawrence, *Not I, But the Wind* (Macmillan, 1934) and 'And the Fulness Thereof…' in Frieda Lawrence, *The Memoirs and Correspondence* (Knopf, 1964); Jessie Chambers, *D. H. Lawrence: A Personal Record* (CUP, 1980); Dorothy Brett, *Lawrence and Brett, A Friendship* (Sunstone Press, 2006), p. 46; Mabel Dodge Luhan, *Lorenzo in Taos* (Sunstone Press, 2007); John Middleton Murry, *Reminiscences of D. H. Lawrence* (Jonathan Cape, 1936); Aldous Huxley, Introduction to *The Letters of D. H. Lawrence* (William Heinemann, 1932); Richard Aldington, *D. H. Lawrence* (Chatto & Windus, 1930).

29. Rebecca West, The Bishop of Woolwich, Richard Hoggart examined, in *The Trial of Lady Chatterley: Regina v. Penguin Books Limited*, edited by C. H. Rolph (Penguin, 1990), pp. 67, 73, 92; Doris Lessing, letter to M. Rubinstein, 1960 ('*Lady Chatterley* Trial Papers', Rubinstein Archive, DM 1679, Special Collections, University of Bristol Library).

30. E. M. Forster, 12 February 1915, in *Selected Letters of E. M. Forster*, edited by Mary Lago and P. N. Furbank (Collins, 1983), volume 1; Forster examined, in *The Trial of Lady Chatterley*, p. 112.

31. Evelyn Waugh, letter to M. Rubinstein, 1960, ('*Lady Chatterley* Trial Papers', Rubinstein Archive, DM 1679, Special Collections, University of Bristol Library); DHL, 'Demon Justice', *CP*.

# Acknowledgements

To engage with D. H. Lawrence is to enter a field of criticism where almost as much is at stake as there was for Lawrence himself in writing his books. Sometimes, reading Lawrence scholarship, my students ask why these critics care quite this much. It's a helpful reminder of the grandiosity of a certain kind of literary scholarship. But I am also grateful to the critics over the past century who have turned writing about Lawrence into so high-wire an art.

My debts to F. R. Leavis and Frank Kermode, to Anaïs Nin, Simone de Beauvoir and Kate Millett, are already evident in these pages. But we have come a long way since these critics urged us to extremes of love and hate, and I have gained hugely from all the contributions from scholars I have heard at the London Lawrence Group, thoughtfully and stylishly curated by the indispensable Lawrence scholar Catherine Brown. Particular scholars whose contributions I have found stimulating here include Terry Gifford, Trevor Norris, Carrie Rohman and Hugh Stevens.

Beyond this group, I am grateful for the scholarship of (and in some cases for conversations with) Masashi Asai, Fiona Becket, Elleke Boehmer, Howard J. Booth, Annalise Grice, Joyjit Ghosh, Andrew Harrison, Stefania Michelucci, James Moran and Julianne Newmark. I gained hugely from collaborating on a project with Laura Ryan, whose ground-breaking work on Lawrence and race will soon be available to a larger audience.

This book would not have been possible without the meticulous editing involved in the Cambridge editions of all

Lawrence's work. I can think of few enterprises of this kind that have been more successful and I have benefited in particular from the editions of the collected letters and from the masterful three-volume biography by John Worthen, Mark Kinkead-Weekes and David Ellis.

In thinking about Lawrence and religion I have profited especially from T. R. Wright's *D. H. Lawrence and the Bible* (2000). In considering Lawrence and nature I have gained in particular from Jeffrey Mathes McCarthy's *Green Modernism: Nature and the English Novel, 1900-1930* (2015), Carrie Rohman's *Stalking the Subject: Modernism and the Animal* (2008), Roger Ebbatson's *Lawrence and the Nature Tradition: A Theme in English Fiction 1859-1914* (1980), Fiona Becket's 'D. H. Lawrence, Language and Green Cultural Critique' (in Howard J. Booth's ground-breaking edited collection, *New D. H. Lawrence* (2009)), Trevor Norris's 'Martin Heidegger, D. H. Lawrence, and Poetic Attention to Being' (in Axel Goodbody and Kate Rigby's 2011 edited collection *Ecocritical Theory*) and Caleb Friedell's overview, 'D. H. Lawrence's Green Modernity' (*D. H. Lawrence Review*, 2018). Raymond Williams has been a guiding presence for me while grappling with nature as a cultural phenomenon, and Jonathan Bate's *Song of the Earth* (2000) has been important in helping me think through the relationship between literature and nature.

I am grateful to Geoff Dyer for showing that Lawrence is best written about irreverently and to Rachel Cusk, Alison MacLeod and Frances Wilson for showing what contemporary women can do in revitalising Lawrence for a new century.

At King's College London, I continue to gain enormously from conversations with colleagues, some of which have now continued for twelve years. At a time when it's hard to feel that universities are getting much right, I've been particularly grateful for the committed backing I've received for a scholarly undertaking that was in some ways very personal, and always imaginatively driven. For several years I have taught an undergraduate course on D. H. Lawrence. It is common to say that we learn a lot from our students but this has I think been particularly the case for me

when it came to formulating my sense of why Lawrence matters
and what we have to gain from tussling with him in our present
moment.

I have depended enormously on the judicious advice of my
early readers Lisa Appignanesi, Peter Boxall, Josh Cohen and
Alexandra Harris. Their balance of encouragement and high
demands has fired up the editing process, while their moments
of bracing rage at Lawrence have reminded me why this project
is worthwhile. This is the sixth book that Alexandra Harris has
read for me, and it has been especially gratifying to feel that
she liked it better than some of the others, suggesting that her
combinations of enthusiastic ticks in the margins and stringent
moral and aesthetic judgements are finally paying off. Along the
way, I have also gained hugely from grappling with Lawrence in
conversation with Kate Kilalea, Deborah Levy, Tessa Hadley and
Hannah Sullivan, and with Merve Emre, Lyndsey Stonebridge
and Rachel Cusk. Alison MacLeod and I avoided discussing
Lawrence until both our books were written but it has been a
source of great pleasure to know that she has been immersed in
Lawrence through these years as well. Since her *Tenderness* was
published, quite apart from being able to engage with Lawrence
as a living, breathing man, I have benefited enormously from her
archival research into the *Chatterley* trial and have been especially
grateful that her novel is so well footnoted.

At Bloomsbury, the book has been seen through to publication
with great poise by those working hard on the ground: Amanda
Waters, Kate Quarry and Francisco Vilhena. This is the fourth
book of mine that Michael Fishwick has taken on, and now that
he has retired, it is becoming clear quite how much I have gained
from his belief in me as a writer. It is the first book that Paul
Baggaley has played a role in, and I am thankful for his insight
and support in publishing it. Tracy Bohan remains the ideal agent
– encouraging, judicious, and very gifted at seeing exactly what
a book is in its early stages – and I have been so glad to have her
working alongside me.

I am, as always, grateful to my parents for encouraging the
kind of passionate adolescent reading that I have, I hope, gone

some way to recapturing in my recent books. My children have lived alongside me and Lawrence so closely during these years that it would be a wholly different book without them. Patrick Mackie has read more versions of some passages in this book than anyone should have to. Patrick likes to quote Milton saying that marriage is a 'meet and happy conversation'. There is a sense in which every paragraph in this book has emerged out of our conversations, both on the page and off, and this book is his very nearly as much as mine.

# Index

'A Dream of Life' 219
'A Propos of Lady Chatterley's
    Lover' 217
*Aaron's Rod* 100–1, 150, 158
'Adolf' 193–4
afterlife, the 169, 228
Aldington, Richard 229
Alps, the 75–6
Alvarez, Al 14
animal writing 193–5
animals, human relationship with
    187–9, 189–95
Anthropocene, the 177
anthropocentrism 176–7
anthropomorphism 186, 194
*Apocalypse* 203–4, 218–19, 220
apocalypse 201–5, 209–11, 232
    DHLs view of 218–20
    and *Lady Chatterley's Lover*
        218, 219
'Aristocracy' 39, 53
Auden, W. H. 3–4, 194, 195
Australia 141–4
Aztec religions 164–6

'The Bad Side of Books' 214
Baden-Baden 198
Bandol 222
'Bavarian Gentians' 224
Baynes, Rosalind 107–8, 150, 208

Beauvoir, Simone de 4, 5, 71, 89,
    99–100, 100–1, 102
Bell, Clive 131
Bell, Vanessa 124–5
Beresford, J. D. 131
Bergson, Henri 24
*Beyond Good and Evil*
    (Nietzsche) 48–51
*Bhagavad Gita* 52, 157, 158
'Bibbles' 194–5
Bible, the 147, 157–8, 202
birds 1, 13, 14, 29, 210, 227
birth 25–6
Black Lives Matter 139–40
blood-brotherhood 125, 142–3
blood-consciousness 19, 21, 24,
    31, 39–40
Bloomsbury Group 124–6, 131, 149
'Both Sides of the Medal' 75
Bowen, Elizabeth 89
Brangwen, Gudrun
    compared to a beaver 187
    Mansfield as model for 136–9
    on marriage 15
    as model 15
    and nature 179–80, 181–2
    and religion 159
    and the unconscious 31
Brangwen, Ursula 82
    chagrin 156

INDEX

chair buying scene 119
compared to a kitten 186–7
and desire 85
eating 37–8
Frieda in 77
on marriage 15, 120
as model 15
and nature 179–80, 181–2
and the rainbow 62–3
and religion 159
revelation of life's potential 15
and sex 65–8, 82
and the unconscious 31
and will 47
breathing 224, 225–6
Brett, Dorothy 145, 222, 229
Brewster, Achsah 158
Broch, Hermann 225–6
Brook Farm 126–7
Buddhism 158
Burrows, Louie 30

Campbell, Gordon 49–50
Canetti, Elias 225–6
Carswell, Catherine 135, 150
Carter, Angela 9–10, 85, 102, 215
Carter, Frederick 203, 220
cats 186–7, 195, 195–6
chagrin 155–6, 205, 223
Chambers, Jessie 11, 48, 229
relationship with DHL 27–30
Chatterley, Constance
cleansed of shame 218
and desire 15, 85
empty womb 99–100
Lawrence inhabits 214–15
Millet on 215–16
and nature 174
and new life 211–13
as ordinary woman 215
passivity 215
pregnancy 218
redemption through sex 150–1

relationship with Mellors
213, 216–17
sexual response 140
Chesterton, G. K. 30
Chexbres 222
child rearing 54–6
childcare manuals 103–4
childhood 98–9
children
DHL's portrayal of 96–102
idealised 98–9
relationship with fathers 101–2
renunciation of 100–2
Christianity 30, 147–9, 147–54, 163–
4, 164–6
climate-change 177
'Cocksure Women and Hensure
Men' 79
communism 124
community and communal life
122–9, 232
American models 126–7
Bloomsbury Group 124–6
DHL's critique of democracy 141–4
families 129
New Mexico 144–6
Rananim experiment 124, 126,
127, 129–39
utopian 123–4
visiting 123–4
writing as 138–9
conflict, and sex 87–9
Congregationalism 160
Cooper, Gertie 221, 222
Corke, Helen 73
Cornwall 211, 227
Rananim experiment 124, 126,
127, 129–39
Cosmic God 148, 151, 152, 158
COVID 19 pandemic 1, 110–15,
139–40, 196–7, 201–5, 210
Croydon 30
culture, and nature 178–9, 196

cunt, use of word 70, 82, 215, 222
Cusk, Rachel 10, 11
Custody of Infants Act, 1839 102

*Daily News, The* 130
dance 152–3
Dante 11
Darwin, Charles 186
'The Daughters of the Vicar' 83
Daum, Meghan 102
death 12
    acceptance of 198
    and rebirth 202
death poems 224–5
'Democracy' 141
democracy 124, 141–4, 232
Derbyshire 194
dialogue 3
Diderot, Denis 13
Dodge, Mabel 43–4, 44, 45, 144–5,
    164, 229
dogs 193–4, 194–5
'Dolor of Autumn' 171

Eastwood 57–9, 61–2, 118, 121, 145–6,
    147–9, 207, 209, 219
eating 34–9
ecocide 180
'Education of the People' 106,
    117–18
Eliot, George 89
Eliot, T. S. 8, 23, 42, 203
Emerson, Ralph Waldo 49–50, 88, 126
'England, My England' 123
*English Review* 30
'The Escaped Cock' 150–1
*Etruscan Places* 167
Extinction Rebellion 176–7, 179, 181

*Fantasia of the Unconscious* 23, 32, 55,
    59, 69–70, 93, 98–9, 101, 105–6,
    107, 122, 150, 158–9
fascism 143–4, 180, 206

female pubic hair, DHLs refusal to
    believe in 28
feminism 102–6
feminist detractors 8–9
'Figs' 36
First World War 7, 53, 130–1, 134–
    5, 202
'Fish' 194
Flaubert, Gustave 208
Florence 221–2
flower picking 110
flowers 175
Floyd, George, death of 139, 224
Forster, E. M. 70–1, 149, 230
fourth dimension, of being, the
    188–9, 191
*Fox, The* 191–2
Franklin, Benjamin 162
Frazer, James 40
French Enlightenment 13
French Revolution 203
Freud, Sigmund 20, 22–4, 25, 31–2, 34,
    39, 41–2, 42, 158–9, 186
'Frohnleichnam' 113–15, 226

Gardiner, Rolf 206, 214
Garnett, David 124–5
Garnett, Edward 48, 75, 76, 80, 145
Gellhorn, Martha 89
Germany 73–5, 81
God 147–9, 151, 152, 153–4, 158, 161,
    163–4, 167–9
*Golden Bough, The* (Frazer) 40
Grant, Duncan 124–5
Greatham 123
Griffith-Jones, Mervyn 229
Gross, Otto 77
Gstaad 222

Haeckel, Ernst 174
Hardy, Thomas 38, 48, 49
Hargrave, John 185
Harlem Renaissance 7

Hawthorne, Nathaniel 126–7
'Healing' 12
Heidegger, Martin 180–1
Hemingway, Ernest 149
Heti, Sheila 102
Himmler, Heinrich 180
Hinduism 157, 158
Hobson, Harold 76, 80
Hoggart, Richard 230
Holy Spirit, the 163–4, 171
homes and homemaking 57, 117, 146
homophobia 69–71
homosexuality 70–1, 83, 125
Hopkin, Sallie 76
Hopkin, Willie 124, 207
horses 183–4, 189, 195
Horvat, Srećko 201–2, 203, 209
Hueffer, Ford Madox 30
Huxley, Aldous and Maria 228, 229

illness 38–9, 155–8
Indigenous Americans 43, 44, 164
Italy 75–6, 80, 80–1, 107–8, 150–1,
    151, 206, 208

Jaffé, Edgar 159
Jesus Christ 147–9, 163, 167, 168, 171
John the Evangelist 202
Joyce, James 23, 149
justice 230–1

Kangaroo 5, 141–4, 151, 161, 162, 166
Kermode, Frank 209–10, 218
Keynes, John Maynard 125
Kindred of the Kibbo Kift 185, 187
King, Truby 104
Koteliansky, S. S. 130, 131–2, 134, 221

Labour Party 124
Lacan, Jacques 34, 52, 85
Lady Chatterley's Lover 204, 214–
    220, 227
  achievement 213

apocalyptic elements 218, 219
chick scenes 211–12, 214, 215
Connie's pregnancy 218
copies seized 223
descriptions of the female body 82
DHL's aim 213–14
DHL's defence of 217
and female experience 208–9
final version 221–2
illness in 38–9
inception 205–8
Mellors 215, 216–18
Mellors's body described 215
Millett and 4–5, 214–15, 215–
    16, 231
Mrs Bolton 216
spring in 211–13
Lady Chatterley's Lover trial 4, 8, 21,
    69, 229–31
Lake Garda 80
landscape, DHL and 58–60
Lawrence, Ada 25
Lawrence, Arthur 58
Lawrence, D. H.
  adultery 150
  afterlives 228–31
  and animals 187–9
  and apocalypse 202–5, 218–20, 232
  attitudes to 7–13
  battles of wills 59
  beds Frieda 74
  birth of the writer 29–30
  and Book of Revelation 220
  childhood 11, 219–20
  and Christianity 147–54
  claustrophobia 73
  comparison with Freud 23
  comparison with Nietzsche 57
  contradictions 42
  courage 4
  courts Frieda 73–4
  crisis of faith 154–5
  critique of democracy 141–4

death 228
defence of the novel 207
detractors 8–10
diagnosed with TB 205
engagement to Louie Burrows 30
enraptured by the male body 82–5
experiments with women 30
false reputations 68–9
fear of Frieda as a mother 105
feminism 103–4
final years 220–5, 226–8
First World War response 202–5
focus on the stomach 19–21, 36,
    38–9, 41, 231
and food 38
and Frieda's children 91–6, 101–2,
    102, 104–5
health 9, 21, 57, 155–6, 198,
    205, 220–5
homes and homemaking 117–22
homophobia 82
houses 57–9, 61–2, 117–18
ideas of leadership 143
identification with Christ 150
impact of Frieda on writing 73–4
impetus to write 121
impotence 222
and landscape 58–60
last trip to England 205–8
late poems 222, 223–5
and love 71, 86–7
Meynell family visit 123
mission 30–1
mother poem 79–80
move to New Mexico 144–6
mythological world 58
name 11
and nature 174–5, 176–84, 187–
    9, 196
paintings 222–3
parenting theory 105–9, 113
pets 193–5
political ideas 5

portrayal of children 96–102
preoccupation with bodies 21–2
as prophet 149–50
and psychoanalysis 22–4, 31–2
racial views 5
Rananim experiment 124, 126,
    127, 129–39
rejection of will 52–7
relationship with Frieda 11–12, 72–
    80, 89, 90, 91–6, 103, 129, 208–9
relationship with God 147–9, 151,
    161, 163–4, 168–9, 170
relationship with Jessie
    Chambers 27–30
and religion 147–54, 157–8, 158–
    66, 168–9
religious vision 144
repellent ideas 187–9
reputation as a writer of sex 68–72
rift with Morrell 139
sense of life 231
and sex 69–71
sexual ignorance 28
teaching job in Croydon 30
theory of the nervous system 23–4
and the unconscious 21–4, 25, 27–9,
    30–2, 33–6, 39–42
view of parenthood 91–6
vision of desire 82–7
wilfulness 57
and winter 196–9
world-view 7
Lawrence, Frieda (nee Weekley) 7
appearance 72
children 91–6, 98–9, 103, 104–5,
    208, 228
DHL beds 74
DHL courts 73–4
and DHLs death 228
homes and homemaking 117, 120
impact on DHL's writing 73–4
marriage breakup 74–5
memoirs 94–5, 229

as modern woman 15
move to New Mexico 144–5
and psychoanalysis 22–3
Rananim experiment 133
relationship with DHL 11, 72–80,
    89, 90, 91–6, 103, 129, 208–9
sexual freedom 90
unfaithfulness 76–8, 80, 205
Leavis, F. R. 2, 7, 9, 214, 230
Lehmann, Ernst 180
'The Lemon Garden' 151, 163–4
Lessing, Doris 8–9, 68–71, 89, 102,
    103, 104, 230
Lincolnshire 205–6
'Lizard' 191
London 197–8
Look! We Have Come
    Through! 15–16
Luhan, Mabel Dodge 7, 10
'Lui et Elle' 36

McCarthy, Mary 89
machines 178, 179–80
McKay, Claude 7
MacLeod, Alison 10, 11
Madame Bovary (Flaubert) 208
male body, the 82–5
male gaze 215
'Man and Bat' 191
Mansfield, Katherine 95, 132–6, 138–9
marriage 15, 71, 120
Marx, Karl 203
Mastro-don Gesualdo (Verga) 207–8
materialism 23, 47
Melville, Herman 16, 162
'The Metaphysics of Love'
    (Schopenhauer) 48
Methuen 130
Metz 74
Meynell family 123
Middleton Murry, John 50, 229
Millett, Kate 2, 4–5, 10, 14–15, 44, 82,
    102, 214, 215–16, 218, 231

modern woman, the 77–8, 79
'Morality and the Novel' 207
Morrell, Lady Ottoline 40, 43, 44,
    118, 124, 125–6, 131, 131–2, 134,
    135, 137–8, 139, 155
motherhood 92, 99–101, 100, 102, 111
Mr Noon 76–7, 84–5, 93
Murry, John Middleton 132–6,
    150, 197–8

nationality 130–1
nature 173–5, 183–7, 195–9
    complexity 198
    connectedness with 180
    contact with 34–5
    and culture 178–9, 196
    destruction of 177–80
    DHL and 174–5, 176–84, 187–
        9, 196
    hierarchy of 188–9
    Highland cattle encounter 181–2
    instant-to-instant alterations 183
    regeneration 177–8
    religious imagery 190–1
    and sex 181–2
    shapes of 184
    vision of man and 179–83
nervous system, theory of 23–4
New Age, The 48
new life 210–13
New Mexico 144–5, 161–5, 184, 187–
    8, 194, 196, 198, 220
New Statesman 131
Nietzsche, Friedrich 24, 36, 48–51, 52,
    53, 54, 55, 57, 78, 107, 134, 158
Nin, Anaïs 7, 9, 102
Norton, Caroline 102
Nottingham 72, 74, 94
'The Novel' 207

Obscene Publications Act 130
Oedipus 72
Oedipus complex 92–3

'On Being a Man' 134–5
'On Being Religious' 163
'On the Balcony' 80
open road, the 162–3
Orage, A. R. 48

Pan 174, 176
'Pan in America' 173, 174
'Pansies' 222, 224, 225, 230–1
Pantheism 176
parenting 54–6, 105–15, 232
Paris 198
party politics 124
Pearn, Nancy 214
phallus-worship 69–71, 71, 215
Pinker, J. B. 131
Plumed Serpent, The 5, 161
    and Aztec religions 164–6
    and blood-consciousness 40
    DHL on 165
    publication 206
    reviews 206
    Toussaint 40
'Poetry of the Present' 14
political ideas 5
Port-Cros 222
prayer 167, 169–70, 232
primeval instincts 184
primordial impulses 53
promiscuity 77–8, 89
property ownership, abolition of 122, 124, 145, 232
psychoanalysis 12, 22–4, 31–2
Psychoanalysis and the Unconscious 20, 23, 46–51, 50–1, 53

Quetzalcoatl, cult of 164–6

racial views 5
rainbow 62–3, 218–19
Rainbow, The 3, 5–6, 14–15, 140, 186–7, 223
    and apocalypse 204–5, 218–19
    banned 130–1, 227
    chagrin in 156
    cleaning scene 128–9
    dance scene 152–3
    eating in 37
    Frieda in 77
    lack of patriotism 130–1
    marital scenes 217
    and motherhood 101
    and nature 177–8, 179, 181–2
    opening 177–8, 204–5
    passage with the sheaves 60–1, 66, 67
    portrayal of children 96–8
    rainbow 62–3
    religion in 151–4, 159
    sex in 78–9
    sexual explicitness 130
    utterances 60, 60–1
    violence of motherhood 111
    vision of God 152–4
    and will 45–6, 47–8
    Will and Anna's marriage 78–9
Rananim experiment 124, 126, 127, 129–39
Ravagli, Angelo 205
'The Reality of Peace' 53–4, 142, 148
'Reflections on the Death of a Porcupine' 187–9, 189–90, 191
Reflections on the Death of a Porcupine and Other Essays 141
religion 53–4, 147–9, 166–71
    Aztec 164–6
    crisis of faith 154–5
    DHLs exploration of 158–66
religious impulse 158–66, 161
Renaissance, the 151
Resurrection, the 150–1
Revelation, Book of 202, 218, 220
'Rex' 193–4
Rhodes. Cecil 139
Rich, Adrienne 102
Ripley, George 126–7

Rousseau, Jean-Jacques 13, 104, 175
Russell, Bertrand 40, 71, 124, 125–6, 131, 202

St Mawr 184, 186, 192, 195
Saint-Nizier 222
Savage, Henry 82–3
Schopenhauer, Arthur 28, 48, 59, 69
Secker, Martin 206
Second Place 45
secularism 149
selfhood 46–50, 49, 52, 82, 100
'Self-Reliance' (Emerson) 49–50
Sense of an Ending, The (Kermode) 209–10, 218
sex
    as an act of remaking 70–2
    bodily contact 66–7
    and conflict 87–9
    descriptions of 2–3, 67–8
    and desire 67, 82–7, 89
    DHLs reputation as a writer of 68–72
    DHLs understanding of 88
    DHLs view of 69–71, 213–14
    dynamic polarity 69–70
    female experience of 217–18
    inner experience 66–7
    lack of satisfaction in 82
    mysticism 65
    and nature 181–2
    Nietzsche and 78
    outlook on 7
    pleasure of reading DHL on 65–8
    redemption through 150–1
    self-formation 78
    and selfhood 82
sex poems 113–15
'Shadows' 171, 224, 225, 228
'She Looks Back' 92
'The Ship of Death' 224–5, 228
Sicily 190

Signature, The 130
Sigourney, Lydia 103–4
silence 174–5
Smiles, Samuel 103–4
'Snake' 190–1
Society of Authors, Committee 131
'Song of a Man Who Has Come Through' 15–16, 227–8
Sons and Lovers
    chagrin in 156
    eating in 36–7
    flower picking 110
    Frieda in 77
    Jessie Chambers portrayed in 26–9
    Oedipus complex 92–3
    portrayal of children 96
    preoccupation with bodies 21–2
    psychoanalytic reviews 22–3
    religion in 160
    setting 59
    sexual squeamishness 28
    spring in 34
    uses of the term unconscious 30–1
Sontag, Susan 8, 225–6
Spanish flu 12–13
Spencer, Herbert 183
spiritual will 51
spring 34, 211–12, 226
stomach, the 19–21, 36, 38–9, 41, 231
Studies in Classic American Literature 16, 17, 24, 126–7, 162–3
suffragettes 15
Sutton-on-Sea 206, 220

Thoreau, Henry David 126
'Thought' 18
Thus Spake Zarathustra (Nietzsche) 24
'Tortoise Family Connections' 107–9
transcendentalist movement 126
Trespasser, The 73
Trinity, the 163–4
Twilight in Italy 39–40

unconscious, the
  and consumption 37–8
  DHLs view of 20, 21–4, 25, 30–2,
    33–6, 39–42
  of different races 39–40
  location of 19, 20, 24, 25, 34, 34–6,
    41, 231–2
  mind/body intersections 41
  union of 134
United States of America 126–7
utopianism 123–4

Verga, Giovanni 207–8
Villa Canovaia 107–8
Villa di Gargnano 80, 80–1
vitalist theories 48
von Richthofen, Else 159–60

Waldbröl 75
Watson, John B. 104
Waugh, Evelyn 230
Weber, Alfred 75, 159–60
Weber, Max 159–60
'Wedlock' 85–6
Weekley, Ernest 72, 74, 75, 91–2, 93,
    94, 95, 101–2, 104–5
West, Rebecca 229
Western civilisation, crisis of 42
'Whistling of Birds' 211
White Peacock, The 6, 29–30, 73, 77,
    213, 230
  and motherhood 100
  spring in 34
  uses of the term unconscious 31
Whitman, Walt 24, 34–6, 36, 42, 114,
    141, 162
Wilful Woman, The (Dodge and
    Lawrence) 44
will and wilfulness
  battles of 59
  children 54–6
  to destroy 54
  DHL's use of 45–6

DHLs view of 43–51, 232
first manifestation 43
lower 46–50
need for 56–7
to power 49, 50–1
power of 45–6
rejection of 52–7
spiritual 51
unconscious 61, 63
universal will 48
in women 57
Williams, Raymond 178–9
Wilson, Frances 10–11
winter 196–9
woman question, the 77, 79
'The Woman Who Rode Away' 44
women
  celebration of 208
  Lawrence worship 3–4
  modern 56
  selfhood 100
  as source of threat and
    possibility 14–15
  will and wilfulness in 44, 57
Women in Love 12, 166, 192
  and anthropomorphism 186
  Birkin on illness 155
  blood-brotherhood 125
  chagrin in 156
  chair buying scene 119
  Crich 44
  cut opening chapter 84
  descriptions of ecstasy 34–6
  dialogue 3
  eating in 37
  Frieda in 77
  Hermione 44
  on marriage 15
  and motherhood 100
  mysticism 65
  and Rananim experiment
    130, 136–7
  religion in 160–1

setting 59
and sex 2–3, 65–8, 70
and the unconscious 31–2, 34–6
and will 44

Woolf, Virginia 14, 89, 125
Wordsworth, William 176

Yeats, William Butler 203

# A Note on the Type

The text of this book is set in Linotype Stempel Garamond, a version of Garamond adapted and first used by the Stempel foundry in 1924. It is one of several versions of Garamond based on the designs of Claude Garamond. It is thought that Garamond based his font on Bembo, cut in 1495 by Francesco Griffo in collaboration with the Italian printer Aldus Manutius. Garamond types were first used in books printed in Paris around 1532. Many of the present-day versions of this type are based on the *Typi Academiae* of Jean Jannon cut in Sedan in 1615.

Claude Garamond was born in Paris in 1480. He learned how to cut type from his father and by the age of fifteen he was able to fashion steel punches the size of a pica with great precision. At the age of sixty he was commissioned by King Francis I to design a Greek alphabet, and for this he was given the honourable title of royal type founder. He died in 1561.